Saved

This is the inside story of how a small community took on the might of a £1 billion development plan that would have destroyed their village, and the protected countryside around it. Funny, shocking and sensational by turn, *Saved* represents a real-life record of a rare victory of local democracy over greed.

DAVID HEWSON was born in Yorkshire in 1953. A journalist from the age of seventeen, most recently for the *Sunday Times,* his first novel, *Semana Santa*, was filmed with Mira Sorvino. His series featuring the Roman detective Nic Costa has been published around the world.

'...this is not a story about Nimbyism. It is about right versus wrong; about transparency versus secrecy; about truth versus lies; about democracy versus authoritarianism. It also indicates why journalists are both necessary to a society and yet so often un-loved.'
Roy Greenslade, Professor of Journalism, City University

'David Hewson writes thrillers. *Saved* is a real life thriller, exposing the sham of "local democracy". A must for all those wanting to save their countryside and communities from the concrete mixers and the planning fixers.'
Robin Page, broadcaster and writer

'This is a fascinating book, full of insights into the workings of local politics, new, web-based ways of campaigning, different en-vironmental tactics, and institutions as powerful as they are unac-countable. As a result of a wonderfully effective campaign, this little corner of an Area of Outstanding Natural Beauty in Kent is safe – for now. But as the author himself points out, the agents of the kind of wholly unsustainable development that is still eroding our countryside will never give up and never go away. With local democracy in such a state of disrepair, in so many parts of the land, many more battles of this kind will still need to be fought.'
Jonathon Porritt, Founder Director, Forum for the Future

Cover photograph © Steve Bloom

Fiction by David Hewson

The Promised Land (May 2007)
The Seventh Sacrament
The Lizard's Bite
The Sacred Cut
The Villa of Mysteries
A Season for the Dead

Earlier work
Lucifer's Shadow
Native Rites
Solstice
Epiphany
Semana Santa

DAVID HEWSON

SAVED

How an English village fought for
its survival... and won

Matador

Matador
Troubador Publishing Ltd
9 De Montfort Mews
Leicester LE1 7FW, UK
Tel:(+44) 116 255 9311 / 9312
Email: books@troubador.co.uk
Web:www.troubador.co.uk/matador

ISBN 10: 1-90588676-4
ISBN 13: 978-1905886-760

Robert Graves' poem 'Marigolds From Fairies and Fusiliers' is reprinted
by permission of Carcanet Press Limited.

Typeset by Troubador Publishing Ltd, Leicester, UK
Printed and bound in Great Britain by
Cromwell Press Ltd., Trowbridge, Wiltshire.

Matador is an imprint of Troubador Publishing Ltd

For the brave hearts who saved Wye

Marigolds

With a fork drive Nature out,
 She will ever yet return;
Hedge the flowerbed all about,
 Pull or stab or cut or burn,
 She will ever yet return.

Look: the constant marigold
 Springs again from hidden roots.
Baffled gardener, you behold
 New beginnings and new shoots
 Spring again from hidden roots.
 Pull or stab or cut or burn,
 They will ever yet return.

Gardener, cursing at the weed,
 Ere you curse it further, say:
Who but you planted the seed
 In my fertile heart, one day?
 Ere you curse me further, say!
 New beginnings and new shoots
 Spring again from hidden roots
 Pull or stab or cut or burn,
 Love must ever yet return.

Robert Graves, *Fairies and Fusiliers*, 1918

Foreword

Journalists in Britain suffer from a bad press. In surveys asking people which profession they most dislike, journalists generally rank just below politicians and estate agents, and sometimes above them. They are inextricably linked in the public mind to newspapers which, despite their claims to act in the public interest, appear to be universally detested and distrusted, even by the people who read them. As a character in the Tom Stoppard play, Night And Day, observes: 'I'm with you on the free press, it's the newspapers I can't stand'. Despite that, Stoppard retains an affection for newspapers and appreciates journalistic endeavour. 'The good stuff is still good', he has written, 'I admire huge amounts of it, mostly people who go out there and file a story.'

I am delighted to state, unequivocally, that this book exemplifies the 'good stuff' of journalism. It offers conclusive proof that journalism can make a difference, a positive difference, to peoples' lives. Yet it isn't about newspaper journalism because it was a campaign carried out entirely on the internet and therefore represents a happy marriage between traditional journalistic skills and the virtues of the improved, instantaneous communication of modern publishing. Old media and new media worked together in harmony.

Sadly, though, it is also about journalistic failure. The main local newspaper forgot the old dictum about the newspaper's proper role being to comfort the afflicted and afflict the comfortable. Instead, it appeared to avert its gaze. Who knows why? It could have been due to editorial ignorance or editorial incompetence, either of which might have been compounded by a lack of sufficient staff. Resources are often stretched in Britain's regional press nowadays. Then again, there must be a suspicion that there were proprietorial constraints on editorial freedom. Was press freedom crushed by the kind of financial, political and social network that Hewson calls a corpocracy? He provides some compelling evidence that should give all journalists, especially those working in Kent, pause for thought.

At its heart, the central story is straightforward. A large academic institution decided to plant a massive development, a new science park, in an Area of Outstanding Natural Beauty, a £1 billion plan that depended for its financial viability on the parallel building of thousands of houses. If it had gone ahead it would have transformed the pretty village of Wye into a town. To bring this about Imperial College, an independent arm of London University, entered into a secret agreement – a concordat – with two public authorities, Kent County Council and Ashford Borough Council. This was accomplished without reference to the people of Wye and, when they were eventually told, the scale and longevity of the collusion – codenamed Project Alchemy – was concealed from them. The Wye villagers were presented with a *fait accompli*.

It was this big secret, along with a host of smaller secrets, that Hewson, a journalist-turned-author, and Justin Williams, a desk-bound newspaper executive who rediscovered his reporting zeal, were to reveal. In doing so, they effectively scuppered Imperial College's plan, thereby saving the village they loved from a development that would have destroyed its character.

But this is not a story about Nimbyism. It is about right versus wrong; about transparency versus secrecy; about truth versus lies; about democracy versus authoritarianism. It also indicates why journalists are both necessary to a society and yet so often unloved. Hewson points to the difference between the well-meaning villagers who pursued a conventional, 'decent' mode of campaigning and 'the new, anarchic, instant form of action' employed by himself and Williams. Hewson explains: 'We had to crack the story. I had no objection to using methods that were shabby, underhand, immoral, deceitful and thoroughly reprehensible to decent, normal human beings who lived by the standards of civilised society.' He admitted that he drew the line at breaking the law, though Williams was altogether less fastidious about the need – in order to serve the public interest – to take that risk. It's a reminder that muckraking often offends the sensibilities of those who benefit from it.

Hewson and Williams ran their campaign through a blog-style web-site set up specially for the purpose. They made effective use of the Freedom of Information Act which, despite its shortcomings and official attempts to frustrate their inquiries, did provide them with their first major breakthrough. In time-honoured fashion Williams – described with affection by Hewson as 'a lone wolf reporter' – also cultivated sources – 'brave-hearted moles' – within Imperial College to secure crucial information. Though the major newspaper in the area ignored the story, the editor of one title did offer support by covering their main revelations. But Hewson and Williams fought for the truth in the face of official hostility, bureaucratic deceit, political cunning and considerable scepticism from many villagers who also opposed Imperial's plans. The infighting among the differing protest fractions was itself partly played out on their web-site, an example of the way in which new media journalism is visible, collaborative, candid and often rude. It's a tribute to Hewson and Williams that they didn't allow this to deter them from their central mission.

By journalistic standards their success was remarkable. Few newspaper campaigns result in unambiguous triumph, usually ending in some kind of fudged compromise, a partial victory at best. Even the *Sunday Times's* famous thalidomide campaign was not wholly victorious. It puts the achievement of 'two blokes with a web-site' in perspective. Theirs was a considerable achievement against the odds, and all the better because, as Hewson writes, 'all that mattered was the journalism, and the fact we were doing all this for free was astonishingly liberating'. In other words, journalism for journalism's sake, uncommercial journalism, journalism for the public good, real journalism. Good stuff, indeed.

Roy Greenslade
Professor of Journalism, City University, London
January, 2007

Introduction

It's not easy to enter Wye. The village sits at the foot of the North Downs, three miles outside Ashford in the valley of the Stour river as it runs on to Canterbury and then the English Channel. The Romans used this narrow, serpentine waterway as an important supply route during their conquest of England. William the Conqueror found Kent much too difficult to subdue when he invaded a millennium later, which is why the county still, to this day, bears the label 'Invicta', undefeated, as its motto, and a warning still to incomers that the locals may, when pushed, turn difficult. The shallow river bed and narrow channel of the river at Wye made it a natural ford in Roman times. Close to the site of a former Imperial era villa there is a narrow bridge dating from the early seventeenth century and, in front of that, a very antiquated level crossing much admired by train buffs.

This is the primary route into the village, with views locals know well through protracted delays at the crossing gates. On both sides the narrow width of the Stour meanders, flashing green and silver, to the west past an old mill race beloved of anglers, and to the east, in the direction of Canterbury, past the gardens and garrulous, greedy ducks of the white-timbered Tickled Trout pub. This old inn's name is relatively recent. Until the 1970s there was a National Hunt race track by the railway line, one so small it was decried by purists as more suited for greyhounds than horses. All the same, the Victoria, as it was known then, used to throng with spivs and bookies and visiting Londoners who crowded the special trains from Charing Cross to the race meetings.

People have always enjoyed visiting Wye, with its crooked buildings and handsome church rebuilt in the 15th century by John Kempe, a gentleman's son of nearby Olantigh who went on to be Chancellor to Henry VI and Archbishop of Canterbury. In the quiet graveyard, surrounded by stones that carry the names of families that have lived hereabouts for centuries, you have the sense of a different England, one that has for the most part escaped the rush of modern times. Walk to any of the many nearby lookouts and you soon appreciate that the church is the focal point of the village, its sturdy spire like the heavy mast of some vast stone vessel left marooned in a sea of meadows flowing in every direction.

The days of special trains are gone. The only rail travellers you'll find at the bar of the now gentrified inn are long distance commuters. Still, the pub has sound reasons for its more genteel name. The river matters; it is a part of this world. Brown trout breed in the clear, relatively pure flow, joined sometimes by larger migratory sea trout and even the odd salmon. The endangered native white claw crayfish still scuttles in and out of the weeds and pebbles beneath the banks. Otters are slowly returning, herons hang ponderously in the air. By dint of geography and the restricted route into the village, Wye is a simple, beautiful, solitary spot.

High ahead on the Downs stands the white outline of the chalk crown first cut by local students in 1902 to commemorate the coronation of Edward VII. This simple, modern emblem is the symbol of the village. It's stitched and printed on the uniforms of the children who attend the bustling Lady Joanna Thornhill Primary School, named after a lady-in-waiting to the wife of Charles II who, when she died in 1708, left an endowment to 'the poorest sort of children' to improve their learning. Until a few years, ago you would have seen it on the insignia of the agricultural college that had, until the mid 1990s, prospered in the village since its inception in 1894, much of it in buildings first founded as a college for training priests four and a half centuries earlier.

I moved to the Wye area in the mid 1980s and found it, like every newcomer, a magical place, a busy, happy village, cosmopolitan, eccentric and unpredictable, an ever lively, occasionally irascible mix of farm hands and academics, artists and office workers, all glad to come home to a place that they all recognised as special. This was a community of people who were reluctant to leave, and those that did often came back in retirement to spend the remaining years of their lives among views that seemed unchanged by the decades. Students travelled from all over the world to study among some of the most renowned academics in their field. In a small lane just a little way up from the church we even acquired a tiny mosque, set inside a wooden building belonging to the college, not the kind of thing you'd find in most small Kent villages.

The young men and women of that era were a mixed bunch: the rich offspring of the landed gentry, male and female, poor sons of tenant farmers looking to find the skills to keep up the work of their fathers, keen, ambitious environmentalists, seeking to discover and develop new agricultural techniques for the distant lands where Wye students often found themselves.

They were funny and different, and their presence lent this village, of just fifteen hundred residents, with another six hundred undergrads in the good times, a unique atmosphere. It was as if a small Oxford college had been plucked out of the city and placed in some of the most glorious and historic countryside of south east England. There were secret societies, gatherings of tittering adolescents dressed as ancient Romans, tarts and vicars, with arcane ceremonies and initiation rituals, one of which involved swallowing a live goldfish with a pint of beer. The summer ball was a riot of lounge suits and evening dresses, fairground rides and tipsy couples stumbling into the bushes. Each November came bonfire night when a procession of students, villagers and goggle-eyed school children wound its way up from the front door of the old archbishop's palace that was now the college entrance, burning torches of sticky tar that dripped onto their clothes, bottles of booze stuffed into pockets, breath steaming in the cold autumn air, flocking *en masse* onto the road up the hill, blocking it entirely for anyone rash enough to think they could drive there on an evening such as this. There was a firework display on the Crown, its chalk outline still carefully preserved by student labour freely given, and the pyrotechnics that burst from the summit of the hill were visible as far away as Canterbury and Folkestone when the sky was clear.

This was the Wye we knew and loved. Then, in the space of less than a decade, it started slowly to fade, like a brightly coloured photograph left out too long in the sun. The summer was always quiet until the students returned. One year, perhaps it was 2001 when we were all a little distracted by other matters, that rebirth never really occurred. The college had changed hands and was now in the uncertain grip of a distant, powerful presence from London, Imperial College, whose intentions towards the small, fragile institution it had devoured were unclear. In this uncomfortably placid, strange atmosphere, the village entered a dream zone of puzzlement and growing disquiet. As the rest of us went about our business, the college slowly dwindled under

Imperial's rule, its professors dispersing, its student numbers plummeting, supposedly in the wake of the decline of agriculture, though no-one quite believed that was the whole story.

We waited, knowing this couldn't go on. The college estate embraced some of the most historic buildings in the centre of the village, from the archbishop's palace to Withersdane, a grand mansion dating from 1815, and encompassed some eight hundred acres of gorgeous fields stretching from the Downs to the Crown, Wye's green moat where livestock munched next to fields of corn and experimental crops and research still went on into that most traditional of Kent harvests, the hop. It was painful watching its decline. It was painful too carrying that worrying nag with us all the time, the one that asked: what will come next?

On Tuesday December 6th, 2005 we found out, and it proved to be worse than anyone could have dreamed in the grimmest of nightmares. Imperial College, which had owned the Wye estate for just five years, had signed a secret 'concordat' with our local authorities, Ashford Borough Council (ABC), and Kent County Council (KCC) to turn the village into a small town, home to a £1 billion 'world class science research' facility. Our community of some fifteen hundred people was, once Imperial's bulldozers had finished their work, to provide jobs for 12,500. A village where manufacturing meant the small and busy cottage enterprise known as the Wooden Spoon, which had, for years, made excellent jam and marmalade for a growing range of customers, would, though this was never made clear at the time, enter the industrial age, with a refinery churning out fuel oil from crops. Hidden from everyone too, though we all suspected it existed, was a plan for new housing, a massive carbuncle of modern brick so large it would turn over the green fields of Wye to concrete even though they, like the entire village, stood inside an official Area of Outstanding Natural Beauty.

The names of the leaders of the local authorities that were, one day, due to sit in independent judgement on this massive project were written already on the concordat placed before us, both pledged to work for its success. It was, on the face of it, a done deal. The Wye we knew seemed dead, its future signed away in secret by the very people we thought were there to represent us.

In modern overcrowded England, where making money out of land and property is often seen as so much easier and profitable than going out and performing industrious work for a living, such stories are far from rare. What makes Wye unique is this. We won, and not a partial victory either, one in which some compromise was struck, a deal that kept a little of the village alive in the sea of industry and housing that was supposed to rise around us. Just 283 days after Imperial College, ABC and KCC announced their intention to take over an entire, happy and successful rural community and turn it into suburbia, the plan was utterly dead, abandoned forever in abject surrender with more than £1 million of public money frittered away on consultants, architects and lawyers.

This is the story of their defeat at the hands of a small band of argumentative and occasionally divided people who took on the might of the new 'corpocracy' running Britain and sent them packing.

The failure of Imperial College and its allies represents, in the short term at least, one of the biggest environmental campaign successes of recent decades. But it's also a lesson in the state of English democracy in the early years of the 21st century, and a reminder of some cold, unpleasant truths. Wye did not win through strength of argument and the determination of its citizens alone, though both played their part. There were darker, less 'civilised' forces at work too, and I'm happy to confess to being one of them. In some ways this is a story which marks the death of English niceness, bitter proof that decent people lose if all they choose to fight with is their decency alone. It is also a reminder that sometimes large truths may lie in small ones, and that staring at a tiny, apparently parochial issue can occasionally give us an unwelcome and alarming insight into the society we inhabit.

I am indebted to many people for their assistance in this work, some of whom will wish to remain anonymous. Justin and Beth Williams and my wife Helen were among those who aided in its writing, though any errors are mine and mine alone. Countless villagers too numerous to mention assisted with their memories of the previous fifteen months. Robin Page and my tireless literary agent Vivienne Schuster provided enormous encouragement in bringing this story to a wider audience. Cliff Whitbourn remained steadfast in his practical support too, as he was from the start. You all have my gratitude, and we all still have Wye. At least for now...

David Hewson

Bleak Midwinter

Our local councillor becomes excited

If I cannot keep my mouth shut, then I will not be invited again. If that happens, other doors will be closed to me and my ability to act as an effective advocate for my village will be severely damaged. No longer will I be able to take the village's views, concerns and worries to the top tables and to the key individual decision-makers.

Ian Cooling, comment on save-wye, June 2nd at 1.08 am.

Though you might not guess it to look at him, Ian Cooling was a product of the Ashford School of Spooks, or the Intelligence Corps as it's more formally known, IntCorps to those who have passed through its secretive ranks, and the 'Green Slime' to regular squaddies who usually haven't a clue what these fellow members of the British Army are up to most of the time. During the latter half of the twentieth century a rather grim army camp close to the centre of what was then a small Kent market town served as the odd location for the headquarters of the British army's primary unit for gathering, analysing and disseminating military intelligence, and for counter-intelligence and security.

It was nothing to look at from the outside, with no hint that, if local rumour was correct, the sprawl of buildings served as some English forerunner to Guantanamo Bay, a place where suspect IRA men might be flown for a little interrogation using the latest 'techniques'. Behind the highly-guarded barriers of Templer lay a proliferation of covert skills. Alongside IntCorps, the Defence Intelligence and Security School and the Joint Services Interrogation Organisation burrowed away at intelligence issues running from Northern Ireland to Bosnia and beyond. UK, NATO and Commonwealth forces logged in here to learn everything from counter espionage to photo interpretation, and the training of 'prone to capture' agents who were at high risk of apprehension and torture. There was a place to set off explosives, a firing range and a Close Quarters Battle (CQB) shooting house that provided the standard training for soldiers and others in the use of firearms at very close range.

One of those who passed through the doors of Templer Barracks was later to reveal, 'It was a fun place to work at. Some of the IntCorps staff were famous for being the sort that would eat their own children dead on a plate of salad if it meant getting a better posting than someone else. They weren't called Green Slime for nothing. Even the local Kent Police used to ask "what exactly do you do up there?" whenever a soldier was nicked for anything.'

But in 1997 IntCorps and its service fellows departed lock, stock and barrel for more modern quarters in Chicksands, Bedfordshire, a famed home for spooks during the Cold War when the base was under United States Air Force control. The sprawling, high-tech Chicksands operation, based around a twelfth century priory, was definitely a step up for IntCorps, like moving from a council house sink estate to the posher part of town. In their place in Kent now stands one more dull identikit housing sprawl, red brick covering the site where intelligence operations around the world were once planned by anonymous cadres of the army's secret squirrels.

The silent squaddies have dispersed, many into civilian life in the Ashford area where few of their acquaintances know anything of their past, though discreet reunions do take place, and quiet nods between men in pubs. Once IntCorps, always IntCorps, up to a point. Their motto – *Manui Dat Cognitio Vires* – means 'Knowledge Gives Strength to the Arm'. Ian Cooling had, after a period of training and service, departed its uniformed ranks for work in even more shadowy areas of the Diplomatic Service. But he remained, as he was wont to tell people, an 'army man' at heart, which was just as well, since he was to have good need to remember his old corps' motto during 2006.

Any community that has had some kind of intelligence operation in its midst is used to the appearance of middle aged men of a certain breed emerging among them then quietly confiding, perhaps over one beer too many, that they were former, and perhaps not entirely retired, operatives from the murky world of espionage. In my years as a national newspaper journalist, at home and abroad, I met my share of such individuals. I also learned at an early stage that you can say this with absolute confidence about the true spy: he or she will never reveal their secret past to anyone, sometimes even a husband or wife. Awkward questions dancing around the subject will always be diverted elsewhere, at best with vague mentions of 'diplomacy' or the arcane administrative structure of the Foreign Office.

Thus went such conversations with Ian Cooling, a man in late middle age, fond of a shabby mac and, in summer, a tweed jacket. He had retired from the Diplomatic Service and returned to the rural area where, as a young man, he had once been in the ranks of IntCorps. To many he would seem a perfect minor character from a John Le Carré novel, genial, slightly scruffy in the way solitary bachelors sometimes are, but with a ready smile and enthusiastic personality, a full head of wayward greying hair, and a constant enthusiasm to be involved in anything that took his interest. Divorced, living alone in a small and somewhat shambolic terraced cottage, Cooling passed his time with a busy round of engagements, some professional, some voluntary, though occasionally, and during 2006 increasingly, it was difficult to decide precisely where the dividing line between the two lay.

His abiding private passion was for cars, Jaguars in particular. Through a web-site labelled 'Ian Cooling's Jaguar Automobilia Collector' he sold 'related automobilia requirements', such as badges and posters, ashtrays and discarded spare parts. On the internet and occasionally at local fairs, he could also be found touting his own entry into print, *The Complete Guide to Jaguar Collectibles,* usually available for £9.99 against £24.99 list price, and blurbed by 'Philip Porter – Jaguar Driver' with the memorable recommendation, for a book listing old car parts, thus, 'You will be strong-willed if you can put it down.' Sales did not, however, appear to extend to sufficient funds for the man to own a Jaguar himself. Instead, he travelled around Ashford in an ancient red Peugeot 206, often in the cause of his second great pursuit: local government.

A few years earlier Ian Cooling had become a member of the local parish council, Wye and Hinxhill, a career largely unmarked by controversy until some tetchy kerfuffle over a strange Wild West show which landed the village with a rather large bill, the blame for which some laid firmly at Cooling's door. He was, however, never one to be dismayed by misfortune. Perhaps it was the IntCorps training or the steel he acquired while working as a 'China watcher' in Hong Kong but setbacks were, for Ian Cooling, simply signs that it was time to find new rungs on a ladder he sought continually to climb. Soon after the Wild West show misfortune, he found himself raised by the local ruling Conservative party clique to become candidate for Wye's seat on Ashford Borough Council. This was as safe a ticket as any in the land.

The Ashford area had been overwhelmingly Tory since hustings began, and now extended to a diverse local authority running an odd, polyglot area of distant Kent beyond the more familiar commuterdom used by Londoners, a land of genteel rolling fields around Wye in the east, extending through the rough, expanding, ugly conurbation of the town itself, on to the beautiful tourist streets and timber-boarded homes of Tenterden where the posh folk lived, among them the council's leader, Paul Clokie.

Elevation to the executive of ABC placed Ian Cooling at the centre of politics in a borough that had been named by the Labour government as the target for some of the most rapid growth in the south east, ordered to create 28,000 new jobs and build 31,000 new homes by 2031... or else.

This was a world away from Wild West shows and flogging old ashtrays from long-dead cars. In the heady melting pot of Ashford politics, as it swam in the promise of a tidal wave of national and European money to back the borough's boom town pretensions, Ian Cooling found himself returned to circles from which he had long been absent. He was talking with national politicians and senior government officials, making policies, chatting to industrialists and the curious mix of landed gentry and quango junkies who hold so many of the keys to power in a sprawling county running from the edge of London to the English Channel, one where, in spite of a gross domestic product larger than some third world countries, important decisions often took place out of sight, in dining rooms and clubs, unelected committees and secretive working parties.

Promotion had come his way too. He now held a grand council title, 'Portfolio Holder for Communications, Partnerships, Forums and Consultation', and was chairing a branding committee which, after much thought, nine months' work, and £60,000 of public money, would come up with the slogan, 'Ashford: Best Placed for Britain'. Sadly this occurred just two months before Eurostar decided to cancel all Ashford services to Brussels and most to Paris, one sign among many that all was not well in this supposed boom town.

But this was in the future. On the night of December 5th, 2005, he was only aware that his village, his constituency, was about to be blessed with a windfall, a £1 billion dream of 'global excellence' that would put the small, sleepy village of Wye on the world map and place him in the presence of yet more powerful 'top tables and key individual decision-makers'.

This was news he needed to share, carefully, discreetly, with those he hoped would one day feel grateful for being allowed a glimpse into the inner workings of the unseen cabal whose hands pushed and pulled the cogs and levers of Kent.

Ian Cooling, Jaguar collectibles connoisseur, former spook, would be mover and shaker in the exciting world of the south east's fastest growing town, needed witnesses, two people innocent of the great storm gathering, unwitting onlookers at the moment that would transform this quiet little community forever.

The concordat from nowhere

Ann Sutherland, the chair of the Wye Business Association, was clearing up after the village's annual Christmas street party on December 2nd when Ian Cooling approached her and offered to put some rubbish in his car then take it to the tip. 'By the way,' he added, almost as an aside, 'what are you doing Tuesday afternoon?'

The college had, he said, an important announcement, '...and you can't invite everyone. If you invite the WI for instance then you have to invite all the others.' His top team list of two turned out to be Ann and John Hodder, chair of the village parish council. They were both told to report to the Old Hall 'in their best bib and tucker' at 2.30 p.m. the following Tuesday for A Very Important Announcement about which Councillor Cooling was determined to say nothing more.

The 15th century Old Hall in Wye College, with its minstrels' gallery and antique furniture, is one of the former palace's grander meeting rooms, often hired out for weddings. It had a very different crowd that Tuesday afternoon, a gathering of serious gentlemen in suits, into whose presence Ian Cooling ushered his guests with an expectant glee. Five of these important men were to figure prominently in the story of Wye that year, but at that moment all were mostly strangers to Hodder and Ann Sutherland, characters from the stratosphere of academia, international business, property development, and the senior levels of local government, rare visitors to the quiet countryside of east Kent.

Professor Sir Richard Sykes was rector of Imperial College. Alongside him stood two colleagues, Professor Sir Leszek Borysiewicz, his deputy rector, and David Brooks Wilson, a beaming, opera-loving, Jaguar-driving and mildly Bunteresque figure who had, through a circuitous career of property development, lodged up in the curious position of estates director of Imperial, though never in the past had his working life taken him much near academia. Next to the Imperial men were the two most important elected local authority members for the area, Paul Clokie, leader of Ashford Borough Council, and Paul Carter, leader of Kent County Council. A PR man in a yellow bow tie and a coterie of lesser officials hung on every word uttered by these grandest of visitors to little Wye.

Canteen staff were quietly handing out tea and coffee, while slices of bread pudding were being served and, Ann Sutherland noticed, keenly consumed by the elderly Charles Findlay, county councillor for the Wye area who lived in the village and was known for two things. He owned a highly small dog which hated the approach of others, forcing Findlay to scuttle into bushes and alleys whenever any other dog owner in the village had the temerity to take their animal out on the street. And Charles Findlay usually said very little indeed about anything, a habit he would not break in the Old Hall that day, or for much of the coming year.

Speeches were made though – by Richard Sykes on 'the Imperial vision', by Paul Carter, who confessed to being 'terribly excited' about whatever was about to occur, and by Paul Clokie who welcomed the arrival of so many new jobs. Then, before the hapless village representatives understood a word of what was happening, a document labelled the 'concordat' was placed on a large table and ceremonially signed by all three men. An official photographer stepped forward to take shots of the trio with some of their colleagues. Afterwards, to their surprise, Ann Sutherland found that she and John Hodder were ushered into the picture with an enthusiastic nudge from Ian Cooling and the words, 'We're on!'

The camera man finished his work. Some polite conversation ensued, and a little later, just as puzzled as they had been when they entered, Ann Sutherland and John Hodder left with a copy of the newly-signed concordat and a press release in their hands.

'We walked down the street angry that we had been set up in a photo shoot,' Ann recalled. 'I said cheerio to John and as I came down Church Street I couldn't help but think that bread pudding was a strange choice for such an occasion. I wondered whether Charles Findlay had slipped a couple of slices into his pocket.'

The men they had left behind believed they had much more than bread pudding in their pockets at this moment. The strangely formal ceremony which Ann and Hodder had just witnessed was the culmination of a covert process which Richard Sykes and his new friends in local government had been working on for more than a year, the blueprint for a new Wye which would be unrecognisable to either of the two villagers who had been ushered into the room to lend it a little local verisimilitude. Though there was no planning application on the horizon, no consultation process under way with local residents, the press release which followed would state baldly, 'Wye will become the home for a new £1 billion, world-class science research and manufacturing facility – creating some 12,500 high-quality job opportunities, bringing prosperity and sustainable regeneration for Ashford, and acting as a major economic driver for Kent and the South East.'

The announcement was couched in the management speak verbiage with which campaigners would become wearily familiar in the months to come. It promised that the primary purpose of the concordat was 'to establish a common and workable framework for co-operation and collaboration between the three principal stakeholders in the Project namely – Ashford Borough Council, Kent County Council and Imperial College London'.

But, for everyone else outside the magic inner circle of the secretive triumvirate headed respectively by Imperial's Richard Sykes, KCC's Carter, and ABC's Paul Clokie, the exact import of what was being set in train was opaque. The correct decoding manuals may have been available to former spooks like Ian Cooling, but ordinary civilians struggled and failed to make sense of such jargon as... 'housing of an appropriate range to cater to a broad spectrum of householders... active participation of global industrial companies in the pharmaceutical, engineering, medical or other sectors as relevant'... and 'sustainable regeneration (to) drive the design, funding and economic aspects'.

These three men and their camp followers knew the answers but were anxious that everyone else should remain in the dark until the facts trickled out in a controlled fashion, through a tightly managed process of consultation which would, inevitably, be steered towards one conclusion only: success. That required care and the utmost secrecy, because the ink on the baffling concordat disguised a truth that would prove shocking, even to those who, in the beginning, believed something remarkable and welcome might be about to arise on the green fields of Wye. What Sykes and Carter and Clokie wanted to do was to pave the way for a massive building project which might one day match the scale of the Channel Tunnel Rail Link, turning the somnolent Wye village into a small town that would, in all probability, one day be swept up merely as a suburb of Ashford, taking many hundreds of acres of green protected countryside with it.

Richard Sykes, a man who moved in the highest government circles, was confident he could square the planning objections this would generate, and the final referral to the minister in charge, at that moment John Prescott, still the deputy prime minister. Earlier that day he had despatched a fawning letter to Gordon Brown, the Chancellor of the Exchequer, selling the idea in such glowing terms he got a warm and welcoming response in return from one of the Treasury's senior officers. Carter and Clokie knew the risks too. They too had been busy dictating a confidential letter to Yvette Cooper, then Minister of State for Housing and Planning in Prescott's office.

This missive was full of bright-eyed and bullish optimism, boasting of a sizeable commercial park and a development that would grow and grow over twenty years, adding the fervent hope that Whitehall would smile kindly on the scheme. But in a throwaway line Carter and Clokie let slip a key phrase: 'A challenging feature of the proposal is that all of Imperial College's landholding at Wye is within the Kent Downs AONB (Area of Outstanding Natural Beauty'.

Richard Sykes, Paul Carter and Paul Clokie could never have guessed exactly how challenging that would turn out to be.

A strange case of synchronicity

Given the secrecy that had surrounded the signing of the concordat, Ann Sutherland was surprised to find the event had garnered huge and glowing coverage in the local newspaper, the *Kentish Express*, which appeared first thing Thursday morning, just a day and a half after the event took place. Ashford's weekly rag was not usually known to move so quickly. Once a spirited publication, part of a group that had won national acclaim, it was now a shadow of its past self, famed for misspellings, late and inaccurate coverage, and a habit of filling its pages with photos of babies, small animals, school children and anything else it could find to take the place of news.

Something else puzzled her too, something followers of the Swiss psychologist Carl Jung would label 'synchronicity' – a 'temporally coincident occurrence of an acausal event'. A whopping great coincidence in other words, and the first of many. At the signing she had spoken at length to another of those closely involved in the concordat, David Hill, chief executive of ABC, the council's most senior officer. She had said to Hill, 'This is what the Victorians must have felt when they knew the railway was coming to Ashford. It did after all change their status from village to town.'

It was an obscure reference and one that would have made sense mostly to those who had lived and grown up in the area and knew a little history. The arrival of the South Eastern Railway in December 1842 had changed Ashford completely, more than doubling its population from 3,000 to 7,000 by 1861, most employed in the locomotive works. This historic industrial development had built more than ten thousand steam and diesel locomotives before it closed in 1981, an economic blow from which the town had struggled to recover.

Hill nodded, interested by the somewhat obscure analogy. Two days later there, on page one of the newspaper, was the headline, meaningless for many, 'Biggest change since coming of the railway', over fulsome, multi-page coverage that carried the awful slug 'exclusive' which, as any hack knows, is, in circumstances such as these, better described as 'planted'. For a newspaper like the *Kentish Express* to have devoted so much space so quickly to a single story was highly unusual, as was the apparent synchronicity between Ann Sutherland's tangential remark in the Old Hall of Wye College and the front page splash headline that week.

I had worked in the regional press only briefly as a journalist before escaping, gratefully, to the freer and better-paid pastures of *The Times*. But looking at the *Kentish Express* took me back thirty years. Over the ensuing decades since I fled the business, most local newspapers had been snapped up by large, impersonal regional chains, milked for profit, and turned into staid, boring, lookalike local rags. Most, I have to say, would have seen a story like the concordat and started to ask some searching questions. But Kent is a different place, and searching questions didn't enter into the *Kentish Express's* coverage that day which was almost uniformly gleeful, welcoming whatever was happening – and it was quite clear they hadn't much of a clue about that too – as the harbinger of prosperous times to come.

This was the first inkling of something I was only dimly aware of at that time. In my adopted county connections matter, and the *Kentish Express* had more connections, very direct ones, to those behind the concordat than its readers might ever appreciate. The paper was a part of the Kent Messenger group which is dominant throughout the county and has been owned since its inception by three generations of a wealthy and highly individual family, the Boormans, who have seen it rise to become a regional giant with a turnover of some £50 million. Edwin Boorman, grandson of the man who had founded the company, was still chairman at the time of the concordat, though about to hand over the day-to-day reins, to his daughter naturally, and ascend to the presidency of the company. Not that this semi-retirement would alter his position as friend, *confidant* and dinner party companion to generations of Kent's power brokers, all helped by his staunch support of the more right wing reaches of the Conservative Party, sympathies that had led him to join the controversial Freedom Association, an outpost for crusty Tories who thought Margaret Thatcher's problem was she was a little too liberal at times.

As I was to learn that summer, connections like these counted. In 1997 they had also gained Boorman the annual position of High Sheriff of Kent, an obscure and archaic honorary title, the winner selected by a bizarre process in which the identities of three contenders are placed before the Queen in Privy

Council for her to choose one by picking out the name of the anointed candidate with a bodkin. There were other more tangible advantages too. While the villagers of Wye were going about their Christmas shopping in a state of utter ignorance of the machinations going on around them, Edwin Boorman had rather more facts than they would glean for some time to come.

As part of the complex preparations to get the joyful message of the concordat to as many important people as possible, Imperial's PR advisers had drawn up a list of two hundred key people and organisations. It included the Deputy Prime Minister Prescott, whose department was seen to be crucial to their dreams, the local Tory MP Damian Green, and former Conservative Party leader Michael Howard, MP in neighbouring Folkestone. Rising Labour stars like David Milliband and Yvette Cooper were on the contact list alongside old troopers like Margaret Beckett, soon to be foreign secretary, and Alan Johnson who would be tipped as a successor to Tony Blair himself before long.

When the trickle of leaked documents from inside the concordat team started to turn into a flood six months later, we finally uncovered that list, and the complex arrangements through which those deputed to spread the word for Imperial – from Richard Sykes, speaking to members of the government, to Ian Cooling, humbly ordered to help David Hill pass on the news to the anglers of the Stour Fisheries Association, but only by letter, and on the day – would go about their business.

Number 103 on the list was Edwin Boorman, to be told by phone call and letter, personally, by Sir Sandy Bruce-Lockhart, gentleman Kent farmer, son of a former deputy director of MI6, Paul Carter's predecessor as leader of KCC, and soon to be raised to the House of Lords and chairman of the Local Government Association. Bruce-Lockhart, a likeable, though some might say rather naive, left-leaning Tory, thought he understood everything there was to know about Imperial's plans, though he was later to discover he was mistaken. Given his quiet chat with Edwin Boorman, the *Kentish Express's* new found ability to be on the nose with the news for once was, perhaps, unsurprising, and nothing to do with synchronicity.

Imperial and its allies had the local media on message and that, they thought, was that. All they needed now was to bring the village on board, and a date was set to jump start that process: January 9th, 2006, with a public meeting in Withersdane, the former country mansion, in beautiful grounds, which had been acquired by the old college after the Second World War and was now distinctly shabby student accommodation, grubby halls of residence set inside the remnants of a stately home shell.

The task of selling the concordat to fifteen hundred of the most awkward and obstreperous people in Kent would fall to the unfortunate Professor Sir Leszek Borysiewicz, a talented medical researcher, Welsh, in spite of the exotic name, and a great rugby fan. Tall and stiff, dour-faced and stern-looking behind wire-framed spectacles, he was not an obvious or comfortable public figure. He'd been knighted in 2001 for his research into developing vaccines, including one to prevent the development of cervical cancer, though quite why anyone within Imperial thought this suited him for a new career as a property developer remains a mystery. In 2001 he joined Imperial as Principal of the Faculty of Medicine, becoming Deputy Rector, number two behind Richard Sykes, another former medical man, three years later. Borys, as he was known throughout the college, sometimes with rather less affection than the nickname suggests, had left behind research for the headier climes of academic management, embarking upon a path that would, if he were successful, surely lead to his stepping into Richard Sykes' role, with its near-automatic seat in the House of Lords on retirement, when it became vacant in the summer of 2008.

Top of the to do list handed down by his superior was sorting out Wye in a way which both men had come to understand implicitly. As scientists who had spent their entire life in the medical field they had an ingrained antipathy towards agriculture, and Wye in particular. They were now in charge of a distant rural college, one inherited from an earlier regime, part of a different, more backward century, not the era of bright new laboratories and 'world-class centres of excellence' which Sykes and Borys wished to establish in the Imperial name. Wye, with its ancient buildings and 850-acre estate, simply did not fit. It was a place for agricultural students who saw nothing wrong in working the fields, mucking out animals, tending crops, or trying to refine the traditional skills of farming for a world in which, increasingly, they were regarded as antiquated and of little use.

For the group of people the village would soon come to know as the 'Imperialists', Christmas 2005 must have been a time of happy anticipation. If all went as the teams of consultants, academics and property developers behind the concordat planned, within the space of the next twelve months this small Kent community and its surrounding protected acres would be as good as theirs.

The past stirs

The press lives by disclosures.
John Delane, editor The Times, *1841-1877*

All this happened while I was in a different country, speaking and thinking a different language, happily convinced my reporting days were far behind me, never to return. Journalism had paid the bills for three and a half decades since I entered the profession as a seventeen-year-old lowly trainee getting a few pence short of £5 a week on the *Scarborough Evening News* for taking down flower show results and the names of mourners outside funerals. Base cunning and naked ambition had allowed me to claw my way to a reporting job on *The Times* by the age of twenty five. But after a long time in newspapers I'd gradually started to switch to writing fiction. My first book had been filmed – terribly, but the money paid off my mortgage. My latest creation, a series about a young Roman detective, was starting to make some serious sales around the world, particularly in the US where I was having to spend increasing parts of the year on promotion.

Six months before I had relinquished my last connection with newspapers, a well-read but rather easy and overpaid weekly column in the *Sunday Times*. I'd been writing it for ten years, covering technology and the 'digital era'. Over the previous year I thought the section had lost its tough, consumerist bite, and I was starting to feel a lone voice among a bunch of 'read this story win an iPod' features that didn't quite mesh with reality. So-called lifestyle journalism, people writing about themselves, screaming 'Me, Me, Me' from every page, had never appealed. I saw its birth on national newspapers in the 1980s and hated it then. In the intervening years papers had got fatter and often lazier, and it was the lifestyle crap that always got called on to fill the expanding wad of newsprint between the ads.

So I'd never been happier. The daily routine of the hacking trade was replaced by the solitary and intellectual rigour of research and writing, something I felt owed through never having been to university. A nagging sense of guilt still lingered though, and it concerned the way my journalistic career had tailed off into idle well-paid punditry. Harry Evans, who was briefly editor of *The Times* during the turbulent period I worked there, once said,

'In journalism it is simpler to sound off than it is to find out. It is more elegant to pontificate than it is to sweat.'

That, in the final years, had been me to a tee: all noise and no fury, and if there was one thing I'd learned in my hacking career it was that fury – a sense of injustice and outrage and bloody-mindedness – lay at the heart of all real reporting. My column on the *Sunday Times* had been called *Sounding Off*. Enough said.

When the story broke I was living comfortably in an apartment close to the Pantheon, spending the nights dining on pizza and pasta, and the days working up a novel that required very detailed amounts of research into the life and works of Caravaggio. I remember clearly calling home while I was walking along the banks of the Tiber, close to the Castel Sant'Angelo and feeling distinctly odd when my wife said, quite puzzled, 'There's something big happening about Wye. It's called a concordat.'

A *what?* I took a solitary dinner in one of my favourite restaurants by the Campo dei Fiori that evening, unable to get this nagging conversation out of my head. Like everyone else in Wye I knew that one day Imperial would surely try to build something. It was only to be expected. Many people would have welcomed sensible, rational development of some of the run-down areas of old labs and research buildings that had been allowed to rot into dilapidation over the years of neglect. Besides, we didn't live in the village. We were on top of the hill, three miles away, beyond the Crown, down a narrow single track lane next to a wood covered in so many tree protection orders I had to get planning permission just to coppice my own modest acre of chestnut every eight years or so. Whatever happened down there, in the place where my kids had first gone to school, with their friends from Malaysia and Ethiopia, we would be fine. I didn't need to travel to London any more. I worked for myself, on books I invented out of my own imagination. Everything was perfect, however much Imperial College might want to make it otherwise down the road. Wasn't it?

Two days later I was home, hunting for the *Kentish Express* the moment I got through the door, determined to make sense of what was going on so that I could put it at the back my mind. It was impossible. Journalists don't see newspapers the way civilians do. We can spot the tricks, the lazy get-outs, the quotes from the other side that never appear, the lacunae that indicate indolence or incompetence or – rather more rarely than readers believe, though it happens – interference from above. The *Kentish Express* that week exhibited possible signs of all three. Here it was supposedly emblazoning the biggest story to hit the Ashford area since the arrival of the railways a century and a half before. Yet the more I read the dreary stories they carried, the more baffled I become. Wondering if this was just me I started to ask others. Wye is a gossipy, garrulous place. Secrets were rarely kept for long. Imperial had only managed to keep everyone in ignorance of the concordat itself by ensuring perhaps only two people in the village – Ian Cooling and Charles Findlay – had any knowledge of it in advance. *Someone* ought to know what was really going on, and the most important detail of all: what did they want to build and where?

For once Wye was at a loss for information. The gossip network Ann Sutherland labelled 'the village tom-toms' was silent. Even those who worked at the college, security staff and people from the kitchen, students and, most of all, the academics, many of whom had been treated brutally by Imperial over the years, knew no more than they had read in the *Kentish Express*. Naturally, the rumour mill invented its own myths, passed with a sage, knowing nod, in all three pubs, the New Flying Horse, the Tickled Trout and the Kings Head, over dinner, on the train and the way home from church. The drugs giant Pfizer would be moving its gigantic base from Sandwich, on the Kent coast, to Wye. All 850 acres of the farm would be sold off for housing. Fuel companies would be coming to the village to set up refineries. It was all guesswork, and the letter Imperial sent round to residents clarified nothing, simply inviting everyone to a public meeting on January 9th with the promise of more information there.

It was interesting, and a little disturbing, to see the way people had automatically assumed it would all happen. Even Wye-Cycle, the bohemian, ultra-green group which had been picking up rubbish from people's doors for more than a decade and recycling it at an unlovely former brick works on the flat road out to Naccolt, seemed to be of that opinion. WyeCycle was a typical village institution, more than a little eccentric under its vocal and visible leader Richard Boden, a Green Party activist. Its three vans, all powered by 'bio-diesel', recycled vegetable fat, pottered through the community picking up waste and vegetable matter to take to Naccolt for processing. Boden, who also played an important part in the development of the popular biweekly farmers' market on the village green, itself college property, was a busy figure in Wye, often in the papers and full of vocal opinions on anything affecting the community, usually ones seen through the very focused eyes of a political activist. WyeCycle was a remarkable story. It collected kerbside waste from 1,100 homes in Wye and Brook, an average of 260 kg per home each year. Most English households produce between 500 and 800 kg, making Wye, Boden boasted, the 'least wasteful community in the UK', a claim no-one seriously disputed.

What did the green lobby think about the concordat? Talk about equivocal, its statement declared, 'The proposal to revitalise the Wye Campus could be the worst possible thing to happen to the environment. It could also be the best possible thing, so long as the following conditions are agreed and adhered to.'

The list of demands that followed varied from the sensible – no building on agricultural land – to the ridiculous, such as a call for a strict ban on any improvements to Wye's existing constricted and congested roads. A £1 billion development would clearly involve huge construction traffic at the very least. Those 12,500 workers wouldn't be arriving by public transport, but cars, and not ones running on chip fat. It was a foregone conclusion that some substantial changes in the traffic infrastructure would have to be a part of any Imperial plan. Without it, there would be gridlock for miles around.

None of this bothered WyeCycle. 'Development along these lines would make Wye a shining example of how society needs to respond to the greatest challenge of the 21st century: sustainable development,' they proclaimed. 'If they are unwilling to do this, the development should be resisted through whatever means necessary.'

So everything was fine provided the development was all green and politically correct, and if not let's bring in the Swampies and the eco-warriors. Like most of the noises made at that time it didn't feel right to me, and the principal reason had nothing to do with the impracticality of some of Boden's criticisms. What grated was the presumption that Imperial, as the dominant local owner, had some kind of *droit de seigneur*, a medieval *jus primae noctis* which allowed them first right to stake out the future of the village then wait for everyone else to fall in with their decisions. It was obvious to me that the college felt this way already, and secret documents we would prise out of the organisation in the months to come made it clear such an attitude under-pinned everything they did. They were the primary landholder. Their permission was needed even for such a small thing as the farmers' market. If you bought one of the houses near the green they still owned the leasehold, and, as part of the lease, imposed on anyone living there a condition that they would do nothing to bring the college into disrepute.

These were hangovers from a different era. Imperial was the dominant land owner, but I saw no reason why we should behave or be treated like serfs. Why say, as so many did, that something was fine in principle when we still had no idea what the primary idea was or its scale? Why give them succour until they deserved it? Why not wait, judge the information as it came out, talk among ourselves, and come to a considered view?

As a viewpoint that turned out to be just as mealy-mouthed, wrong-headed, vapid and 'nice' as everything else going around at that time, because Imperial and its allies were already several steps ahead of us. I hadn't learned the key lesson that was going to be imprinted upon me repeatedly in the months to come. When you are fighting organisations which are big and powerful and rolling in money, corporate giants who will do anything, and obfuscate any awkward fact, simply to get their way, the only people who play by the Queensbury rules are those who end up on the losing side.

I scanned the papers again and still found nothing. I bearded my local contacts until they got bored with my questions. I even tried the local, privately-run web-site, wye.org, which was essentially a directory of local services and businesses, one put to-gether in such a haphazard and ham-fisted fashion it managed to look old-fashioned in the way that only a modern, fast-moving medium, when misused, can achieve. It was hopeless.

Nine months before, when I was getting increasingly frus-trated with my inability to get into the *Sunday Times* the opinions and topics I thought important, I'd had one more row among many about a story idea. I wanted to write about the potential of blogs as community publishing ventures. It hadn't gone down well. Blogging was all the rage at that time, and the paper had already run down the well-worn path every other newspaper had followed, questioning whether the rise of individual columns by so-called 'citizen journalists' spelled the end of professional media as we'd come to know it. This subject bored me intensely, as did most blogs out there, which seemed simply to be over-inflated opinion pieces, often based on a shaky grasp of real world facts, spouting at excessive volume to little effect. A more exaggerated and less professional version of my own newspaper column if you like.

What did interest me was the opportunity blogging software might give a community to voice a variety of opinions, to share and develop ideas quickly and easily through a web-site. I'd spent years listening to all the PR guff the computer world churned out about the social possibilities of the internet. This, it seemed to me, was a rare example of genuine opportunity, something real, the ability to produce a kind of online local newspaper, instantly at very low cost, using free software produced by the enthusiastic, altruistic geeks who made up what was known as the open source movement.

Over the holiday I became more and more morose about the information vacuum into which Wye had fallen. Four days after Christmas I signed up for a web hosting account which included installation of one of the most popular blog platforms, Wordpress. Imperial was to spend more than £1 million on consultants and PR men over the next nine months before giving up the ghost. That internet account cost me just over £30 and included a free domain name. I thought hard and picked save-wye.org. Then I wrote and published our first article, one that I hoped would spark a flood of free thought, information and interaction among the residents of the Wye area keen to understand and influence the development heading their way.

More light, less hype
Thursday, December 29th, 2005 in Opinion by David Hewson

It is now three weeks since the residents of Wye and its surrounding area woke up to a bombshell. Without the slightest prior warning, two organisations supposed to represent their interests – Ashford Borough Council and Kent County Council – had secretly signed a 'concordat' with a third public body, Imperial College, London, to transform our charming rural area into a hotbed of futuristic research and development, or, as others might put it, home to a bunch of new and sprawling housing and industrial estates which will transform our lives and the heritage of this region forever.

Why is this happening? What exactly *is* happening? As I write this, it's hard to say. The information released by ABC, KCC and Imperial is skimpy at best, though we are promised more at a public meeting on January 9th. But here are some facts that are known. Wye is an attractive and largely content rural community at the moment. No-one, prior to this announcement, was heard bemoaning the lack of industrial or housing development, let alone on a scale that will bring in thousands of new jobs and homes, with their associated traffic and impact on the environment.

There may be good reasons why Imperial wants to proceed with these plans, since they will involve the sale, doubtless at great profit, of land it inherited through the purchase of the old Wye College. But the loss of a working, vibrant rural community seems a high price to pay for the ambitions of a London university that seems to have little genuine interest in its small east Kent outpost, particularly when this 'offer' is backed up by the threat that Imperial will abandon Wye altogether unless it is allowed to do whatever it likes.

Any project with such far-reaching consequences for a settled, prosperous community like Wye deserves facts, explanations, research and consultation, all things that have been remarkably absent to date. This web-site exists so that people who are interested in and affected by these proposals can air their views, from both sides, and allow the residents of the Wye area to make an informed opinion about their future. We also intend to host all the public documents we can on this project so that anyone interested in it can find them in one place. You can see what we have so far here.

If you would like to contribute in some way, please use the contact form and get in touch.

I don't look back on this debut piece with great pride. In it I was just as equivocal, vague and clueless as everyone else. Deservedly, this sorry excuse for an article scarcely caught the attention of a soul. During the closing stages of this saga, save-wye would attract two thousand or more visitors a day from around the world. In the two weeks that followed this anodyne debut I got about thirty, and no-one hung around very much, naturally, because there was nothing to read. It was going to stay that way too, because not a soul came up with an article, though I approached people I'd known for years, begging them to write something, anything, whatever their views on the Imperial announcement.

The excuses were astonishing. They didn't understand the internet. They were too busy. They didn't want their names out there on articles that Imperial, ABC and KCC would see. And, more than anything, they wanted to 'wait and see'. I'd covered enough planning issues to be horribly familiar with that last one. Usually when I talked to people who waited and saw what had been cooked up while they were sitting on their hands.

Finally, one villager took me to one side, looked at me as if I were a touch soft in the head even to have come up with such an idea in the first place, and said, 'The problem, David, is the title. *Save* Wye. So... judgemental. It presupposes there's something we need to be saved from, and we simply don't know if that's true.'

My entry into the world of electronic publishing had been still born. There were murmurings among the middle classes about setting up some kind of group alongside the parish council to discuss and, if necessary, oppose Imperial's plans. But the wild, open spaces of the internet, where everyone could have a voice and hear and discuss those of others, were not the territory upon which this slowly assembling army of lawyers and accountants and their fellow professionals wished to pitch their tents.

Still, there was the public meeting on January 9th. I had one more opportunity, perhaps a last chance, to put some fire into save-wye's young and fragile belly. And I was about to blow that too.

False starts

Set back from the high road leading to the Downs, imposing and grandly secluded, Withersdane Hall was the kind of country home the landed Victorian gentry adored. By the 1840s, some thirty years after its completion, it was occupied by Captain Arthur Davies who farmed three hundred acres of the estate, employing sixteen outdoor labourers, and, for his wife and nine children, a tutor, a governess, two male and four female servants. Davies clearly enjoyed Wye, and became involved in local charities and village affairs. Alongside most of his substantial family he now lies in a pink marble tomb by the north wall of the village churchyard, a place so beautiful even an old atheist like me can envy his good fortune. Withersdane in those days was a substantial, three-storey gentleman's mansion with beautiful grounds and views in all directions, to the Downs, the farmland east and west, and the village half a mile away towards the river. After Davies' death in 1867, the property moved into the ownership of the local squire, John Sawbridge-Erle-Drax of Olantigh where John Kempe, creator of Wye's archbishop's palace, was born four hundred years earlier. The Drax family lived there briefly after Olantigh was destroyed in a fire, then the property passed into the ownership of one Andrew Bigoe Barnard, an officer of the empire, who had recently retired from the post of Deputy Commissioner of Police for Bengal.

The Barnard family was to be the last private owner of this substantial and, in their time, elegant property. After Andrew died in 1928 it was inherited by his son Norman, known to everyone as 'Chippy' who presided over a gilded era of garden parties and social events straight out of the pages of P. G. Wodehouse. Wanley Erle-Drax, who had inherited the Olantigh estate, produced pageants by a summer house close to an area known to the Barnard children as 'The Wilderness', once playing Bottom in *A Midsummer Night's Dream* himself. Quintin Hogg, the future Lord Chancellor and mentor to Margaret Thatcher, was a visitor, as was the author Anthony Powell whose *A Dance to the Music of Time* series took place in the very kind of social circles typified by visitors to Withersdane in the 1930s.

This golden era was not to last. Chippy was a career soldier who had been working in the Committee of Imperial Defence at the outbreak of the Second World War, living with his family in London. The following year, as a German invasion and air attacks on the capital seemed ever more inevitable, he was deputed to work in the underground War Cabinet rooms, and moved his children out to Withersdane where they were billeted with a group of young evacuees from east London. The conflict was not entirely distant; gas mask practice was frequent and at one point an enemy bomb exploded in a neighbouring field killing three sheep.

Then, on Monday April 22nd 1940, Chippy and his wife May visited the children on a rare day off, planning to drive back after dinner. At Charing Hill, on the return journey, he blacked out. The car hit the kerb and left the road. May suffered a broken leg. Major Andrew Barnard, 'known and loved by everyone' said the Wye Parish Magazine later, died of head injuries in Ashford Hospital later that evening. He was buried next to his father in Wye churchyard. The following October Withersdane ceased to be a private residence and became the Divisional Headquarters for the operation to repel the expected invasion of Kent, home to first the 43rd Wessex Division, then the 56th (London) Division, housing the divisional general and the intelligence section, all surrounded by barbed wire, with underground shelters and all the latest state-of-the-art telecommunications wartime Britain could find. When peacetime came Chippy's widow gladly accepted the offer of £10,000 for the house and estate from Wye College. It needed the room urgently for accommodation to house the female students of Swanley College who were moving to the area because their own quarters had been bombed.

From this point on, the grand mansion where novelists and future politicians had once been entertained at glorious weekend dinner parties would be a university hall of residence and soon, with the addition of an ugly modern wing, reduced to the rather shabby circumstances such places seem to regard as a natural fate.

Not all its historic links disappeared, however. Anne Barnard, daughter of Chippy, who had grown up through the delightful times of the 1930s, and the turbulent ones of the following decade, married and settled in the village once Withersdane had been sold. She and her husband lived there still, even as Imperial College issued letters to villagers inviting them to hear everything of their plans, at a public meeting in the meeting room known as the Swanley Hall, named after the girls who had been moved there sixty years before because of Hitler's bombs. Anne Barnard had become Anne Findlay, wife of the very same Charles, county councillor and silent devourer of the bread pudding served as Sykes signed the Wye concordat designed to steal away the village forever. Geographically, Kent is the tenth largest ceremonial county in England, but socially and historically it can sometimes seem very small indeed.

The meeting at which Professor Leszek Borysiewicz wished the village to hear 'our exciting plans' was set for 19.30 to 21.00 on the evening of Monday January 9th and, while I knew it was a important opportunity for the floundering save-wye.org, I had grave reservations about whether to attend. It was my 53rd birthday, not that I could, with any great conviction, use that as an excuse. The real reasons for my reluctance were two-fold. Two years before I'd suddenly lost all hearing in my left ear and discovered, to my shock, that deafness could sometimes be a very noisy experience indeed. While I was able to manage conversations with small numbers of people without difficulty, I struggled and felt deeply uncomfortable in large, noisy rooms, where the multiple voices become distorted and usually impossible to understand. The thought of sitting there, with a notebook in front of me for the first time in years, would have been daunting enough in normal circumstances. To do that with an ocean-like roar running through my head – which as any tinnitus victim will tell you is inevitable in these situations – was unthinkable.

But then a part of me insisted this whole idea was unthinkable. The web-site had been live now for almost two weeks, and had made no impact whatsoever. I was thirty thousand words into a new novel which needed my attention badly, since this is the point at which things can begin to go wrong in the structure of any story. Even when I'd been a rank junior sitting in the offices of the *Scarborough Evening News* wondering what menial task I'd get next I'd had a bigger audience for my work. Its readership of 13,000 was something like a thousand times larger than anything I'd managed to get using a system Chippy Barnard, with all the technological miracles of his day in the depths of the War Cabinet bunker in 1940, would have thought belonged to some distant and unimaginable future.

This was important, *is* important. Some people write out of ego, a need to show that they can. I'd lost that years ago. I wrote because I liked to communicate, to put across in words something another human being might find interesting or entertaining or both, whether it was a piece of fiction or a real-life story. Writing demands readers. Without them it's a needless, pointless exercise in self-inflation. Having someone looking down at the page adds an extra, essential dimension. If I couldn't get an audience soon, there really was no point in carrying on.

It's a ten minute drive from my home on top of the Downs into Wye, past the high lookout of the Devil's Kneading Trough and the Crown, visible reminders throughout that year of why I thought I was doing all this. But not in winter at seven o'clock on a cold January evening. It was as black a night as I ever remember, and as I reached the foot of the hill I saw something else I'd never seen. The road outside Withersdane was jammed with traffic, cars struggling to get in, cars struggling to get out, clearly realising there were no more spaces left in the parking area. Vehicles littered the narrow road into the village. Even though the meeting was due to start in only ten minutes cars were still struggling to get up the narrow and always difficult stretch of Scotton Street that led to this outpost of the college. This was the kind of jam we used to get in the past, for the old college's summer ball, when a fairground ride might be among the vehicles trying to fight its way into the grounds of Chippy Barnard's old mansion. It seemed as if half of east Kent had turned out to hear Professor Borys speak glowingly of his vision and his excitement for the future ahead.

I didn't even need to think twice. I let a few people past, struggled onwards, taking fifteen minutes or more to cover half a mile. Then I parked outside the New Flying Horse, walked into the empty bar and ordered a beer.

There's a practice in journalism called 'picking it up'. It means getting a story without being there, by asking someone who was or, if you're friendly enough with other hacks who were present – and I rarely was – pulling a favour from their notes of the event.

There was no good reason why I couldn't pick up the Withersdane story. I didn't have a deadline. I didn't even have a readership, for pity's sake.

Cliff Whitbourn, the landlord of this flagship pub hotel owned by the very individual, if not downright eccentric, Kent brewery Shepherd Neame, and a man who would come to play an important part in the battle to save Wye in the months to come, served me.

'Not going to the meeting?' he asked with his usual acuity. Classical music buff, rabid fan of Bath Rugby Club, and a first time father just turned fifty, always impeccably dressed, usually with a bow tie which gave him more the air of a bright and busy advertising agency executive than a pub landlord, Cliff never missed a thing.

I mumbled some miserable excuse and rambled on about the web-site, and whether it was really worth continuing. The detail of what he said is lost to me now, though I recall it was to do with different ways of skinning cats. My little experiment interested him. Though, like me, he wasn't local, Cliff had taken on a touch of the raw Kent spirit embodied in the old motto, 'Invicta'. He wasn't a committee man and nor was I. We both understood how elements of the village would react, through the slow round of formal meetings and outraged dinner parties, the traditional, sluggish means by which the English middle classes expressed their misgivings. We both, I think, instinctively appreciated this was somehow insufficient given the scale of the threat the village might face, one in which a developer, Imperial, wished to embark upon a project of colossal scale, and had somehow managed to get on board our two councils before the public even knew such an idea existed.

I do know this though. That night I came home and started researching something that had never been around when I was a reporter, a piece of legislation called the Freedom of Information Act that gave public bodies a duty to cough up information to the public on request, provided it passed a few hurdles. Six days later I felt sufficiently comfortable to be able to lodge, by e-mail, a request for information under its auspices to the FoI team at Kent County Council, asking for 'the chance to see documents relating to discussions pertaining to the recent Wye concordat signed between KCC, ABC and Imperial College. I am particularly interested in documents which detail when these discussions began and any outline planning documents to do with the subject'. I had no idea at the time that I was laying the groundwork for the story that would finally put save-wye on the map, and set the tone and the direction of our coverage for the rest of our short existence.

Before all that though, I had to pick up on what had happened in Withersdane. It just took a few calls the following day to find out, and what I discovered was, in a subtle and yet significant way, quite sensational. While I was sitting in the bar of the New Flying Horse, having a stimulating and, it proved, highly useful conversation with Cliff, Professor Sir Leszek Borysiewicz was managing to offend and outrage, deeply and in the eyes of many irrevocably, the very community he was trying to win to his side.

Borys upsets the Numpties

> Having reflected on the claims made for Imperial it struck me that I do not recall any major scientific contribution to the second world war coming from Imperial College. It was Florey and Chain who ensured that penicillin was available in time for D-Day. Not quite what Borys claimed, but perhaps he was keeping the story simple for the 'turnip tops'.
> *Emerson Oetzmann, comment, July 4th at 10:13 pm*

Even after the entire project collapsed, Imperial College was paying to keep alive an internet video of Professor Borys's speech to Wye that evening. The joyous cocktail of amateurishness and arrogance which prompted such grand gestures from this most self-important of academic institutions was a recurring feature of their stuttering campaign over the next nine months. Reduced to a postcard size web movie, his presentation continued to carry the same charge of failure and disaster that it did as he delivered it in person in Withersdane's Swanley Hall that night.

The audience was the largest Wye had ever seen for a public meeting, much to Imperial's surprise. The turnout far exceeded the legal capacity of 550 of the Swanley Hall so that a good proportion of the grumpy, suspicious residents, already warming up for a scrap, found themselves watching everything on a TV screen from an adjoining room. The message with which Borys began his talk – that Imperial was a first class college of international importance, one where Alexander Fleming had developed penicillin, and ground-breaking scientific breakthroughs appeared to be made almost on a weekly basis – fell on somewhat deaf ears among people whose first impression was that Imperial couldn't even organise a decent public event. The hostility was there from the outset, and it would never go away from this night on. After Borys had boasted of how Imperial's scientists had recently penetrated the very depths of outer space, one wag chirped up, 'If you're capable of studying the rings around Saturn, do you think you could sort out the level crossing?' He didn't reply. He didn't have to.

The turning point, though, came after a long and tedious illustrated presentation about Imperial's achievements, when he was about to begin his section on Wye.

He peered at his audience through his wire-rimmed specs and said, somewhat haltingly, 'This is going to be an inexorable process but one thing we need to be very clear about is that once we set out on this particular road there is absolutely no turning back. And there are good reasons why there is no turning back because to make it a success this will have to be a large scale venture.'

Then, with great timing, he delivered what a thespian would call a 'Pinter pause', a momentary hesitation to emphasise the effect of the words to come.

'But to put it in terms you'd understand...'

There was an audible gasp from the audience. Then laughter. Then fury. Later, Borys would apologise, at the prompting of the parish council chairman John Hodder, for this extraordinary lapse. What had he done? There's a wonderful word I first encountered in east Kent: numpty. It means village idiot, turnip top, local yokel, boggle-eyed moron.

'He thinks we're all numpties!' one of those present complained to me afterwards, summing it up neatly. In that one unbelievably thoughtless sentence, Borys lost the village from the start, talking down to a group of mainly middle aged, middle class people who were temperamentally inclined to know their place until the moment someone who thought he was their superior reminded them of it.

Borys would never be allowed to forget the short sentence he uttered from the platform in the Swanley Hall. Even though I wasn't there, I was able to make sure of that. Months later, when the concordat was slowly falling apart, a reporter from *Kent on Sunday*, the only local paper to cover the story regularly, reminded him of the words and the offence they caused. It was only one sentence among many, Borys harrumphed. No it wasn't. It was the first sign of a chink in the enemy's armour, the moment when the tenor of the relationship between the village and the college was set as I indolently and in ignorance sipped my beer and chatted to Cliff in the New Flying Horse.

Imperial College had never made much effort to get to know Wye since it took over the old agricultural college in 2000. The quiet consensus was that this standoffish London college thought this distant little village sat somewhere beneath the salt in the estimation of its ennobled and self-important leaders. Borys's off-the-cuff remark confirmed it, in local eyes, as an arrogant, metro-politan institution, one more bunch of London toffs looking down on country people who'd spent the last decade dealing with crises such as BSE, foot and mouth, and, for some, but by no means all, the loss of fox-hunting, and thinking, as they saw us... *numpties.*

It wasn't just insulting. It was plain wrong. Wye was a univer-sity village. Many of those in the audience were current or former academics themselves, seated alongside farmers and office work-ers, lawyers and retirees who had abandoned urban life for rural peace and were determined not to lose it. They didn't just feel insulted. They knew when Imperial got it wrong. Borys's boast about Alexander Fleming was, as an avid and knowledgeable reader was to point out in a comment on save-wye, simply wrong. As Borys struggled to persuade his audience that the focal point of the new Wye's research efforts, the transformation of crops into 'bio-diesel' to reduce global warming, would make the pain worthwhile, Richard Boden must have sat in the audience bewil-dered. The process of turning vegetables into car fuel was scarcely rocket science. He and his colleagues at WyeCycle had been do-ing something similar for years on their scruffy little eco-junkyard out in Naccolt. If Borys needed to know how it was done, he could simply have hopped into the chip fat-powered WyeCycle van outside and seen it for himself.

The difficulty for me, as I picked up the story of Swanley Hall through phone calls and conversations over the following days, was that this important shift was a subtle one that took some time to work through the community as Borys's unfortunate words were passed from individual to individual, each adding a little of their own ire to the mix. What I wanted to carry from the meeting was the very thing that was missing from the story so far: facts. Forecasts, time scales, details of what was being put forward and, most of all, what everyone wanted to see: plans. We were all desperate to know where all this building, of labs and houses and manufacturing facilities, would take place. There were parts of the Imperial campus where most people would have wel-comed development. The so-called brown field sites off the Olan-tigh Road were, in the main, abandoned and ugly, ideal for mod-est and sensible renewal. What no-one wanted to see was building on the green fields of the farm estate running beneath the Downs, with its glorious views and walks.

David Brooks Wilson, the college's estates director, appeared to rule this out at the meeting. As Imperial's own records of the event later stated, 'He emphasised that rural regeneration in this area is not about building houses on farmland, but about reviewing existing assets and looking at replacement of some of the existing buildings. He suggested that this would be to the good for the village and the area.'

Within the space of six months this same man would be presenting to the management board of the college, and receiving approval for, a plan that would have caused a riot had it been disclosed that evening. The blueprint would have created as many as four thousand homes in the fields surrounding Withersdane, in and beyond the gardens and the Wilderness where the young Anne Findlay had played as a child. In front of the old mansion, over that night's choked car parks, would have risen office blocks and laboratories. Across the road, in the meadow leading to the Crown, there would have been industrial and manufacturing facilities, among them a substantial refinery for bio-fuels that would have dwarfed many times over Richard Boden's home-grown effort in Naccolt. So huge and ambitious was this secret project to destroy the old village and put a new town and commercial estate in its place that Imperial's own consultants would conclude it could only meet sustainability targets by erecting two wind turbines, each fifty metres high with a blade diameter of twenty metres, and a dedicated power station burning 'friendly fuels'.

None of this could have been guessed at from Borys's presentation that night, which focussed on vague concepts, not details, and introduced a refrain that Imperial and its supporters would chant repeatedly over the coming months as they assembled their forces for the attack upon the village. This was 'a vision not a plan', an idea which the local authorities concerned backed vocally from the outset in the person of David Hill from ABC and another interesting personality, Pete Raine, a former environmental campaigner who had risen to be strategic planning director for KCC. Both these public servants were introduced by Borys as 'colleagues', which seemed a little odd given that their authorities were supposed to take an unbiased view of any planning application they received.

Hill, a cautious, unassuming individual who looked as uncomfortable in public as Imperial's deputy rector, told the meeting that 'there was no further information other than that discussed during the presentation this evening. It would be inappropriate to imply that Ashford approve the development where there isn't a planning application, or even a firm proposal. But it does acknowledge the enormous positive potential of this vision for Wye, and for Kent.'

Raine was far more forthcoming. A striking, talkative man, quite unlike most dry, serious council officials, he loved the media and still had something of a fan following from his days as director of the Kent Wildlife Trust for whom he had co-authored a book entitled *Wild Kent*. What environmental street cred he still possessed would rapidly dissipate over the coming months as he turned into one of the chief public spokesmen talking up Imperial to the world at large. At Withersdane he was word perfect throughout, reading, like the others, from a script of 'key messages' which had been provided to everyone, from Paul Clokie to Paul Carter, by the consultants Ernst & Young.

The Imperial account of the meeting documents Raine's message at Withersdane. 'Mr Raine pointed out that the lack of plans at this stage is a well-known planning Catch 22, and commented that he doesn't see a way round it. He gave his undertaking that such plans do not yet exist, pointing out that, whilst critics object to the current lack of plans, the invitation that had been extended is to discuss a concept. He suggested that if the community could engage in the consultation process, there is a chance of keeping Wye as (a) world class institution, thereby minimising inevitable changes.'

There, in a nutshell, was the local authority case. Trust us to go away and decide what's best or you'll lose the college altogether, and it could all be so much worse.

These subtleties were largely lost on a meeting that continued to fume over Borys's 'to put it in terms you'd understand' remark. But for me, reading the notes and watching the video in the cold light of day, they stood out a mile, raising awkward questions that screamed for answers. The language, with its implicit, hidden messages, was deeply revelatory.

The line that this was 'just a vision not a plan' sounded too much like a transparent deception, a convenient myth to which Imperial, ABC and KCC had to cling because if the truth were known – that they had already agreed in principle about what was to take place – there would have been even more outrage than had emerged already. Yet the signs were there in the language of all of these men. In Borys, saying, very frankly, 'This is an inexorable process'. One, in other words, that couldn't be stopped. From the mouth of Pete Raine who never once in the months to come qualified his version of the future. For Raine, Imperial's plans for Wye were always exciting, and always something that 'will' – never 'might' – happen.

As far as these people were concerned the war was over. All they needed to do was subdue the local populace sufficiently for the bulldozers to be sent in to finish the job. Borys and Brooks Wilson gave the game away towards the end, when the audience's concentration was wilting. To begin with, Borys said, there would be a hundred to a hundred and fifty 'principal investigators' in labs, costing £150 to £200 million for 'a few thousand square metres' of floor space. After a further £300 to £400 million was spent 'kick starting' the development, a critical mass would be reached that would bring in business partners to build the rest. The project, said Brooks Wilson, would run for twelve years, from 2006 to 2018, with an investment of £80 million a year, totalling £960 million.

In other words, they hoped to start work later that very year, and had a projected budget in mind already. There was certainly a vision. But to have such precise numbers and such a close time scale in mind, surely there must be something, some outline blueprint, a document, a piece of paper, perhaps even a map, to allow such apparently precise forecasts to be made?

It had to be there, even in a rough form, already, and close to completion if the statements these men were making in January of 2006 bore any resemblance to the truth. The tame hacks of the *Kentish Express* weren't going to dig to get it. Nor, I suspected, would any formal, conventional campaign group. Uncovering the truth about these people had to be the job of save-wye, if only because no-one else would try.

And here I was, too deaf to sit through a public meeting, my shorthand shot to pieces, my reporting skills rusty from years of idle neglect. I needed help, and quickly.

Fresh talent

All successful newspapers are ceaselessly queru-
lous and bellicose. They never defend anyone or
anything if they can help it; if the job is forced on
them, they tackle it by denouncing someone or
something else.
H. L. Mencken, American journalist, 1880-1956

In 1986, at the tail end of my Fleet Street staff career, when I'd
departed the newly-launched *Independent* having discovered my
opinion of its then editor coincided with his opinion of me, I'd
toyed with the idea of joining the *Daily Mail*. They seemed to like
my writing and usually gave me plenty of space if I pushed free-
lance ideas their way. Then I spent an evening in their editorial
office, at that time under the iron fist of the legendary David
English, and knew it was never going to work. I was used to the
idea that journalism was a tough calling, but the *Mail* was the
toughest place I'd ever seen. Its aggressive, uncompromising outlook was something that, as a professional, I could only admire.
What I wasn't prepared to accept was being Mailed. Everyone I'd
ever worked with who had passed through the paper's doors had
re-emerged a different person. Hacks who have been Mailed
stood out in any newspaper office. They were the ones you didn't
mess with, the ones who told you what they thought, usually with
a free, frank and rich vocabulary well before they were asked.

I didn't mind getting my hands dirty to nail down a story back
when I was a daily reporter and it was necessary. But Mail hacks
looked for the dirt first then sifted through it out of curiosity in
order to find out if there was anything there. It was a talent of a
kind I never wished to emulate, though my reawakening journalistic skills were starting to tell me it might come in very handy
indeed if only it could be found for save-wye. By one more
strange instance of synchronicity just such an opportunity was
about to occur only half a mile from my home.

Justin Williams was fifteen years my junior but old enough to
have experienced provincial journalism back in the days when
people 'went out' on stories instead of sitting in an office busily
writing them from press releases, e-mails and rushed phone calls
because there were so few reporters to go round. In his first week

as a cub hack on a provincial newspaper in Sussex he'd been sent on a 'death knock', ringing the doorbell of some unfortunate family that had just lost someone to a road accident, then asking for an interview and some nice photographs of the freshly deceased, please. He'd been told, in an unambiguous fashion, to clear off because somebody from the paper had already been round pestering. When he got back to the office his chief reporter admitted trying to get the interview herself over the weekend. She'd sent him round to nag them again because she believed being told to eff off was good experience for any trainee hack.

I hated death knocks. So did Justin though as I came to know him I began to suspect it was with rather less fearful antipathy than I felt myself. While I'd fled to the better-paid and death-knock free pastures of *The Times* as fast as my feet could take me, he had hung around, discovered Ashford, and become for a short while editor of the *Kentish Express* in its heyday before moving on to national journalism. After a spell on the *Mail* he had risen to be a senior executive on the *Sunday Telegraph* which was where he was berthed when we first made contact through the distant and impersonal medium of the internet.

With his wife Beth he'd bought an isolated cottage two miles out of Wye down a dead-end lane that had once been the main horse track from the heights of the Downs into the village. He knew I lived in the area too, visited my *Sunday Times* column in the paper, grabbed the e-mail address there and then started nagging me about when he could get the broadband connection then denied to everyone on our local, tiny exchange, as it would be for the length of save-wye, to infuriating effect. I'd no idea why a complete stranger thought I was privy to the internal plans of BT when it came to the technical infrastructure of rural telephone exchanges and tried, politely, to tell him so. But Justin didn't take no for an answer. Every so often he'd e-mail me on the subject again, not that I was ever able to help. It did make me feel I was owed somewhat though, sufficiently, when save-wye was struggling to get someone, anyone to write articles, for me to dig out his address and despatch a message asking him for something for a change.

A few days later, after the Withersdane meeting, and a pretty anodyne report of the event on the web-site, we sat down for a beer in the Timber Batts, a remote and once dilapidated pub in the nearby hamlet of Bodsham that had become a very popular

French restaurant, evidence of a rural regeneration that needed no concordat and not a penny of public money. I'd never spoken directly to Justin before and it only took a second or two for me to realise he'd been Mailed through and through, and would stay that way for life.

As this story progressed I began to divide those on the village side into three categories: the Planners, the Plotters and the Frothers.

The Planners were those gathering together under the auspices of what would become the formal campaign organisation, Wye Future Group (WFG). They were decent people willing to put in extraordinary amounts of work, sometimes to no effect whatsoever, in order to oppose Imperial College and its backers through the system, by raising possible legal and planning challenges, and by sitting down in interminable meetings to engage with the consultation process set up and, to a large extent, controlled by the triumvirate. The Planners were good, honest citizens who believed in due process and democracy. A fair proportion, it seemed to me, would have welcomed a victory achieved through compromise, a watering down of whatever gruesome future Imperial had in mind to one that was not quite as bad. Mostly they felt this way because common sense indicated the majority of campaigns such as theirs ended in abject failure, and anything other than that could be counted a win. This was, in the circumstances, a very sensible and understandable position, and one for which I felt no sympathy whatsoever, for a very simple reason. What was going on, I was fast coming to believe, was something outside the normal democratic process, an unprecedented and extraordinary conspiracy that required an unprecedented and extraordinary response.

The Plotters had reached this conclusion too and replaced the slow, tedious process of building a campaign with a feverish network of rumours about 'what was really happening' and who knew what and when. Ian Cooling, who had once been on the payroll of Imperial College as a consultant, was the focus of much of their gossip, which was his own fault given that he'd been remarkably quiet in public since leading Ann Sutherland and John Hodder to eat bread pudding with the high and mighty. But everyone was fair game, including us, when the theorists started to pass round their latest Chinese whispers.

Some villagers were Plotters from the start. As the weeks and months passed, their ranks were joined by disaffected members who either got bored with WFG's tortuous bureaucracy and in-fighting or left altogether. One thing I soon learnt about the Plotter mentality was that words were often more important than deeds. Over the breadth of the campaign there would be any number of plans under discussion, most of which would, like the Future Group's internal e-mails, find their way, unwanted, into Justin's and my inbox minutes after they had been despatched. The Plotters, when they could agree among themselves, would create their own web-site, publishing the stories and, most im-portantly, the comments save-wye had spiked, usually on the grounds that they were libellous, not that this mattered to their infuriated authors who, since they were anonymous, would ensure we were the ones who'd get the writs. Later some were on the verge of launching their own organisation with the dark threat of 'direct action' on the horizon.

Nothing happened, of course, though Plotters were by no means without use to us at times. Two of those on the edges of everything were to become a crucial research and intelligence unit, our own secret squirrels burrowing to get information we didn't have the time or resources to chase ourselves. But if save-wye were to have any lasting influence it had to establish a repu-tation for facts and genuine disclosure, not gossip and pub chat-ter. Planners wouldn't give us this because, increasingly in those early days, they regarded save-wye with enormous suspicion. Plot-ters felt the same way.

Frothers, on the other hand, showed promise, if only because they needed, *craved* someone to listen to their complaints as they foamed at the mouth with genuine and heartfelt fury. Brendan Pierce, who'd grown up in Wye, attended Lady Joanna Thornhill as a short-trousered schoolboy, worked as a Metropolitan Police officer, eventually as a Royal bodyguard, then returned to the vil-lage in retirement, was a Frother *par excellence*. Like many resi-dents, he was quiet and ordinary on the surface, complex and interesting underneath. Brendan was always discreetly silent about his Royal connections, though willing to indulge an audi-ence with Sweeney-like tales of the Met in the 1970s when the occasion suited. The content depended entirely upon the audi-ence. One night my daughter, an English student and avid con-sumer of literature, came home from the New Flying Horse after an evening working behind the bar. Anything happened? I asked. Dead quiet, she said. Spent most of the time discussing Iris Murdoch at length with Brendan. Not that he had ever once let on to such tastes to his bloke pals.

The reason this former policeman was a Frother was because what was going on *offended* him, deeply, constantly, raising a red mist every time something reminded him of it. He was a local boy, one who wanted to retire in the place where he was born. He didn't expect it to be unchanged. He didn't expect it to be destroyed either, and he was smart enough to read between Imperial's lines and understand that was what was on the cards. This was justification enough. We'd have conversations where I'd explain some of the issues and how, when you bumped into people with doubts or possibly even intelligence to pass on, it was important to focus on detail, pressing councillors and those involved about specific issues and listening closely to what they said then trying to spot the holes. This, I tried to say, was better than descending into an argument, which was what they wanted, because then they could, as they soon did, wag a finger and say, quite without reason, 'Nimbies...'

Brendan would nod, taking in every point, full of good intentions. Inevitably I'd hear, a few days later, of some flare-up in the bar, often with Cooling around, one that ended with a heartfelt cry from Brendan along the lines of, 'How could you even think of it...?'

When next we met I'd go through the patient routine about focusing on detail again. Brendan would shake his head, look deeply guilty and say, 'I know, I know. I meant to. But it just makes me so bloody mad...'

A part of him, the old Met copper, told him there was a system for these things, and decent people on both sides were supposed to work through that. Another part told him that wasn't happening, for reasons none of us could understand, and that part, the frothing part, couldn't and wouldn't shut up in the face of obvious injustice. Frothing was a part of Brendan's personality, as it was of mine. But neither of us could froth like Justin, not in a million years. For him the Imperial saga was more than a travesty of the planning process. It was a personal insult, something he woke up swearing about in the morning, and cursed till he closed his eyes that night. Even without knowing a jot of Imperial's plans, Justin found himself utterly opposed to them, for the same reasons that fired up all good Frothers, like Brendan and, in his own quiet, detached way, Cliff in the New Flying Horse. Like me too, because hacks are invariably Frothers at heart. On top of everything Justin had been Mailed. He could froth for the nation, for the entire world, given the right subject. When I put this to Beth she objected that this facility had been there always, probably from birth. Surely he was different after the *Mail*, I objected. She thought about it then observed, 'In that his indignation became more organised and his rage better channelled, yes.'

And here was the perfect object for all that indignation and well-channelled fury: the concordat. Our councils had sat down with an institution that wanted to change the shape of Wye radically, and they had cut some kind of a deal, one worded so vaguely it was impossible to penetrate. Both Justin and I had covered planning issues in the past. We knew there was never meant to be an Iron Curtain between a developer and a local authority. The law was clear on this point. It was good for both sides to talk and settle problems before the time and expense of an application was entered into.

This was not what had happened here. Ashford and KCC had spoken at length with Imperial. Then they had signed a piece of paper saying that, whatever it was this distant London college wanted to do, it was A Good Thing. Without consulting the very people the plan would affect. Without, supposedly, even knowing the details themselves.

A fundamental element in all real journalism is curiosity. In truth, reporters are simply members of the public who are willing to ask the awkward, nosy questions that polite people shrink from. At save-wye we had no special rights whatsoever. Most of the organisations involved refused throughout to recognise us as news media at all. The only thing we could do was try to ask good questions, examine what answers we got, then go back and ask some more. That is the sum of the journalistic process, and here we had such huge and interesting questions, all of them going unanswered. When did these discussions begin? Who was involved? How can they be sufficiently advanced to enable David Brooks Wilson to quote financial estimates, but insufficiently developed for any of us to understand how much protected countryside might disappear when it all happens?

Talking to Justin I realised I'd found a kindred spirit. He saw the situation exactly as I did. Like all good hacks, his approach was essentially anarchic too. We didn't discuss 'roles', who was number one, who was number two. Nine months later, with the battle won, save-wye contained 281 articles and close to a thousand comments from readers, around 300,000 words or nearly three of my Roman crime novels. But I still didn't feel I was its editor, or that Justin was somehow a junior partner. Hierarchy and structure were irrelevant. All that mattered was the journalism, and the fact we were doing all this for free was astonishingly liberating. Our aim, not that I think we ever needed to articulate it at that moment, was to find out what lay behind this extraordinary thing called the concordat, to make those facts public, and hope they would allow people to reach better, more informed decisions about something which we all assumed was inevitable.

There really was no more to it than that. If anyone had suggested the whole plan would be dead before summer was out they would have been regarded as lunatics. Total victory was something no-one even dared think about in those bleak winter days. It was about staving off the full horrors of total defeat, and that was going to be hard enough.

Justin and I went away from that meeting determined to do what we could. Between those beers and the end of the month we posted nine articles, mainly opinion pieces, well argued, trying to set some kind of agenda for the facts we felt ought to be made public. It was good, solid stuff. The visitor statistics trickled into three figures. We felt isolated. The Future Group was coming together and still regarded us as upstarts. We didn't even live in Wye, did we? Someone, on the train into work, turned to Justin and asked if we might not be some kind of 'fifth columnists' really working on behalf of Imperial.

The problem was that we lacked what all journalism craved. Facts. Disclosure. Truth. You can only ask questions for so long. After a while you have to start providing answers.

By the end of the month the readership was trailing off again, and we were wondering how many more opinion pieces we could write alongside the trickle of minor news stories we were managing to assemble. After the brief burst of life Justin had introduced, save-wye was slipping back into lethargy again, with few readers, and not a new contributor in sight.

For the first twelve days of February we didn't publish a thing. Then, on the morning of the 13th I looked in my inbox and felt a sudden surge of excitement I hadn't experienced for twenty years.

I was looking at an exclusive. A scoop. The biggest there'd been since the stage-managed day this story broke in the *Kentish Express*. An astonishing development that would lift save-wye out of the doldrums and, for the time being, get everyone interested in Wye racing to read us as quickly as they could.

Someone had coughed up a hard fact, and what that told us about the concordat confirmed everything we'd suspected all along.

Finally, we were in business.

Spring: A Glimpse of Hope

The breakthrough

He said that there were no extant plans and pointed out that had Imperial come to the Wye people months ago, it would have caused even more confusion. He assured the audience that the College came straight to them immediately after a main Board meeting at the College, and as soon as the (non-binding) concordat was signed.
Official report of remarks by David Brooks Wilson, Director of Estates, Imperial College. Withersdane, Wye public meeting, January 9th, 2006

...the truth is that Imperial – at our suggestion – brought their thinking into the public domain at the earliest possible opportunity.
Paul Clokie, leader of Ashford Borough Council, March 23rd, 2006

I wasn't the only one new to the Freedom of Information Act. Kent County Council, like all other public bodies, only found themselves legally compelled to deal with information requests from the public from January 1st, 2005. Their FoI team was just a year old when I put in that exploratory request after sitting out the Withersdane meeting and chatting to Cliff instead. As the months wore on, and we bombarded public bodies up and down the country with FoI requests about Wye, we noticed a steady tightening up of the flow of documents from this source, using the standard get-out clause that to release the information we wanted would 'inhibit free discussion' between the parties involved. Very soon it became pointless putting in requests to the triumvirate of Imperial, KCC and ABC because they would be routinely kicked into touch. Given that an appeal to the Information Commissioner might take eighteen months, that effectively amounted to a total rejection.

But this wasn't the case that happy month of February. For whatever reason, and it's difficult to put it down to anything else but inexperience, KCC briefly felt a little talkative about the concordat's past, until Imperial came in and ordered them to shut up. By that time something Richard Sykes and his team had hoped to keep quiet was out and loose in public view. This revelation was a beauty, and would establish save-wye in a way we could never have achieved with a series of biting opinion pieces.

The secret this first KCC release revealed was astonishing. In spite of what David Brooks Wilson said on the night of January 9th, and Paul Clokie reiterated two months later, the college had not come straight to the village as soon as the concordat was signed at all. They and their council cohorts had waited nearly nine months because there were, in reality, *two* concordats, the public one, witnessed by Ann Sutherland and John Hodder, and a secret, more far-reaching one, that had been agreed and signed the previous spring.

KCC's FoI response detailed everything. How the then council leader Sir Sandy Bruce-Lockhart had first met Richard Sykes to discuss Wye's future in November 2004, thirteen months before that show signing in the Old Hall. How some of the key players in the race to develop Wye had assembled soon after: David Brooks Wilson and his assistant Nigel Buck meeting with Pete Raine, KCC's strategic planner, and David Hill, chief executive of Ashford, in the early part of 2005, prompting Imperial to appoint the international consultancy Ernst & Young to 'lead investigations into potential infrastructure costs and funding opportunities and to suggest how the concordat should be worded'.

Bruce-Lockhart and Paul Clokie of ABC signed the first, secret concordat on April 29th, 2005, after hearing Imperial warn that, without their active support, the supposed science park scheme could 'go abroad', spelling the end of academic activity in Wye altogether. Sykes, for reasons that have never been explained, didn't get around to putting his initials on the document until May 19th. After Bruce-Lockhart departed KCC en route to the House of Lords the new county leader Paul Carter took his place and the team nailed down the final timetable for the revelation of the plan in public at the end of the year.

I headlined the story, 'Signed and Sealed... nine months before you knew' and it put us on the map. Hundreds of visitors flocked to the site over the ensuing days. We were, in our own eyes, on a roll. The only place you could read this story, and the official FoI release on which it was based, published in full, was on save-wye. The *Kentish Express*, naturally, thought such a revelation was of no importance to its readers. But its independent rival, *Kent on Sunday*, saw things differently. It followed up on our story and gave us a credit. It got a quote from David Hill too, which was more than we could manage. He told the paper, 'We believe the report's chronology is broadly correct... The concordat launched a vision, not a plan.'

Hill never revealed why there had been two concordats, not one, or why preliminary talks about a property development needed such an unusual, if not unique, written agreement between the developer and the authorities who were supposed to be impartial in such matters. ABC was rattled by this unexpected revelation from its larger counterpart. Imperial was utterly livid. Soon all three groups would be co-ordinating every subsequent FoI request they received to make sure there were no more unfortunate surprises. Before the month was out we would feel the effects of that decision.

But KCC's brief show of frankness lifted our spirits just at the moment when we were both wondering whether it was worth continuing. Justin was positively seething that all this had been hidden from the public, and carved up among a bunch of people who were supposedly our representatives. He was even more outraged when, at the beginning of March, KCC coughed up more documents as a result of our original request and we finally managed to get hold of a copy of that first concordat, the 'real' one in our view. It went a lot further than the anodyne PR stunt Ann Sutherland had watched while Charles Findlay munched on bread pudding.

Justin handled this story and pointed out the differences in a way that no-one in Wye could miss. He wrote...

It is similar in outline to the version released to the public in December but differs in several important respects:

• The first is far more enthusiastic on the part of the local authorities, committing them to regular meetings and putting their 'personal and organisational support to this exciting plan'.

• The 'concordat' signed in April and May commits the parties to secrecy saying that 'the sensitivity of the proposals is well recognised and we will maintain the confidentiality of issues raised and discussed at all times'.

• In the April and May agreement, KCC and Ashford council go further down the road in agreeing to large-scale housing development. The document states: 'The parties to this concordat will work together to secure external funding recognising that the total costs of Phase 1 will be circa £300 million. Imperial College will need to sell part of its estate in Wye to fund any "gap" and the Local Authorities understand this fact'.

• Further proof, if any were needed, that the local authorities were willing to act as unpaid PR consultants for Imperial. 'We will agree as part of our action plan a communications strategy for all stakeholders including Central Government'.

Everyone had been grumbling about conspiracy theories, and aware, too, that this was a dead-end path without evidence to substantiate them. The consensus, which we were to later prove was incorrect, was that Imperial had only entered into negotiations to take over the old agricultural college in 1998, concluding them two years later, because of the development potential of the estate. Another theory, which was to prove equally fallacious, was that the initial collapse in the student numbers after the take-over was deliberately engineered to bring on a financial crisis that demanded radical change. In fact, it was largely due to a huge administrative error that demolished a single year's intake of undergraduates. When the Sykes regime took over the helm of Imperial during 2001 it found Wye stumbling already, and did nothing to correct the drift. But a conspiracy from the outset... no.

Two concordats, though, one public and vague, the first secret, signed almost nine months earlier, and full of dark words about the sell-off of land to raise money, told a different story altogether. To the village this was tantamount to proof the triumvirate had been working on a covert plan to stitch up everything in advance, then roll out some quick, meaningless form of local 'consultation' before bringing in the builders. There seemed no other explanation. There *was* no other explanation. On David Brooks Wilson's initial timetable work on the project would begin in 2006, twelve months after the whole idea was made public. He could only have penned a start date like that if he felt confident everything would swim through the planning process without serious obstacles.

KCC then did something else quite extraordinary. On February 27th, their FoI team sent me a list of new documents which would, they said, complete everything they were willing to disclose about Wye and Imperial in response to my request. Their FoI officer agreed all these documents would be sent by e-mail. They never turned up. I nagged. And nagged. After a week of excuses – the computer's down, they're too large, the right person's not here – I got a message saying they had been posted on KCC's own web-site, in a rather obscure location. I looked, finally found them, and checked them off against the list of documents I'd been told by the council they intended to release a week before.

Most of the material, including the first concordat, was there. But the list was different and it took me a while to work out why, and even longer to get an explanation of what had occurred. On February 27th, KCC had been willing to let me see thirty four documents. The following week, according to a new schedule, which carried exactly the same name, perhaps in the hope I'd never notice, this had been reduced to thirty two. Naturally, the two that were missing were the most important ones of all.

At the beginning of February we got a huge boost from scooping everyone with something the council had decided to disclose to us under the FoI, the existence of the first, secret concordat. A little less than a month later we had our second major exclusive based on what they were trying to stop us, and the public, seeing, even though only the week before they'd said it was fit to be released.

It was the easiest thing in the world to compare the original list with the second and see which two documents were missing. The first had been produced by GeraldEve, the property consultants the college brought in to help draw up the masterplan for Wye. All we knew of it now was its title from the first schedule of documents we were supposed to received. That was enough: 'GeraldEve Draft 23/1/06 31 page briefing note considering the key policy criteria and issues which we must satisfy to justify development in the AONB for the research and commercial enterprise (also dated 20th January 2006)'.

Thirty one pages of guidance on how the triumvirate would try to get round the problems of building in an Area of Outstanding Natural Beauty. It was no surprise they didn't want us to know this document existed or, as we later learned, that Imperial had furiously demanded KCC withdraw it from the release list, even though the council's own officers had marked it for publication.

The second item which had been snatched from our hands by Imperial, just as KCC were on the point of passing it over, was called, 'Ernst & Young document – 4 sided A4 User Guide entitled Project Alchemy QuickPlace'. A search on Google quickly established what 'QuickPlace' was: a big company corporate information system from IBM used by Ernst & Young to manage large development projects among diverse teams or, in this case, different organisations. And Project Alchemy? There I must confess to hazarding a guess and publishing it as fact, for the first time since save-wye came into being.

Project Alchemy, we surmised, was the code-name used for the Wye scheme from its inception and, as it turned out, synonymous with the team of officers and council members, all of them signatories to the concordats or paid high-level consultants to Imperial, who had been meeting for more than a year to get the development's initial phase off the ground.

The story had everything any hack would pray for: secret code-names, the shredding of information which KCC itself had earlier said the public could read, and clear evidence of a long and concerted organisational process leading up to the December announcement. We went live on March 7th, after I'd spent days screaming at KCC to give me the files they had originally promised, all in vain. It was headlined, '"Project Alchemy": the story you may never read'.

That had a *Daily Mail* ring to it I thought, feeling a bit proud of what we'd achieved.

This all helped with the nagging question, too, the big one, the conundrum which, if only we could answer it, would surely unlock the answer to everything. How could these people have gone to such lengths, employing expensive, international consultants, spending more than a year in secret meetings as the Project Alchemy team, and still insist this was all 'just a vision not a plan'? It didn't add up. Something more concrete than vague aspirations and talk about 'sustainable regeneration' surely existed. Otherwise what had they been talking about all that time? The weather?

We needed to get nearer to that secret. We needed, too, both to extend and focus our coverage. The story no longer concerned a little local fuss over a development project. It went to the heart of bigger issues, the state of democracy in Kent, the transformation of a renowned scientific college into a grasping, highly aggressive, neo-corporate institution, and the defence of the status of an Area of Outstanding Natural Beauty – throughout England, not just in Wye – against rampant greed backed by the connivance of two important local authorities.

I don't recall ever discussing this with Justin. Shifting the nature of our coverage simply seemed to be a natural progression, one so obvious we just went ahead and did it. We did something else too, and whether it was his background or mine I don't know but, again, it was so entirely logical and, in journalistic terms, so entirely defensible I never gave it a second thought. This was a big story, in local terms the biggest ever. It was only right that we should personalise it, making the individuals involved part of the issue too, just as much as the institutions they represented.

Political coverage was about people as well as policy. This was no different. We had a duty to bring the individuals behind Project Alchemy out into public view, making them visible and responsible for the actions. Richard Sykes, Borys and David Brooks Wilson, along with their council henchmen, were embarked upon an attempt to transform – we would say 'destroy' – an entire community. The public had a right to know who these men were, why they thought they had the right to inflict such uncertainty upon a peaceful rural village, and how they had come to be in such positions of power in the first place.

These two stories changed the nature of the site. We were still maintaining the line that save-wye was a vehicle for information and opinion, open to everyone, even those who supported Imperial, if we could find them. Had Borys or Sykes wanted to write an article explaining their position I would happily have carried it. Instead, they pretended we didn't even exist, which was ludicrous.

But to the public we were becoming part of the campaign all the same. For some, those who hadn't liked the look of the interminable meetings and the middle class make-up of Wye Future Group – which Ian Cooling had labelled cruelly, though not inaccurately, the 'Oxenturn road dinner party set' after the area where many of the members lived – we were starting to look like *the* campaign, and that made us feel very uncomfortable indeed.

These two very visible successes, which were followed up in *Kent on Sunday*, with credit for the source, were to cause problems we didn't foresee. Though we scarcely knew it, and weren't, in truth, much interested, the 'proper' opposition, the formal campaign organisation was still stumbling into being, troubled by internal dissension, silent outside its own ranks, almost invisible in the village that so badly needed it.

A campaign takes shape

Sod the theories. To a simple mind like mine, whilst too many well intentioned folk sit on their committees and do bugger all, the time for pitchforks and burning barricades draws ever closer.
Cliff Whitbourn, comment, March 23rd at 6:47 pm

Wye Future Group's inaugural meeting took place at the Village Hall on February 1st, chaired by John Hodder of the parish council who stood aside to attend later meetings as an observer. The organisation's new chairman, by common consent, was to be Ben Moorhead, an amiable, bright London lawyer who, like me, lived outside the village, near Bodsham, but, unlike me, had an extraordinary patience with the tedium of trying to hold together a sprawling organisation that encompassed many individuals and opinions. Moorhead had made a speech at the January 9th meeting, a great one that won him many admirers. At heart he was a Frother, but an innate sense of decency guided him towards the traditional path of campaigning, which turned him into a dedicated and enthusiastic Planner who would work tirelessly alongside many similarly devoted WFG members over the coming months. This was not going to be easy.

In his typically sensible and perspicacious way, John Hodder had referred obliquely to the problems such organisations can face when he issued the letter inviting villagers to get together to take part in the new group. The aim, he said, was to establish a pool of people to help, on a purely voluntary basis, in dealing with the challenge from Imperial. This pool would be 'headed and managed by a small group of people (Wye Future Group), separate from, but including, some members of the Parish Council'.

I knew nothing about military campaigns but a gut sense told me it was best to have one general, a handful of commanders in the field, and a good army of loyal, committed troops. Hodder, it seemed to me, was suggesting much the same. What the Future Group became in reality was a militia of minor lieutenants, drawn together under Moorhead's kindly but, in the eyes of some, indulgent leadership, a noisy gathering of voices out of which it was difficult at times to distinguish a single, clear message.

It was also, from an early age, throttled by bureaucracy and an obsession with endless, frequently tedious meetings. By the end of February the membership had risen to somewhere in the region of seventy, mostly professional men and women. They had been divided into three groups labelled, with the same insane logic that, surely, had led Imperial to code-name its plan 'Project Alchemy', Orange, Green and Indigo. Orange was responsible for 'fund-raising, support and community'. Green took control of 'planning, infrastructure and environment'. Indigo, which was to prove the most quarrelsome of the lot, was in charge of 'communications, PR and politics'.

Justin and I knew all this almost from the start because it took scarcely the blink of an eye for arguments to rise within the organisation and supposedly confidential e-mails to start flying to us and other parties the moment they were issued from the WFG bunker. We just junked them. We wished WFG well but, as we kept emphasising, save-wye wasn't a campaign, just a news and opinion service. When they got around to having some news and opinions we'd happily publish them. Unfortunately they never turned up. The group, at this stage, was a bunch of hard-working, well-meaning people who were essentially looking inwards trying to make sense of what to do next. It was responsible for some important efforts on behalf of the village, managing to scare Ashford Borough Council in particular with threats of legal action and other complaints that Paul Clokie took seriously and personally. But as a campaign it was terrible at communicating internally and, more importantly, externally, to the community and the world at large.

It was also determined to pursue the case through established means of argument, discussion and consultation. One of Moorhead's early acts was to have lunch with Cooling at the latter's club in London, reporting back to members that their borough councillor was 'on side', a comment made remarkable by the fact that it had to be issued in the first place. This was the tone almost from the outset, one of civilised middle class English protest. No-one ever issued an edict that ordinary working class villagers or retirees were unwelcome in its ranks. Some of them made it there. Still, there was a feeling in some quarters that this was a bunch of professionals, of 'toffs' who 'thought they knew best', and Cooling's jibe about the Oxenturn Road dinner clique certainly hit home.

The poor souls who had volunteered for Indigo, Green and Orange also found themselves inundated with a bewildering mountain of material to try to absorb. Reports covered everything. There were discussions of Indigo's publicity posters in Ann Sutherland's shop, Ticketyboo, and 'Rex's window', a pane of glass on a private house in Church Street. Members also received frequent detailed and highly technical papers on the intricacies of AONB legislation from Diana Pound, a professional in the planning business who was one of the more vocal members of Green. From the outside this seemed to be a wailing sea of white noise, and talking to people on the inside it was clear it often appeared to be that way to them too.

My concern was their web-site. They had none. This was the responsibility of Tatiana Cant and Kamal Sayany who ran a small computer business in the village and had put together wye.org, the 'village web-site', though it was actually a private business for which donations were solicited in return for adverts from time to time.

Tatiana had once lived near Justin and expressed an interest in journalism. He and Beth had lent her a few books on the trade. Not long after she got the pin money job of village correspondent for the *Kentish Express*. Tatiana had no real clue about how journalism worked. Why should she? She'd never been through the mill of years of training that had been mandatory for people like Justin and me. But that didn't stop her becoming the Future Group's supreme spin doctor, with Kamal working as the 'technical genius' at her side.

This still didn't get the organisation a web-site, only a mention in a section on wye.org which I found hard to read and difficult to understand. Kantara, Tatiana and Kamal's company, used old web design software that was ponderous to update. Every new story they published took ages to produce, since it demanded a new design for the page. We, on the other hand, had deliberately gone with a blog system which formatted articles automatically. That meant we could get up new material in a matter of minutes. It was simply a question of writing the words, inserting any graphics, then hitting publish. There was no other way we could work. Readers would only come back if fresh articles appeared regularly. Wordpress let us publish pieces the moment they were written. We were using an automatic weapon that we could reload and fire again in minutes. Even if we missed the target – and we did – the immediacy still made a lot of noise. Kantara, and by association the Future Group, were lumbered with an ancient blunderbuss that needed endless coaxing and stoking in order to let loose a single shot, then a long rest afterwards. It was no way to reach the public.

I quietly contacted a friend in the group and made a suggestion: they could have a free web-site of their own, based on Wordpress, like save-wye, which I would host at my expense, though it would be theirs to run as they saw fit. I also offered to set up a smaller, open source version of Imperial's Project Quick-Place system so that people could communicate easily through a single, secure web-site instead of having to wade through a sea of repetitive e-mails. Both approaches went nowhere. Unknown to me, we had mortally offended Tatiana and Kamal by setting up save-wye in the first place, and would never, in their eyes, be able to make up for such impertinence.

The return suggestion from one group member was that we hand over save-wye to them and run it ourselves 'under the guidance of Tatiana'. I was briefly attracted to this notion if only to see the effect it would have on Justin. By its nature Wye was a voluble, quarrelsome place at times, with more than its fair share of quietly bubbling feuds and vendettas. Even without the stress of the concordat on our doorstep, it sometimes resembled a death-free episode of *Midsomer Murders*, and I calculated that handing over our now burgeoning site to Tatiana and Kamal could probably get us to real blood in no time flat. Nevertheless, I politely declined.

Tatiana's loathing of save-wye extended to refusing to let us have anything that the Future Group produced, even the rare press releases, though we were by now the single most popular place anyone went to in order to read about Imperial and Wye. Kamal's antipathy was made clear when, as the man running the private e-mail network for the the busy membership, an unnecessarily complex system which eventually fell over completely, he ordered save-wye's name be excised from all future e-mails. We were the primary information source on the subject for which their organisation was created and we were now unmentionable.

Their view of what did make for good media relations was revealed in an enthusiastic round robin sent by Tatiana to WFG members, 'the first of many reports on WFG press activity', she believed, which turned out to be credulous in the extreme.

From "Tatiana Cant", February 14, 2006 10:23 PM
Listen up! An interview with Ben was pre-recorded today by KMFM who will be running bulletins tomorrow (Wed 15th Feb) on the morning news bulletins – 'on the hour every hour' with lengthier coverage on the 1pm and 6pm slots.

The frequency is FM 107.6. Orange – could you arrange for some-one to record these broadcasts please. If you could decide who's doing it and then let me know, that would be great.

BBC Radio Kent is waiting to see developments on this issue before running with the story. The system seems to be working well and we will reach out to TV and national media as soon as we're ready. A word of caution, please remember that a consistent message is vital. We have now established clear lines of communication with the press which they, and we, need to respect. If you want to get a message out to the press, please come via the WFG press office (grand name for Kevin and me) in Indigo. Equally, if you're approached by the press, don't allow yourself to be drawn into making comments on behalf of the WFG – just send them to us – we'll field them in the right direction – possibly straight back to you!

It was a measure of the popularity of KMFM – owned, naturally, by Edwin Boorman's Kent Messenger group – that recipients of this e-mail had to be told where to find it on the dial. BBC Radio Kent, which took little interest in Wye throughout, was widely known to have a reliable audience of three pensioners in Chatham and a goat. And the goat was probably there under duress. Being turned down by them was like having the hirsute wallflower at the village hop reject your offer of a dance. I'd refused to appear on the station since 2003 when a planned live interview they – not me – wanted to do on the appearance of my latest novel, a crime story with the word 'dead' in the title, was cancelled at the last minute because the station manager thought its use might upset people during the middle of the Iraq war. Cutting edge broadcasting it wasn't. In public relations terms sucking up to stations like these was on a par with singing loudly in the bath and hoping some distant neighbour might hear.

The tragedy was Tatiana and Kamal simply didn't know. They didn't get it. Not any of it. When we broke the two big FoI stories that month, instead of welcoming some actual news and revelations which the Future Group were to use to their advantage later, she began to pontificate about how we screwed up the story. At an Indigo meeting shortly afterwards she told them, as if this were fact, that KCC might have sent out the rest of the documents if only we'd held back, waited and been nicer to them. The truth was I'd spent four days arguing with KCC trying to change minds, even though I knew that it was hopeless. FoI decisions were not made on the basis of how politely the people asking for the information had been. They were confined to a strict interpretation of the act and, since KCC had received a rocket from Imperial for letting out news of the first, secret concordat, a determination to keep the lid down on information as much as possible.

Tatiana was also incensed by a profile we had run of Richard Sykes as part of our process of personalising the story. The piece was headed 'Arise Sir Richard, Emperor of Imperial', and illustrated with a graphic which superimposed Sykes' head on a famous portrait of Mao triumphant over the masses. It was standard journalistic stuff, quite mild compared to some of the things we were to produce later. Given the size of Sykes's ego and what we knew of his ruthless management techniques, it was scarcely *Private Eye*. I'd done much more hard-edged stuff on *The Times* back in the 1980s. But it wasn't for Tatiana. What we did was 'insulting'. It was wrong to attack 'personalities'.

There was also the question of attitude. The control freakery and desperate emphasis on the need for 'respect' on both sides might have come straight out of some *Dummy's Guide to Public Relations* penned by Alastair Campbell over a rainy weekend when there was no good footie on the telly. No-one wanted to talk to the Future Group, let alone listen. In circumstances like those, the organisation needed to cultivate contacts, develop stories, and establish lines of communication with journalists who were too busy to waste time listening to the minutiae of policy or gripes that sounded deeply Nimby in nature on occasion. We offered to help with a few tips but no-one returned the call.

To be candid, we didn't really care. By mid-March Wye Future Group had been around for six weeks, enough time we felt to make an impact. They hadn't, and most of what we heard on the grapevine was criticism. The organisation that had been formed to defend Wye against Imperial's marauders was still mired in its own bureaucracy, struggling over such things as a lengthy and detailed constitution instead of speaking to a village that desperately wanted to hear what it had to offer. In spite of all the hard work and endless meetings, it was a classic case study in how good intentions can so easily go astray.

We didn't write about any of these tensions, though there was an increasing number of people who felt they ought to be brought to the notice of the village at large. This idea made us nervous. We didn't want to be seen criticising a group of hard-working people whose hearts were very much in the right place. Besides, there were bigger issues to tackle. Out of the blue, one popped up at the beginning of that month very soon after we published the second FoI story on how Imperial had killed the release of the documents KCC had promised us.

Ian Cooling, up till then as much the silent man of Wye politics as his counterpart Charles Findlay, was about to make his position clear. To my utter astonishment he didn't just want to use save-wye to do that, but to come on board as a regular contributor too as part of our philosophy of a friendly free exchange of ideas and opinions. Now, it seemed we were three.

I noticed a certain darkness in Justin's eyes when this became apparent. I was overjoyed. This was exactly what I'd wanted, a nice, open, liberal-minded forum on the web where we might debate the great village issues of the day.

In the end it damned near finished us for good.

Getting personal

By the beginning of March we were starting to find our rhythm. It was time to branch out and move the story beyond planning issues and unanswerable questions about the early, secret days of what was now becoming officially known as 'Wye Park', since both 'Project Alchemy', the working title, and the term 'concordat' were starting to have unfortunate connotations for the locals.

What we needed now was someone who could be made to personify the project, becoming a figurehead for everything it represented. Imperial provided us with the perfect character in the form of the man who was to be the college's primary link with the village, deputed to be its public face in so-called consultation with the parish council and the Future Group while, at the same time, deeply engaged in secretive meetings with ABC and KCC, as he had been since the early days.

He was the estates director, David Brooks Wilson. A double-barrelled name raises eyebrows with any half-decent hack, particularly after we discovered that he only gained the 'Brooks' part when he joined Imperial in 2002. The man was a gift to us, and his influence was, as we discovered later, far greater than we initially appreciated. He was also a very busy individual, widely known on the power network of Kent in ways which left a very useful audit trail of his past through Google which I and, in the future, our two home-grown intelligence agents could pick up and develop repeatedly.

Targeting Brooks Wilson worked wonderfully because, from the very outset, he had clearly been a key player in the battle to develop Wye. Indeed it was probably his past experience of the area that got him the job in the first place. While he may have been occupying an office in London at the time the concordats were being secretly negotiated, managing the college's extensive property holdings with a brief to 'realise the value of the portfolio' when necessary, Brooks Wilson knew the Ashford area intimately, in a way that simply didn't fit with someone whose primary brief appeared to be the management of the substantial property holdings of a large London academic institution. A glance at his CV showed very clearly that, had Richard Sykes been seeking the right man to develop Wye, it would have been difficult to think of someone better suited for the job.

Brooks Wilson had been a senior executive of the property arm of Eurotunnel, the company that built the Channel Tunnel and owned and developed, under his control, huge areas of commercial and industrial land around Ashford where he had been based and was, in some circles, very well known.

Before the Channel Tunnel project arrived, Ashford had been a sleepy, rundown town in an area with some of the highest unemployment in Kent. The Tunnel had not generated the economic rewards to the area many had predicted, but the size of the development brought Ashford to national attention, and would one day help persuade John Prescott that it deserved to be named among his list of top towns for rapid growth in the first three decades of the 21st century. Brooks Wilson had been instrumental in the growth of Ashford from dilapidated former railway town into the sprawling, ugly, uncertain community that it became during the 1990s. On the way he met, and managed to cultivate, many of the most important people in the county, in councils, quangos and professional bodies.

This was a man who had spent more than a decade trying to turn worthless agricultural land around the rail line in Ashford into hard cash. It hadn't been wonderfully successful. Many of the estates that Brooks Wilson had developed still had large vacant plots which could easily have been used for the research facilities which Imperial supposedly wanted to develop. But that would not have enabled the college to argue for the release to commercial housing of its valuable protected green fields in Wye, more than eight hundred acres of them. Brooks Wilson must have seemed ideally placed to deliver what Sykes wanted.

Through his connections, too, he moved in the same circles as many of those who had come together under the umbrella of Project Alchemy. We spent many long hours searching minutes and membership lists, finding information that went a long way towards suggesting an answer to the question: how did this whole project begin?

On Saturday, March 11th, we placed Brooks Wilson's name in the frame as a man who could certainly tell us. After the style of *Private Eye* we would frequently refer to the man from this point forward as 'the very interesting Mr David Brooks Wilson', in recognition of his intriguing past and multiple connections with the people who mattered in Kent.

The Very Interesting Mr David Brooks Wilson
Saturday, March 11th, 2006 in Profile by David Hewson

There are many unsolved puzzles surrounding the hazy inception of the Wye Concordat, and few people willing to put their head above the parapet to bring some clarity to this foggy tale. Funnily enough, some of those who know more than any about this story have little public profile at all, though behind the scenes they appear to wield very considerable power.

Take Mr David Brooks Wilson, for example, who goes under the modest title of 'director of estates' for Imperial College. Most of us would think that someone with that kind of job description is essentially some sort of property manager. Not the bloke to phone when you see a fence has blown down exactly, but the one who gets the bill after it's fixed. And there you would be very wrong indeed, for Mr Brooks Wilson is a powerful and key figure in this whole story, as you can guess from the way he tends to get copied into virtually every important e-mail from the local authorities involved.

Who is this man? You can find a hagiographic profile of him in the Imperial College online magazine. We also reproduce (elsewhere) the biography produced in 2002 when he was elected vice chairman of the South East England Regional Planning Committee (a position he no longer holds).

Mr Brooks Wilson is certainly above phoning builders these days. He's there, so Imperial's own publication states clearly, to get value out of the college's considerable property portfolio which, after the take-over of Wye College, now includes 800 acres of unspoilt Kent countryside. Let me quote from the article...

> For the last few years, his challenge has been to consider the transformation of £1.25bn (reinstatement value) of College estate stretching 550,000 square metres – the equivalent of 3.5 Canary Wharf towers.
>
> 'I try to walk around College sites each month,' he says. 'There are still little corners I've not seen. I've had two years to understand where everything is, how it really operates, how it ticks.'

He seems very well qualified too. Before joining Imperial, Mr Brooks Wilson was property service director for Eurotunnel during its formative years, then managing director of its property subsidiary, Eurotunnel Developments. He must surely know a lot more about land, and its value, in the Ashford area than you'd expect from someone in a job based in London, and, from the outside, somewhat administrative in nature.

We must also add to those talents an extraordinarily broad range of interests for someone whose business card looks like that of a university administrator. That 2002 bio lists a seat on the south east region of the CBI, membership of the London and South East Regional Industrial Development Board, and chairmanship of the Kent Developers Group, 'an informal group of the managing directors of the major developers in Kent', not that one would have expected Imperial to fall into that category, at least back then. Plus he was a director of Locate in Kent and the 'Euroregion Round Table' consisting of 'business and political leaders from France, Belgium and Kent'.

He is, or has been, a Freeman of the City of London, a Liveryman of the Worshipful Company of Gardeners, a Fellow of the Institute of Treasurers, a Fellow of the Institute of Chartered Secretaries and Administrators and a Fellow of the Chartered British Institute of Management. As if all that wasn't enough, that 2002 bio describes Mr Brooks Wilson as chairman and CEO of his own company, Noble Wilson Ltd, a 'transaction based property and real estate advisory company' based in the City of London, with offices in Hong Kong and Seoul. It makes you wonder where he finds the time to turn up to the office in Imperial.

Where did this chap learn his skills and acquire such prodigious energy? Let's go back to the Imperial profile...

His vision could partly be due to what he learned about business from four mentors – former bosses Sir Nigel Broackes, chairman of Trafalgar House Investments plc, Geoffrey Sterling, former chairman of Bovis plc and P&O plc, John Ritblat of the British Land Company Ltd and Sir Alistair Morton, Co-Chairman of Eurotunnel.

'Sir Nigel Broackes was very instrumental in moulding my career, suggesting I follow the course of training to be a chartered secretary or company secretary for a plc company which involved my spending a day a week in each department of the organisation over five years.

'Geoffrey Sterling, now Lord Sterling of Plaistow's attitude to takeovers and acquisitions, was very, very instructive and enabled me to put together the entrepreneurial instincts I had learned with Nigel Broackes and use them as a springboard into my longer stay at British Land, where I worked very closely with John Ritblat.

'He probably taught me most of what I know in terms of property trading, property negotiation and property financing. Alistair taught me nothing was impossible.'

Now there's an interesting cast list of influences, one which includes some of the biggest property names to prosper, sometimes controversially, during the Thatcher era. The late Sir Nigel Broackes was the boss of Trafalgar House, the property and shipping conglomerate that, at one time, owned the Daily Express. Geoffrey, now Lord, Sterling ran P&O until last year. I met the late Sir Alastair Morton (and that is Alastair, by the way, not Alistair, as Imperial have it) when I was a business journalist 25 years ago; he was a likeable, irascible character, with a slightly bonkers side on occasion. Sir John Ritblat continues to chair British Land, which includes the gigantic Broadgate estate near Liverpool Street in its portfolio, and has also stirred quite a furore with its plan for the tallest office block in London at 122 Leadenhall Street.

How have the corporations run by Mr Brooks Wilson's 'mentors' fared over the years? Like this…

• P&O, after 168 years under British ownership, has just been taken over by the Dubai-based DP World.

• Eurotunnel has lurched from crisis to crisis and last year lost £87 million. In February 2006 it warned that it may not survive due to its current debts of £6.4 billion.

• After a few sticky years Trafalgar House was taken over by the Norwegian company Kvaerner in 1996.

• British Land is doing very nicely indeed, thank you, and sent shares throughout the UK property sector soaring last month when it unveiled pre-tax profits of £1.4 billion for the first nine months of its financial year.

Noble Wilson Ltd has some way to go to catch up with any of them. You can find the latest set of accounts for the company below (with Mr Brooks Wilson's address as director given as Imperial College). According to that 2002 bio, remember, Noble Wilson Ltd is 'a transaction based property and real estate advisory company, it specialises in property development, property management and the creation of inward investment. It is based in the City of London and has offices in Hong Kong and Seoul and advises companies on property matters in Europe, United States of America and Asia.'

The accounts reveal that at the end of 2004 the company had no profits, no fixed or tangible assets, some £5,000 in current assets, £3,000 in cash, and current liabilities of £11,000. With all the other bits and pieces that adds up, say the auditors, to a negative net worth of £5,402.

A few weeks later, on April Fools' Day, I put together a spoof story of 'revelations' about a report detailing the future of Wye. They included a supposedly leaked mock-up of the final development, which was actually a shot from a Lego brochure depicting a fake city, a doctored photo of the second concordat signing masquerading as a shot of the first, secret event, but with Michael Jackson, Mr Bean and Darth Vader in attendance, and a scene of the church with an amphibious vehicle negotiating the river that now ran along what used to be Churchfield Way.

I photoshopped an evil-looking bird onto the lamp post near the bus stop and described it thus...

Among the new species expected to prosper in these changed times is the obscure and vaguely sinister Brooks Wilson Vulture (Avarishus Avarishus) which can be seen on the lamp post here. This bird, which survives on nothing but carrion scavenged from any source it can find, has already been spotted in the Wye area on several occasions. Keen observers of alien breeds remain on sharp lookout for its return, since it is thought to be a threat to indigenous species, in particular the endangered 'East Kent Farmer' (Iratus Bucolicus) which has lived largely undisturbed, and genetically unaltered, in this habitat for centuries.

Brooks Wilson had already been out and about in the village for some weeks. His gleaming Jaguar XK150, with a Panama hat on the back seat, which Ian Cooling must surely have drooled over, was always evidence of his presence, provoking suspicion and puzzlement among most of those he met. From the gleeful com-ments that came in after that story appeared I knew we had our *bête noire* for the duration of the campaign to come.

A councillor calls

On March 22nd I announced we had a new contributor. I'd been trying to get politicians and local councillors to write for save-wye from the outset. All I'd managed was an anodyne few paragraphs from the Ashford Tory MP Damian Green, a man who managed to stay on the touchlines of the Imperial project throughout. Everyone had rebuffed me pretty much, apart from Peter Davison, the leader of Ashford Council's Independents, who earlier in March had uttered the first sustained public display of dissatisfaction with their secret deal.

Davison was an interesting man, a former Tory who had still been in the Conservative group when Paul Clokie arrived from Kingston to be raised to the leadership of Ashford Council's Tories soon after. For a time Davison had been groomed as a potential deputy to Clokie. But the two never got on, and soon after Davison quit to stand as an independent, though he would never elaborate in public on why he had decided he could no longer work alongside the new man who had come in as leader. At heart he was a natural Conservative; after a short time under Clokie's leadership he became convinced there was no role for party politics in local government.

On March 20th we published his comments about the concordat. He told us, '...ABC councillors should be fully informed by the leader of the council at all times. As it is we had to read about the announcement in the press and ever since we have had to play an unsavoury game of chasing him for information which he has been reluctant to provide or has just refused to do so. Unless, of course he is ignorant himself. This is all simple stuff about the breakdown of democracy in Ashford.'

The political bodies of the area were dominated by Conservative members, so any dissent within the ruling wing would never be heard in public. Oddly, though, the few independent, Labour and Lib Dem representatives on Ashford Council rarely raised a controversial word on anything. For Davison to speak out so frankly and with such apparent heat was unknown, and Clokie was determined to make him pay for such impudence. From this point on, any utterance by him on Wye Park was met with threats of being reported to the Local Government Standards Board or accusations of 'playing politics'. I was astonished. This was a big local issue. It was incredible to think that councillors would be threatened if they dared to mention it in public, but that was, indeed the case. Strangely, Paul Clokie never felt he was breaking any rules by supporting Imperial on every possible occasion.

In March, this silence from our elected representatives was to be broken. Ian Cooling contacted me and said he wanted to take part as a regular contributor to save-wye, writing articles and answering questions. I ran a piece announcing his arrival. Given that in the space of a couple of months he would be complaining to anyone who'd listen that we had been conducting a campaign of character assassination against him for months it is worth recording this introduction verbatim...

We're delighted to tell you that Ian Cooling, Wye's borough councillor, is to contribute his own opinions on the Imperial College development issue here on save-wye. His first piece will be his open letter to villagers which will be distributed around the Parish shortly. This will lay out where Ian stands at the moment, give an outline of the results from a series of wide-ranging discussions he has had across the community over the past three months and offer his thoughts on how he can best work for the community in the weeks and months to come.

You can comment on it in the usual way, and Ian is keen to answer your questions if you post them through the site too. In case people are still in any doubt about the nature of save-wye let me reiterate: Ian's appearance here in no way indicates his support or agreement with articles by other people on this site. I'm sure he disagrees with things he reads here, and he's absolutely free to say so.

Save-wye is a focal point for dialogue, not a campaign group trying to steer any of you towards any particular conclusion or consensus. We simply want to see the facts out in the open for all to see and mull over. We're really pleased that Ian has become the first elected representative to choose to open up his views to the public through save-wye. If any other councillors would like to have a similar platform they need only ask.

I meant every word, even when I got the piece he wanted us to run. It was enormous, more than two thousand words long, and capable of being reduced to half that length by any worthwhile sub-editor. But this was citizen journalism, so I let through every flabby sentence... and the site statistics started to leap to new records. I knew Cooling was a controversial figure. I never appreciated just how much. What he said was so anodyne and predictable I couldn't understand why he'd stayed silent for more than two months. He was for development, but only on the brownfield sites. The first he'd known about the plan was on November 18th when he was briefed by David Hill. He was 'very angry' about being kept in the dark, and critical of Imperial's skills, adding, 'Unless Imperial engage effectively and directly with the community here in Wye (not just parachute in and zoom out again) they will dig deeper holes for themselves.' He also sought to quash the rumour rife in the village that he still had some commercial link with the college. He had been a consultant to the conference and catering departments, but his last contract had ended, he said, in July 2004.

The village's councillor also had some warning words for his constituents, contained under the somewhat over-dramatic headlines, 'Beware "helpers" and "supporters" from elsewhere' and 'Beware halls of mirrors'. The first cautioned against 'certain individuals and organisations' from outside 'jumping on the bandwagon'. The second advised against conspiracy theories, noting darkly, 'Too far down that road and distrust will spread in the community. Then communication, understanding and tolerance will corrode and die.'

Unfortunately, Cooling's open letter fanned those conspiracy theories instead of pouring water on them. He never sought to explain his own silence or why, if he had been 'very angry' on hearing about the concordat on November 18th, he had been so enthusiastically introducing Ann Sutherland and John Hodder to it two weeks later. Worse, those on the parish council still had a copy of the e-mail Cooling had sent at the odd hour of 03.26 on the morning of December 8th, beating, by a few hours, the *Kentish Express* to the story. This was a glowing paean to the deal and boasted, 'I have seen my prime role in shaping the vision for this project, as being to make sure that the need to take account of local interests has been flagged up and heeded... The mentions of the local community in the press release, are a direct result of my intervention.'

It then went on to talk up the potential benefits and suggest the parish council begin the task of assembling a range of conditions to demand from Imperial in return for approving the project.

'In the meantime, I suggest that we might start to think about putting together a community "Wish List"... that should aim to define some of the benefits we as a community would like to see from the project – automatic access to sports and leisure facilities? Creation of a mini Arts Centre/Heritage Centre? Improvement of road access? Sorting out the level crossing? Creation of a "Gateway Centre" for one-stop access to public services? and so on.'

No-one had ever thought Wye suffered from the absence of an arts or heritage centre, or a 'gateway centre for one-stop access to public services' for that matter. Nor could many people see why a £1 billion housing and commercial development was needed in order to sort out the problems of the level crossing.

Cooling's open letter, once dissected, seemed deeply ambivalent, the sort of thing one could write to keep everyone, constituents and Imperial, happy at the same time. It also contained one oddity, a report that a villager had welcomed the news with the statement, 'Great – good jobs for my kids and in walking distance'. This anonymous comment seemed decidedly strange. No-one knew what, if anything, would be in walking distance, because there was, we were repeatedly told, only a vision not a plan. Nor had anyone spelled out any possible employment in detail except for Imperial's claim at the January 9th meeting that they would employ one hundred to one hundred and fifty 'basic principal investigators', scientists specialising in the field of bio-fuels and non-food crop research, subjects yet to appear on the curriculum of the Joanna Thornhill primary school or any other educational institution nearby.

Lots of things didn't add up, and the comments that started pouring in pointed this out. Many we simply couldn't use because they were libellous. The blog software we had was pretty basic when it came to allowing people to add their own observations to pieces. As it was set up, anyone could write a comment using a pseudonym and a false e-mail address. This then went into a queue for an administrator – either Justin or me – to approve or delete. We had no automatic way of forcing people to use real names or real e-mail addresses. It could only be done manually, by checking, and we didn't have the time. Besides, we reasoned that some individuals would wish to stay anonymous for good reason.

Imperial was still a big employer in the village, and landlord to several local businesses. There could be plenty of people who didn't want their names known as opponents of the college plans.

For several days after Cooling's open letter appeared I went to the computer at seven each morning and found a stack of often quite nasty and abusive comments there. While they had no name attached, the system did log the network addresses of the people sending them, many of whom had been in touch using their real names about other issues in the past. Usually it wasn't hard to work out who was saying what, sometimes under two or three different names. I felt shocked on occasion to see what men and women I knew, church-going people, who'd smile and say hello to anyone they met on the street, might type into a computer when they thought no-one would know who they were. Sometimes it was quite disturbing. At one point, three pseudonymous individuals started having a blazing online row about a minor topic that had fallen out of a Cooling thread. I knew full well they were one and the same individual, and that I had far better things to do with my time than deal with such nonsense.

But we weren't the only ones with web-site problems. The festering resentment within the Future Group about the failure of communications there had burst into a huge, semi-open row, one in which Ben Moorhead was muttering threats of resignation. We'd given Cooling a vehicle with which to address the village, and opened a vast can of worms there. Now we had to face up to the first real challenge to our credentials as a local news service. Wye Future Group, an organisation whose goals we absolutely supported, was in a serious state of disarray with accusations flying everywhere. Did we cover the story, as our journalistic instincts told us we must? Or did we hush it up and hope the village at large, and Imperial, never found out?

Trouble in the ranks

Hardly a time to start throwing toys out of the pram. I expect this spat has brought amusement and a little relief to Imperial at a stage when as much pressure as possible should be being brought on them and their cohorts in local Government. A cautionary word from Milton Berle, 'a committee is a group that keeps the minutes and loses hours'.
Cliff Whitbourn, comment, March 14 10:19 am

From the outset I was determined that save-wye would be as professional as my meagre technological talents could make it. One thing I'd insisted upon was accurate statistics showing how many people were coming to the web-site, what they looked at and, whenever possible, where they came from.

This was useful in a variety of ways. The stats showed we were developing a large audience within Imperial, KCC and ABC, as well as regular return visits from a hard core of individuals. When someone came to the site from a corporate network our system was smart enough, usually, to tell us its name. We watched this like hawks for the very obvious reason that it could often produce stories. When Justin noticed a large consultancy firm spending serious amounts of time on save-wye, for example, he simply called their office and, in a classic piece of journalistic practice, asked, 'Can you confirm you have been hired to work for Imperial on the Wye project?' A little taken aback, they instantly did, and he had a great story about one more big name lining up on the side of Wye Park. That's not a stunt you can pull with a newspaper.

At the beginning of March I began to notice something very odd. We were a tiny site with a very distinct focus. We didn't expect millions of hits, and I'd had to deter politely one enthusiastic supporter who, at his own expense, had paid for promotional clicks on Google so that people searching for Imperial College got a little ad directing them to us. We weren't about numbers, we were about quality, reaching the right people. One other way of determining that was seeing which other web-sites were linking to us, sending visitors our way. Very few people did this, so it was easy to spot when it occurred. Then it started happening in a way that caused me intense concern.

I'd been hearing for weeks of the unhappiness within the Future Group about the lack of a decent web-site for the organisation. Tatiana and Kamal had made it clear to Indigo that any site was their responsibility, to be handled under the wing of the flightless bird that was wye.org. I'd grown blue in the face pointing out the problems with this, which were both editorial – Tatiana happily excised any opinion with which she disagreed – and technical. Two months into their campaign, all WFG had in public view was a set of lacklustre pages which only available through wye.org, not directly as an individual site.

I wasn't the only who thought this was a wasted opportunity. A couple of members, Chris Pound and Garth McCleod, had come up with a plan: design a new site in secret then offer it to the organisation as a done deal. Unfortunately, their formative design included working web links to both us and wye.org, which were clearly visible to anyone at the receiving end. The site was called www.wyefuturegroup.info, a tortuous title chosen because it transpired Tatiana and Kamal's company had already registered the three most common site names based around the term wyefuturegroup. Another test site was also being worked up using the odd address www.vanillaweddings.co.uk. Both of these supposedly covert efforts were highly visible. I dashed off an e-mail to someone who knew what was happening behind the backs of wye.org, warning them that it was impossible to keep secret what was going on. But it was too late.

The truth came out and Tatiana sent round an e-mail saying brusquely she was quitting the organisation and had been 'greatly insulted' that the site had been set up without her or Kamal being told. Furious e-mails started to fly around, all of which landed in our inboxes, naturally. Equally naturally, Justin came on saying we had to cover the story. The village had the right to know that the organisation formed to defend its interests was in a state of civil warfare over such a crucial communications issue. How could we call for more openness on the part of the local authorities and Imperial if we were willing to hush up something that was clearly of public interest on our own doorstep?

Neither of us enjoyed the idea of using save-wye to document, finally, the tensions inside the principal campaign organisation fighting Imperial. But it would have been irresponsible to have shirked covering a story that was manifestly of importance, particularly when Ben Moorhead weighed in and warned, in an e-mail we soon received, 'If this situation continues, I will seriously consider my own position. I find it extraordinary that I have to say that when the cause we fight is greater than all of us.'

I left the story to Justin, and was grateful for that. Naturally he e-mailed Moorhead, as chairman of the organisation, and asked for a comment, as any good reporter had to. In return he got the one ill-tempered response Moorhead sent us throughout the entire nine months, though I'm sure we tested his patience on many occasions. He replied, 'If you believe discussing Tatiana on your site will improve relations then I am surprised. Of course the decision is yours but I cannot see it would be interesting to anyone interested in serious news.'

In the real world journalists faced this kind of dilemma all the time. Do you run a story and live with the consequences? Or do you bury it and hope everything will work out fine in the end? We didn't even have the discussion. This *was* serious news. We could, if we'd wanted, concoct an argument that said publicity would, in the long run, assist the Future Group by generating pressure on the organisation to deal with the serious fundamental problems afflicting it. But we didn't have that discussion either. We'd turned a blind eye to the fissures within the group for weeks, we'd been deliberately excluded from its press release lists and, in formal terms, treated like pariahs. None of which mattered. All that did was the simple question: did the public deserve to know that the organisation created to defend the village had lost its press officer and might see its chairman resign soon too? Of course. Justin wrote the story. Formal relations between us and the group became even chillier, if that were possible, though individual members continued to say kind words about our work, and the flow of leaked e-mails grew ever stronger.

We had raised the pressure all round, on ourselves, on the Future Group and, as Imperial, KCC and ABC became regular readers of the site, on those behind Wye Park too. We were fast, we were noisy and we were aggressive. No-one had done anything like save-wye before, least of all us. I was unsure where it was going, and so was Justin too I suspect. All we knew was that we would, from this point on, carry any relevant story, whether it was good or bad for the Wye cause or not. We weren't a campaign. We were an oddly focussed news service. What mattered was the truth, as much as we could discern it.

It only took a couple of days for this same dilemma to raise its head again. The Future Group had organised its formal launch for April 1st. I planned to be on a brief working holiday in Venice by then, leaving everything to Justin. The absence of a press officer meant that we got no official information whatsoever about the event, though a stream of e-mails, some bizarre, some angry, some simply exasperated, ran through our inboxes. Lots of people wanted us to take yet more prods at WFG. We were determined to stay clear of another awkward story if it was at all possible. Most of the tales being sent to us were bitching and gossip... rows about the siting of the event, which couldn't take place at the market, as originally planned, because that was on Imperial property, niggling concerns that the balloons that were to be released had to be bio-degradable, a reluctance on the part of one of those involved to go near them at all because he hated being in proximity to any kind of gas.

Then one popped up that we simply could not let pass. For some bizarre reason, the Future Group had asked the mayor of Ashford, Malcolm Eke, to launch 84 balloons, each representing ten of the 840 acres of Imperial's Wye estate, at the opening ceremony. Eke was an independent, but he was still a councillor and, as mayor, public representative of a local authority that the organisation had, separately, threatened with legal action over the signing of the concordat. It was unthinkable that he could effectively strike a bottle of champagne against the bows of a group bringing in lawyers to attack the authority he represented. As mayor he had accepted the invitation without understanding what it was about. Four days before the launch, he pulled out of the event completely. We ran the story because if we hadn't people turning up for the launch would have expected the mayoral car to have been parked outside. Once again, it was a matter of public interest, not that we endeared ourselves to some for carrying the news.

All this very public display of attitude started to get us noticed in unexpected corners. Strong, independent journalism has that effect after a while. People with a story to tell or something else to contribute come to you because they find their voice goes unheard elsewhere. In the end, our independent stance would find us the material that would prove crucial in delivering to Wye

Park an astonishingly early demise. But in these early days it did something entirely unexpected too. It got us two new recruits, ones we never expected, people who were willing to work for us with the proviso that their identities could never be revealed, even now.

Soon, I had a name for them too.

The Two Connies

In John Le Carré's spy novels, Connie Sachs was the eccentric, irascible keeper of the secrets, the fount of all knowledge for George Smiley and his spooks as they went about trying to discern the moves and motives of their Russian enemy. If there was a fact Connie didn't know, she'd have some way of finding it, most of the time anyway. A useful person to have around. By the end of March save-wye had its own Connie Sachs, in our case two different people who scarcely knew one another before the concordat saga began but were drawn together by exasperation at the state of affairs inside Wye Future Group and a need to act.

They were Frothers *par excellence*, seething daily over what was happening at all levels, and both, too, had links with the trio behind the concordat. This meant they were simultaneously desperate to assist in any way they could but adamant their identities had to remain secure. They still felt like that after the war was won. All I can say is this: if you think you know who the Two Connies were you're probably wrong.

They could be incredibly exasperating at times, despatching long and rambling e-mails filled with bizarre conspiracy theories linking Wye to other issues elsewhere, and making desperate connections between people and events that frankly didn't stand up to a moment's rational analysis. They would also work endlessly, tirelessly and with an unpredictable grasp of deadlines which could drive any professional journalist mad. We learned to live with it because, through personal and professional connections, they were often indispensable. If I wanted to know how many students there'd been at Wye in the 1980s I'd only to despatch an e-mail and an answer would be there in an hour or so. If I wondered whether there had been anything in the minutes of a council or a quango suggesting some connection with an obscure part of the Wye project, one of them would spend ages on the net going through public records and trawling interminable official documents trying to pin down a single sentence or statistic.

Like the original Connie Sachs, they were a vital source of knowledge in areas where we lacked intelligence, covering historical time scales when Justin and I didn't even live in the area. One of the two later admitted to 'feeling like a member of the French resistance in the old BBC comedy 'Allo 'Allo. But their contribution, hidden from the world at large, available by e-mail seven days a week, evenings too, was much more serious than that, and would continue to grow in the months to come.

Outlandish as some of the Connies' suggestions were at times, they had an instinctive Frother's feel for the nature of what we were up against too. They didn't want a compromise, some half victory supposedly made acceptable because Imperial might be forced to climb down a little on their outrageous plans. They were after a win, nothing less. They also had deep misgivings about Ian Cooling and were, though they were much too timorous at this stage to mention it, extremely concerned about his arrival at the heart of save-wye as a contributor. As one of them was to put it months later, 'We thought Cooling was trying to start an argument between you and Justin right from the start.'

Whether they were right or not, the rows certainly started, and Cooling was always the subject. His open letter continued to provoke vast numbers of comments, about fifty per cent of which were usable. Justin and I had the rotten job of sorting through each and deciding whether to run it. When the things were carried, Cooling would invariably respond, usually at interminable length. Not that this would have mattered if his responses were interesting. But they weren't. They were repetitious, often vague, and frequently circumvented the point of an earlier correspondent. Cooling didn't answer questions he 'addressed' them, which, in practice, meant that he was able to drone on for several paragraphs without uttering anything of substance whatsoever. This naturally infuriated the anonymous frother who had foolishly attempted to trip him up in the first place, and quickly prompted a never ending round of, 'Yes you did', 'No I didn't' that continued until Justin or I intervened and said that was enough of that.

Justin felt that Cooling had begun using the site as a personal bandstand, campaigning for himself, not fielding genuine questions. He was doing this, without a doubt. But, between his used car parts and his stewardship of an old soldiers' association for retired members of the Green Slime, Cooling was a politician. Not one quite as adept or street-smart as he considered himself, perhaps, but someone who hungered after public approval and acclaim all the same. Asking him not to grandstand on the site was like demanding some old actor stop preening himself and hamming it up when there were fans around. It needed to be kept in check, but in principle it didn't bother me. And we did, after all, have a different voice on the site now which, under its original founding principles, was something we needed.

Was I being naive? A little, though I still failed to appreciate the personal animosity Ian Cooling could generate in some quarters. I'd never lived in the heart of Wye, and sometimes it showed.

It didn't take long to get a flavour of why people felt this way. On Wednesday, March 29th, three days before we were due to catch an early morning flight to Venice, I noticed some odd things happening to the site's statistics. There was a strange number of visits that involved huge amounts of data consumption. On a normal site such as wye.org this wouldn't have mattered. But save-wye was a Wordpress blog, effectively a software program that was 'run' every time someone visited it. The limits on how much bandwidth we could handle were huge and could never be exceeded. But there were also controls on how much processing power we were allowed to consume through the use of that database.

Ordinarily these limits would never be reached. Something very out of the ordinary was going on. I waited for it to disappear as the glitch I imagined it to be. The following day, in the middle of the morning, the site disappeared entirely and came back online only for brief periods before disappearing altogether.

I couldn't work out what to do. Then an e-mail came through from the hosting service. It said that save-wye, a tiny blog, with a couple of hundred visitors a day at most, had been so exceeding its database limits that the company would close us down unless we desisted. We stood to lose everything for no obvious reason. We hadn't been hacked, we'd been stormed, by a version of what's known as a denial of service attack designed to shut us down completely.

All this happened at around midday on Thursday, March 30th. Some forty hours later I was committed to my only family holiday of the year, one I badly needed. At noon, as I thought about how to respond – by phone, by e-mail, by trying to set up some last minute alternative – the shutters started to come down. Without the slightest warning, our hosting service gave up the ghost, decided we were 'abusing' our contract, and said they would close us for good.

Crashed

I'd prided myself on the fact that save-wye was a 21st century web-site, hosted entirely on some remote server on the net, safe and secure from the viruses, glitches and hardware failures that assaulted those people who still designed sites on their own computers then uploaded them for all to see. Talk about hubris. Two things I had never counted upon: getting taken down by some malevolent geek, then discovering that the company hosting the site really didn't give a damn now it had pocketed the fee for an annual contract. Throughout that Thursday the site kept appearing only intermittently and I was involved in a string of increasingly hectic and baffling e-mails with the technical support service of the hosting firm, ones that soon made me realise I was going to need a new home for save-wye and fast.

The hosting company's position never changed. The number of people accessing save-wye may have remained in the hundreds, but someone, somewhere was hammering the site so hard it was slowing down everyone else on the same shared server. They had to stop us to let the others breathe. I protested loudly and repeatedly that we shouldn't be blamed for an outside attack. It was all to no avail. The site would be closed, the company said, then transferred, at its leisure, to a new server. By the time they came out with this news I'd been cutting and pasting every last article I could onto my own computer whenever save-wye briefly appeared. The smart, 21st century solution I'd chosen, hosting the entire site in a remote database, not as vulnerable individual files on a local machine, fell apart entirely once that link to our server, hosted somewhere in California, was broken. Nor was it easy to transfer one Wordpress site to another host. If this had been a local site, like wye.org, I would just have uploaded my files elsewhere and pointed users to the new destination. But Wordpress stores its files in a single database which is impenetrable to all but the highly technically proficient, which I wasn't. All I could do was grab as much material as I could while save-wye flickered briefly on the net and hope I'd be able to reassemble it somewhere later.

By late that afternoon, just a few minutes before the site disappeared forever on its original server, I had everything except the comments copied to my machine. Then save-wye was gone.

Anyone trying to access the site got an error message. My inbox began to fill with heartfelt complaints from users. I was a day and a half away from going on holiday to a place where there was no internet access. This was not a happy time.

I had one lucky break, though. My personal web-site was with another host on a plan which allowed me to run other sites there too. If I could upload the material to that then point the save-wye address there then we might be back in business within a day at most, the amount of time it takes for the internet at large to register the fact that a site has changed location and find its new home.

Around six I tried uploading the backup database. The new site rejected it on the grounds my old service had been using out-of-date software. That meant there was no easy, automatic way to restore everything, comments included. I would have to try to rebuild every article manually, cutting and pasting over my sluggish net connection.

I finally finished at four the next morning. We'd lost all comments. Some picture links were broken, and a few documents were missing. But the heart of the site – the articles – was there, and within a few hours we were back online. I was exhausted... and baffled too. When the original service went down it took with it all our statistics, denying me the chance to see if there was any way I could track down who was responsible for crashing the site. There was only one clue: early that day there had been an extraordinary amount of activity from a single machine somewhere in London. It had consumed a highly unusual amount of bandwidth for such a small site as save-wye, though not enough to have brought us down on its own. I tried to track down the user but with no success. We had insufficient information, and it was possible the culprit lay elsewhere. Without more detailed statistics – which were not forthcoming from the old host – we would never know who had decided to hit save-wye so hard we apparently breached the terms of our contract.

I don't believe for one moment this was a concerted, deliberate hit by any of the parties involved in Wye Park. That would have been illegal and unthinkable, even though we knew by this stage they were taking an active interest in our coverage. We were the victim of an amateur hit, possibly at random, one made ten times worse by the ineptitude of the bargain basement hosting company I'd picked in the first place.

We got a nice set of 'welcome back' comments once the site came back online at its new home. Then Ian Cooling, never one to miss an opportunity for a little *schadenfreude*, piped up...

But David, surely this was all triggered by Imperial sympathisers in MIT backed by someone who sat on a UN committee with David Brooks Wilson with funding supplied by one of Paul Clokie's maiden aunts and a former patient of Prof Borysiewicz.

Furthermore, the whole operation was clearly being run under the cover of one of those KCC educational jaunts to the States that Paul Francis (political editor of the *Kent Messenger*) covers so well elsewhere.

Indeed, could this be where you first read that the Kent Messenger Group is itself a player? Paul is obviously employed to generate the smoke-screens and this would also explain why Kentish Express coverage of the whole Wye saga is so low key.

This was posted the previous evening but, because of the technical problems, didn't make it into the comments queue until five thirty the following morning when I was still at the keyboard. Between gritted teeth I typed a brief response explaining that we had indeed been brought down by a deliberate attack, and 'I must admit my sense of humour on this matter is failing somewhat'.

Cooling's ability to offend people for no good reason was, I soon learnt, quite remarkable. It was as if the man simply couldn't walk past a slumbering wasps' nest without giving it a kick. This unfortunate habit was made many times worse by his inability to give a straight reply to the simplest of questions. Perhaps it was his IntCorps training but nothing was ever straightforward in Ian Cooling's world. Even the most basic of issues was liable to prompt a woolly response, one carefully prepared so that it would not, he hoped to ensure, trip him up when repeated many months later. While he was inveigling his way into save-wye the man was making friends inside Imperial too, winning their confidence by briefing men like David Brooks Wilson about us and members of the Future Group. I was slow to appreciate this. Justin seemed to understand it implicitly almost from the very beginning, as I was to discover during my so-called holiday in Venice.

The absence of an internet connection scarcely mattered. Justin and I, both hamstrung by poor net access at home, had got into the habit of administering the entire web-site on occasion through nothing more than our smart phones. It was hard to write more than a couple of sentences but we could easily deal with e-mails and approve or delete comments while sitting on a train or, in my case that week, in a rented apartment just over the bridge from the Accademia. The flood of messages and comments never stopped. My phone bill for those seven days exceeded £100, more than I'd spent on the whole of save-wye so far. The subject of almost every e-mail and every comment was Cooling. His remarks often seemed calculated to inflame the anonymous frothers who made up our commenting community.

Justin made two phone calls to me in Venice, neither of which I appreciated. The first was just plain ridiculous, a suggestion we indulge in a spot of illegal hacking of our own in order to crack Project Alchemy. I told him not to be so stupid. The second, late at night, waking me up, was about Cooling, complaining again that he was using the site for his own ends. The cause was a story Justin had written about KCC approving an outline bid for a new road from the M20 motorway to feed Imperial's science park, a project that, if it ever went ahead, would have proved as controversial as the original idea itself. The road proposal was nodded through at a KCC meeting attended by Wye's county councillor Charles Findlay who, true to form, had said not a word throughout, to the surprise even of some of his Conservative colleagues. Cooling, though a borough councillor, not a county one, immediately leapt in to attack the story, claiming what had happened was merely a 'budgetary exercise' not a planning application, as if this somehow diminished its importance. Then he went on to defend Findlay, whose absence from any discussion of Wye Park was beginning to cause serious annoyance throughout the area.

> Shouting names at Charles Findlay, however therapeutic, is therefore a pointless and probably self-defeating exercise. I have known Charles for many years. I and others who know him (possibly better than the name-callers?) have a great deal of respect for him as a skilful, behind-the-scenes operator, with excellent political antennae.
>
> We also recognise him, with some relief, as the sort of politician who does not feel the need spend his time pon-

tificating away on soap-boxes (there's quite enough of that from Cooling!). Make no mistake, we shall need Charles' knowledge and experience of the KCC players and procedures to pilot us effectively through those shoals as we engage on the roads issue.

Charles Findlay's contribution to the defence of Wye was to become only too apparent by the close of the game. For now, though, Cooling simply hoped everyone would take his reassurances on trust. By the end of March, he was happily settled in the role he had set out for himself, talking in enthusiastic but vague terms of the need to fight any development of the greenfield land, but equally keen to attract substantial new 'controlled' development by Imperial too. It was a position he seemed to find extremely comfortable. Had Imperial won he could have turned to the village, shrugged his shoulders, and said, 'I did my best.' Then watched as Wye was transformed into a small town under the guiding eye of its resident borough councillor. And if the great venture stumbled, then he could turn round and hope to claim his part of the credit too, as he did, though not without one final, astonishing admission.

The lengths to which he would go in order to appear equivocal over Wye Park would become clear at the first meeting of the 'consultation panel' set up by Imperial in order to fulfil its statutory duty to talk to the community it wished to destroy. That took place on April 4th and the confidential minutes reveal one more odd intervention by our village borough councillor.

Brian Roberts, a parish councillor, had told this first panel meeting that he thought the village worked uniquely well already, and the best way to maintain its characters 'was to keep it the way it is'. Cooling leapt in with instant objections. As the minutes record...

Cllr IC responded that this was not the view of the village. He had spoken to numerous people in the village and the majority view was that there were some problems with parking, traffic and other issues. His impression was that people accepted there needed to be some development, and that this should be on brownfield sites and in the style of the village. Whilst he accepted that some people want no change, and some welcome any change, his view was that the majority believed that some development was necessary.

IC observed that the village had been haemorrhaging jobs for the previous twenty years, and many people in the village, particularly those with children, wanted jobs for the village so supported some development.

This was exceedingly disingenuous. Wye did indeed have problems with traffic and parking, but no more than any other busy village of its size in the overcrowded south east. The idea that it had been 'haemorrhaging' jobs for two decades was highly debatable. One pub had closed, leaving three busy ones alongside three restaurants, all in a community of fifteen hundred people. There had been some small shop closures, but the Co-op had expanded as they disappeared. The retail picture was largely shaped by the growth of out-of-town supermarkets, much as it had been elsewhere in the country. The principal job losses had come through the rundown of the college by Imperial, nothing else. Not that Ian Cooling seemed minded to say this at the consultation panel in the presence of Professor Borys and David Brooks Wilson. A steady and private correspondence had now been struck up between him and officers of the college, among them the estates director, the very man who had been deputed to build on Wye, and the figure we had set out to target as the focus of much of our coverage.

Quietly, at every opportunity, Cooling would now make the case for development to bring in new jobs and commerce, carefully adding that this should not be on the greenfield part of the estate, although it was rapidly becoming clear that Imperial would not deliver one without the other. His assertion that this represented the majority view of the village was baffling. Everyone we spoke to, everyone who e-mailed us, said the very opposite. Wye was not populated by Nimbies. The bedraggled laboratories of the existing estate could have been redeveloped with local support. There were those with doubts about our opposition, and a good number of people who wanted to 'wait and see'. But the idea that there was widespread support for some vast scientific and manufacturing scheme was hard to justify. Most people simply felt they lacked sufficient facts to make a judgement, and regarded Imperial's silences on all important questions with deep suspicion.

This didn't stop Ian Cooling. In private meetings he would repeat the possible benefits, his shopping list of a 'heritage centre', a 'one-stop shop' for council services, adding in the possibility of 'affordable housing' too, not that this could in any way be reserved for local young families, as most villagers naturally assumed when they first heard the idea.

I returned feeling depressed. The book I was working on needed more work, and another research trip to Rome. Normally that would have been a welcome task. But not now. I was facing a substantial rebuild of the story, and Wye wouldn't get out of my head. Even in Venice, with nothing more than a mobile phone linking me to the outside world, it was ever-present, nagging me with questions and decisions.

Justin felt the same way too, not that we talked through the issue, and I was particularly concerned about the way the site had come to be the focus of so much of his life. We were doing a good job but we were small, isolated and had careers to work on too. Yet both of us would check the site constantly, monitoring comments and where visitors came from, scanning the net and our sources for new stories, many of them well beyond our original brief. Imperial's other failed ventures, the history of the college's management structure, and articles dissecting red herrings such as Cooling's bait of so-called affordable housing all began to fill save-wye's digital pages. It was astonishing to see how we could sometimes produce articles almost on a daily basis when the apparent focus of save-wye was so narrow. It was also incredibly exhausting and time-consuming.

I was taught as a junior reporter to question everything and accept nothing at face value. It was standard practice in those days, though these skills seemed to have been lost in some areas of conventional local journalism over the decades. So we examined every statement, checked its antecedents and, using the invaluable reference services of both Google and the Two Connies, tried to work out what was true and what was spin. It was utterly absorbing, a dark tunnel of intriguing connections and possibilities that drew us inexorably into their midst. Without noticing we had both become hooked, obsessed. For the duration of the campaign, which would, to our astonishment, last only a further six months, I don't think either of us was entirely sane or able to shake off this fixation. Wye Park collapsed, thankfully, just a short while before we would have. But at this stage I could never have dreamt of such an outcome. I thought save-wye would be around for years, and for that to happen we needed more contributors, more voices.

Ian Cooling's arrival did not have the desired effect. Instead of broadening the range of views and the quality of debate, it increasingly threw an unforgiving spotlight on our original mission to be an open forum for a variety of viewpoints, Though I never appreciated it at the time, these conflicts demanded some decisive resolution, before they would come to threaten save-wye's existence altogether.

The dinosaur returns

One day Justin announced, 'We need something in the village on paper, not just on the net.' I squawked something about him being a 'print dinosaur', and argued that we didn't have the time or the money to start being a proper publisher. This was the 21st century. Broadband had entered Wye. A lot of people were now spending more time online simply because we had appeared. If they wanted free, up-to-date news it wasn't a lot to ask that they found their way to a computer from time to time. Also I really hated the idea of going back to the labour and expense of page make-up, paper and distribution.

I was adamant: if he wanted to do it, fine, but I didn't have the time or, any longer, the skills to get involved. Justin's work on the *Sunday Telegraph* meant he retained the ability to lay out pages. I'd long since lost that, and knowledge of the software used for the job. There was also the question of distribution. I could run off a few copies in black and white on my own laser printer. These could then be run down to Wye News, the small newsagents opposite the church, and given away for free. Beyond that, we really didn't have much of an idea.

Then something unexpected occurred. As so often with the story of save-wye, a solution offered itself out of nowhere, one we couldn't have dreamed of ourselves. It was Cliff Whitbourn, landlord of the New Flying Horse, who set the ball rolling. Cliff had taken an active and engaged interest in the site from the earliest of days. Occasionally he commented in messages that were short, pithy and always to the point. He, almost alone, insisted on placing his real name on the message, and found it astonishing that others sought to hide their identity behind a pseudonym. Cliff was a very visible figure in the village and worked for a Kent company with close connections to people on the power network in the county. Bobby Neame, the grand old man of the company, had recently moved from the post of chief executive to president, much like his friend Edwin Boorman at the Kent Messenger group. Like Boorman too, his name had been pricked out by the Queen's bodkin to make him High Sheriff of the county. He had once been leader of the Tory group on the county council, though it was the expansion of his highly individual brewery that had occupied his time now for a good two decades.

I never expected Cliff to become actively involved in our work. Many others in the village refused to be named when they contributed to the site, with much less reason. But Cliff was a Frother and nothing was going to stop him. As well as commenting from time to time he'd taken to printing out articles he found interesting and distributing them round the bar. I watched these get snatched up by customers and realised Justin was right. We didn't have the funds or the means to generate a printing press, but we could let others get involved. During the Cold War, banned books were copied and distributed using the 'samizdat' process where individuals would make a few copies then pass them on to others with a request to do the same. This would be our model. Justin was able to produce a two-page A4 paper version which we would print out for Wye News and the New Flying Horse then place on the site as a downloadable .pdf file that could be viewed or printed out locally too.

People got the idea from the beginning. Households that were on the net and had the equipment started taking Justin's newsletter and printing it out for elderly neighbours who had never entered the computer age. Brendan Pierce used to run issues hot off his home press to a pair of old ladies in their nineties who followed every development. After a while I bought a colour laser printer to increase the circulation and found people leaving anonymous envelopes behind the bar of the New Flying Horse, containing donations for toner and paper. Finally, when demand was outstripping anything I could meet, one anonymous supporter in the village bought a commercial A3 printer which was used to output four-page digests and news specials the moment they were posted on the site. These were then distributed covertly using intermediaries sworn to keep secret the identity of the machine since its owner had connections that might have made its existence embarrassing.

Producing a weekly digest was, increasingly, a lot of work, and I worried that Justin was taking on too much. He had a job and a home life too. We both did. Not that there was much point in tackling him on the subject. If he simply couldn't cope I'd try and leap in and produce something that looked rather less professional but at least got the job done. We didn't manage to keep up with our target of one news bulletin a week, but we came close. And finally I remembered enough about page make-up to produce a two-page print document myself. It was entitled, 'When democracy goes bad' and attempted to explain Wye Park in simple terms for those who were new to the story and wondering what it all meant. This sat on the bar of the New Flying Horse until events overtook its contents towards the very end, reprinted countless times, picked up by locals and visitors, business people and tourists staying in the rooms on their way to the Channel for a holiday abroad.

Here is what I wrote...

Wye is a large village between Ashford and Canterbury, an unusual place in that it has, for many years, been a tiny university community too, home to an agricultural college that is renowned around the world. All that changed in 1999 when Imperial College took over the institution which was wracked by financial problems.

In December 2006 many observers felt they had finally worked out why a big London college like Imperial was interested in little Wye, and its 800 plus acres of farmland, most of which lie in an Area of Outstanding Natural Beauty (AONB) on the North Downs. Out of the blue, Imperial announced that it had signed a 'concordat' with Kent County Council and Ashford Borough Council for a £1 billion science, housing and commercial development which would, the college later revealed, transform this largely rural community into 'a small University town'.

Tough luck on Wye? Perhaps, but in the months following the concordat more details about this idea began to emerge. What was once simply a local furore with Nimby overtones has rapidly escalated into an astonishing series of revelations about the way projects which affect the lives of thousands of people, and impact upon some of the loveliest countryside in Kent, are dealt with, in secret, without the knowledge of elected representatives. And all to achieve what may, in the end, be nothing more than one more commercial property development that leaves the interested parties considerably wealthier, and the east Kent countryside ruined forever.

There is no room to go into detail about what we know of this story here. For that you will need to go to our web-site where, on a daily basis, we are trying to peel back the layers of secrecy from this murky story of underhand deals, put together in ways that are deliberately calculated to keep the public in the dark. Were it not for the recent Freedom of Information Act we would know even less than we do now. But here are a few tasters of what has emerged of the dealings between three public bodies, funded by British tax and rate payers' money...

- The concordat was not signed in December at all, as claimed, but agreed seven months before in writing, using a secret wording that went further than the public one.
- Kent County Council has killed the release of crucial documents on what was known internally as Project Alchemy (see overleaf), simply because Imperial ordered them to.
- The proposal would involve a new motorway junction and road into Wye.
- So keen are KCC to see the proposal go ahead, they have written to Government ministers offering to lobby on Imperial's behalf.

Disquiet is growing throughout the whole of local government in Kent over what has happened with the Wye Concordat. Members of all political groups are increasingly disturbed at the way a project of such scale has been developed outside the view of any but an inner circle of senior members and officials.

The leader of Ashford's opposition party, Peter Davison, spoke for many when he labelled the Wye Concordat 'the breakdown of democracy'. Please take a little time to read more of this story and see if you agree. It could be your home next.

Justin's idea took save-wye to a different, wider audience and gave us a degree of credibility we could never have achieved on the web alone. By bringing in volunteers, visible ones like Cliff, covert ones such as the samizdat army of secret printers, we broadened our base of support at a time when we badly needed to spread the load. It was a brilliant concept, one that mixed new technology with the old, and got us talked about and visible in ways I could never have imagined myself.

Through the statistics software for the site I could see this primer on Wye Park wasn't just popular with the public either. It was being actively downloaded within Imperial, ABC and KCC. There was a message in there I wanted to get over to these people. It was hidden in the line about growing concern about the concordat among the county's political community, a line that was hyperbolic in the extreme since most of the county's tame

Tories didn't give a damn about Wye and would vote any way they were told.

Sometimes you have to wish hard for what you want. Imperial and its backers had spent more than a year preparing to unleash their onslaught on the village and press for a quick victory before sending in the bulldozers. There were signs that all was not well, though, hints and murmurs leaking out from behind the firewall they had tried to place between themselves and the public. Imperial and its fellow travellers never faltered in their constancy. Wye Park was something, they always said, that 'will' happen, never 'might'. After a while, that started to sound rather hollow.

I recall Justin and I met for quick drink around then, a rarity, since we were both so busy most of our communications were electronic. We discussed what had been going on, the vagueness that was still apparent in Imperial's rare statements and the quiet feedback we were beginning to get from the other side.

'This isn't going to happen,' Justin said, putting my own thoughts into words. 'It's going to collapse.'

Such an outcome seemed unthinkable. Imperial had world-class consultants engaged on turning Wye Park into reality. Big name companies such as Ernst & Young, the lobbyists Pottinger Bell, and the American architects Skidmore, Owings and Merril, which numbered the World Trade Center replacement among its current projects. It was easy to see why they felt the momentum of the scheme they had dreamed up in concert with their backers in KCC and ABC was surely unstoppable.

Yet some gut instinct told us it wasn't entirely insane to believe this was possible. For that to happen, though, we had to sow the seeds of doubt deep within the very people who were trying to make Wye Park a reality. Though few in the village ever truly understood this, our core readership was no longer the residents of Wye. It was the tight cadre of people at Imperial, inside KCC, and at Ashford, who would decide whether Wye Park would really fly.

If they could be made to believe they were building a house of cards then perhaps one day the entire, flimsy edifice might come crashing to the floor. Our opinions couldn't achieve this. We already knew what they thought of those. What was needed, as always, was hard fact, a proven development, impossible to deny, that might give David Brooks Wilson, more than anyone else, a sleepless night and an awkward meeting with his Imperial bosses.

I'd no idea what that might be. But we had been putting out feelers for weeks, quiet pleas for information from people on the inside we thought might be sympathetic, as well as a flurry of routine Freedom of Information requests to any government department we could think of. I left the former largely to Justin. I didn't think I had those skills any more, and I was right. I knew he did, but how much time and opportunity he would have to use them alongside a busy career on a national newspaper I doubted. There I was happy to be proved very wrong.

Still it was, once again, the lucky dip of FoI requests that brought us a breakthrough, delivering a story that must have ruined David Brooks Wilson's lunch for that day and perhaps several more to come.

Bafflement in Whitehall

Any scheme the size of Wye Park would need government approval. Given that KCC and ABC had already effectively signed up to Imperial College's ambitions, some reference to the responsible minister for a final decision seemed inevitable. That prospect was viewed with widespread dismay within the village because of the identity of the politician responsible, John Prescott.

The Deputy Prime Minister had few friends in the area. It was his decision to make Ashford a focal point for the government's growth plans for the next thirty years. His civil servants had come up with the targets – 31,000 new jobs, 28,000 new homes, all by 2031 – which Paul Clokie had seized on so gleefully since they promised to unlock hundreds of millions of pounds in central aid to the area. This bubble would soon burst. By the autumn of 2006, with a string of failed developments on its hands, Wye Park among them, Ashford was faced with the news that it would require a staggering £2.8 billion of public and private investment to meet the ridiculously ambitious goals set in the Prescott era.

None of this was apparent in the spring of that year. Ashford, with Clokie at the helm, was hell-bent on being the fastest growing town in the UK, and rushing through enormous swathes of new housing estates, though struggling to find any jobs to go along with them. The general feeling – one that Justin and I shared – was that Prescott's team must have had early warning of Imperial's plans and given them a quiet nod. After all, hadn't the college itself been boasting of support from central government from the start? Not for the first time, we were to discover there was a huge gap between the statements emanating from the college and hard reality.

In the middle of April, anticipating a response to my FoI request to the Office of the Deputy Prime Minister (ODPM), I had run a speculative piece asking the question, 'So is Mr Prescott calling the tune?' I didn't offer an answer, but I was not optimistic. Much of the piece concerned another struggling pipe-dream, the Kent Science Park near Sittingbourne, some forty miles north of Wye. This was earmarked for expansion too, against the wishes of locals. While Ashford's MP Damian Green had been almost as silent as Charles Findlay over Wye, Sittingbourne's Labour member Derek Wyatt, facing meltdown at the next election with a majority of just seventy nine votes, had become a vociferous opponent of expansion on his own doorstep. Don't build it here, he said in the Commons. Build it in Wye instead. Thanks mate... we thought, and wondered if someone had tipped Wyatt the wink. They had, but not the people we thought.

An anonymous comment of the time summed up the widespread conspiracy theory in the village, referring to Prescott's car preferences, David Brooks Wilson's own Jaguar, and the part-time business interests of Ian Cooling...

So the hierachy is:
1) Two Jags
2) New Jag
3) Bits of other people's Jag
Rememorabilia, April 6th, 2006 at 4:31 pm

The idea of some government conspiracy rapidly disappeared the moment our FoI request uncovered the actual e-mails, complete with spelling mistakes, shared among members of the Government of the South East (GOSE), the regional quango working to the then ODPM, after news of the concordat broke.

Tony Howells, a member of the Kent growth team within GOSE who had been closely involved with yet one more quango, the South East England Regional Authority, often home to many of those behind the concordat, told his colleagues on December 12th, 'A bit of great news just before Christmas, its (sic) enough to warm the cockles of my heart.'

Not for long it wasn't. We had the original messages, with their timings. Two hours after Howells was feeling so chuffed he got knocked back by the then acting regional director, his boss, Colin Byrne who observed, 'Not to deflate you before Xmas, but there are significant planning obstacles to this ie it is in the AONB and they will be extremely difficult to overcome. Jim is in the loop on these.'

'Jim' was indeed in the loop. He was Jim Palmer of the Kent planning team within GOSE, and he'd been making clear his misgivings thirty minutes before Byrne had found time to issue his observations. Palmer's e-mail went straight to the core of the issue. It had never been seen outside Whitehall until we published it, and the contents must surely have sent shivers down the spine of Brooks Wilson, KCC's Pete Raine and Ashford's planners too.

Palmer noted that Imperial and the councils had written to the ODPM seeking backing for the scheme and added...

> Any major development in the AONB is contrary to national policy in PPS7 (Planning Policy Statement No.7). Neither does it sit very well with the proposals in the Greater Ashford Development Framework, which is being taken forward in their LDF Core Strategy (this had its public consultation stage a couple of months ago).
>
> The councils recognise the "challenge" of developing in the AONB and are clearly trying to get the Minister onside before anything comes to us formally. However, the Minister should avoid commenting on the planning aspects of the case at this time, because this might prejudice any future decision.
>
> I see no problem in the Minister making encouraging noises in principal (sic), but you might want to say something like: "You recognise the challenge of developing in the AONB. I cannot comment on the planning aspects of the case at present because it might come to the Secretary of State formally in the future. But no doubt you will be feeding these proposals into the Local Development Framework for Ashford so that the sustainability aspects of scheme can be properly considered".

That was exactly the tone of the reply the triumvirate eventually got. They had tried to bounce the government into giving Wye Park direct support. Using a script written by Ernst & Young called 'key messages', to be broadcast by Project Alchemy members like Clokie, KCC's Carter and the Imperial team on all occasions, the scheme's supporters claimed their vision was 'also shared' with GOSE and ODPM – which was manifestly untrue. There were huge misgivings in Whitehall, and they didn't go away.

Later in the year I returned to the Department for Communities & Local Government, as the ODPM had become after Prescott's resignation, and placed another FoI request. This shed an interesting light on Derek Wyatt's involvement in trying to shift development away from his own constituency to Wye. By this time Imperial had hired a very expensive lobbying service from the top-name agency Bell Pottinger. They had watched keenly as Wyatt, perhaps with a little help, had pushed Wye's name in the House of Commons.

When the government's representative, Jim Fitzpatrick, failed to respond Bell Pottinger's spin machine swung into action and asked for a meeting to press Imperial's case. The unnamed lobby lizard employed for the job wrote to the then ODPM...

> I noticed last week that Jim Fitzpatrick responded to a debate by Derek Wyatt about the possible downgrading of the Kent Science Park, Wyatt spoke approvingly of Imperial's plans for Wye but in his response Jim didn't even mention it which surprised some of us.
>
> Would you mind considering if this is something you might want to do and if so who else we might include in a group briefing – I appreciate that in the future this will turn into a planning issue which is why I have avoided suggesting colleagues from Planning.

This ham-fisted attempt to curry favour in the very department that would, had Wye Park proceeded, have made the final decision on whether it might go ahead did not go down well. Mike Seager, who had direct responsibility for Ashford in the New Housing and Communities Directorate, immediately e-mailed his colleagues...

> I did not know about the Jim Fitzpatrick response to the debate ... As you say, there appears to be a well-organised campaign getting underway against the Wye development, led by David Hewson (a Wye resident who is also an author of international repute) and the Kent on Sunday newspaper has, at least for the last few weeks been reporting on the anti-development campaign (I have copies of the articles if you want to see them). I am also dealing with a Freedom of Information request from Mr Hewson who has asked for copies of correspondence etc between Ministers and officials here and Imperial College, KCC and Ashford BC.
>
> Given this, we ought to tread carefully and ensure that we don't compromise Ministers' positions on this, par-

ticularly as it looks likely that any planning application will be referred here for a final decision.

Imperial knew none of this. All they had was the glowing and expensive report on ODPM from Bell Pottinger which crowed...

> The overall message was that Imperial can be reassured that on the basis of the current proposals, the Growth Areas section of ODPM is broadly supportive in principle of Imperial's development plans for Wye. On that basis, they feel that at this stage Imperial should be focusing their energies on the regional level stakeholders such as GOSE, SEEDA, SEERA, KCC, ABC and the regional representatives of the Environment Agency, English Nature etc.

Mike Seager's attitude did not reflect such an optimistic outlook at all. He told colleagues on June 26th, 'Latest article in yesterday's *Kent on Sunday* on the Wye College proposals attached. Bet you're glad we're keeping out of this one (for now at least!) study into going ahead or not.'

We could scarcely have asked for a better story with which to begin our steady bid to unsettle Imperial and its supporters, planting doubt where previously there had been certainty. It was intriguing, too, to learn that we had been in the college's sights from the start. One of our FoI requests had gone to GOSE and drawn a blank. This didn't stop an unnamed GOSE officer telling Bell Pottinger, against all government privacy rules, that we had been in touch with them, and informing Imperial's lobbyist that they 'were sceptical of the impact of negative coverage in the local press and of the effectiveness of the Save Wye Group. GOSE had received a Freedom of Information request from the Save Wye group but had not been concerned by it as they genuinely had no information to provide'. After complaining about this flagrant breach of standard practice, I was later to receive a fulsome apology from GOSE for this act, and an admission that, when they said there was no information to release to us, they had been mistaken, and had failed to follow the correct internal procedures.

Imperial had been paying substantial sums of money to Bell Pottinger for their lobbying services, and it had got them nowhere. Nor were all of the promised leads in Whitehall ever successfully followed up. The lobbying costs may have been a small part in the £1 million plus bill the public picked up for Imperial's ambitions for Wye, but at times they were very bad value indeed. The company had boasted of direct contact with two named officials of the Department for the Environment, Food and Rural Affairs to sell Wye Park. When we asked for a full FoI release of all exchanges that happened with Defra over the project, a somewhat bemused information officer told us, 'I have searched our paper and electronic records and have established that Defra does not hold any information on this specific project. Our Head of Division did receive a phone call about this project from a PR company unknown to us. He asked the PR company for further information but this was never received.'

We read these replies and wrote them up with glee. Imperial came to Wye boasting, in words straight from the 'key messages' script, that 'deliverability' was not an issue given the 'intellectual and financial strength' the college brought to the project. 'The weight, importance and determination of IC will – with KCC and ABC – drive this project forward', these briefing notes added, with not a single whisper of doubt about planning, economics or local opinion.

Justin and I had covered other public sector Titanics in the past. We knew now the truth was very different. Imperial had done a fantastic job of working the Kent power network to get some impressive names signing up to the deal. When it came to putting the project into action, they were, like us, making it up as they went along. Very soon this fragile effort might, with a little outside help, start to fall apart, in ways David Brooks Wilson and his team could never, surely, have expected. The rocks upon which Wye Park might crash were there, we felt sure. All that we needed was a fair wind, a little luck and a touch of journalistic expertise that was way out of my league.

Pete Raine puts his foot in it

Increasingly now we saw signs of fissures, divisions and uncertainty within the triumvirate as they attempted to turn the vague 'vision' enshrined in the concordat into sufficient reality to place a planning application on the table. We knew there had to be firm ideas taking shape behind the scenes, blueprints with, to use the jargon, 'scope and scale', the amount of land that would be needed and what it would be used for. We'd come to suspect that the key to the project was housing, lots of it. Imperial said it needed to raise £300 million to £400 million to kick start the scientific research unit into bio-fuels that was the nice green, environmentally friendly lure that was supposed to justify the destruction of some of the most protected countryside in the land. At current market values that could represent more than three hundred acres of housing, thousands and thousands of new homes, all demanding new roads, such as the one KCC had quietly slipped onto the agenda, and years of construction work.

And all to produce what exactly? This still wasn't clear. During his now infamous 'putting it in terms you'd understand' speech Professor Borys had rambled on and on about the joys of biofuels, green diesel from crops, planet-saving technology that would spare us all the further ravages of global warming. Most people in Wye liked this idea. We were a green community, which is why Richard Boden's WyeCycle had proved so popular. But we still didn't understand what exactly Imperial were up to. Research into this area had been going on for years. It was no longer rocket science. By now we also appreciated that Imperial's academic plans for the village had expired altogether. It had decided to hand on its remaining undergraduates, all studying for business degrees, to the University of Kent. They would stay in Wye College accommodation and be taught by the same tutors, but in the name of a different university which simply rented the rooms.

Wye Park hadn't saved Imperial's presence at Wye at all. The college was determined to leave in any case, becoming simply a landlord to a range of tenants until it could get its science park and housing plan in order. Nor was there any academic reason to site a bio-science park in Wye. Once upon a time, when the college still had high level academic staff with an agricultural background, perhaps, but they had been steadily dispensed with under the Imperial regime. Now every new bio-fuels expert would have to be imported. Wye was, we understood very clearly, chosen for one reason alone: its land could be freed up for housing, making Imperial a very fat profit.

That jobs figure kept nagging me too. Twelve thousand people was an awful lot of bodies, more than the student population of Imperial College itself, impossible to imagine through an academic institution alone. Like most hacks I am essentially innumerate but I do have a feeling for scale. To get employment of that nature normally means some kind of manufacturing – something that had been mentioned in the early days of the concordat, then painted out of the picture as the controversy began to grow. Was it possible that what Imperial actually wanted to do in Wye was not simply research bio-fuels but manufacture them too? That what we would actually get on our doorstep was some kind of oil refinery, perched on the green land of the AONB beneath the hill?

This was denied all round by everyone at the time. It was the absolute truth. When Justin's labours finally bore fruit we would discover the reality of the 'preferred land option'. It would include a 2,000 square metre bio-mass 'fermenter', effectively a small refinery, and perhaps the first of many. This was how the original oil refinery business began, with the largely accidental siting of onshore local facilities in the early days of petrochemicals, growing through natural momentum to become the vast industrial complexes we see today. Did some lunatic dreamer within Imperial really think those 12,500 jobs would be the by-product of turning Wye into the UK's first bio-diesel refinery farm?

We couldn't prove any of this at the time. Imperial were keeping quiet, even at the so-called consultation panel, sticking firmly to the 'only a vision not a plan' line, and starting to downplay the 12,500 jobs figure somewhat too. Thankfully they had an ally who couldn't keep his mouth shut. He was Pete Raine, the former environmentalist and author, now strategic planning director for KCC and a man so in love with the idea of Wye Park he was willing to shout its benefits from the rooftops, even when it managed to cause huge embarrassment all round for the cause he sought to champion.

In mid-April Raine decided to share with the world his thoughts on the future of our village, setting straight doubters and critics like ourselves. He chose a presentation to the county's environment overview committee to do it. By some amazing quirk of fate there was a competent *Kentish Express* journalist around to chronicle what he said. Imperial had gone out of its way to hide the extent of its ambitions. Raine blabbed about almost everything, revealing the project was potentially the biggest development in Kent in twenty years, after the Channel Tunnel rail link. He rounded down the jobs estimate to 12,000, though this applied to posts 'in and around Ashford and the rest of east Kent', which surely backed the manufacturing idea to the hilt. Parts of the Area of Outstanding Natural Beauty would be 'irreparably' damaged, he forecast, adding, 'There is a level of housing that will be necessary as a result of the jobs being created. Inevitably, you are going to change the face of the village.'

In Wye itself, there would be between two and three thousand jobs – more than the present population. And finally a real cracker for the files. 'This will use up most, if not all, the available brown field sites in the village and at that point you are straight into AONB and planning problems.'

The language was simply incredible. By this stage we were used to the idea that Imperial never harboured any doubts that it would manage to railroad through the project. But here was Raine, senior representative of the county authority, displaying the same certainty that all of this would come to pass...'It is impossible to estimate how many jobs *will* be created... This *will* use up most, if not all of the available brownfield sites... There is a level of housing that *will* be necessary...'

It was a remarkable thing for anyone to say given the paucity of public information and the growing controversy about the project. But from a public servant bound, ultimately, by the political decisions of elected representatives, it seemed even more astonishing. Why would any council employee feel this way? In passing, at the meeting, Raine dropped a big hint, revealing, 'If we had not (signed the concordat) we would not now have a relationship with Imperial College.'

This was a gift we couldn't turn down. Closing our report of the meeting, I wrote, '...at least we now know what that relationship is. Imperial says, 'Jump!' Straight away both KCC and Ashford Council chirrup in unison, 'How high?'

Slowly, things were going our way.

A conflict of ideologies

Modern warfare is fought on multiple fronts, something save-wye's small but vocal band of critics within the Future Group singularly failed to appreciate. Imperial was tackling the parish council through the slow, formal and largely meaningless consultation panel it had set up as part of the essential prerequisites of moving towards a planning application. The Future Group had now consolidated into an organisation with funds of several thousand pounds, a growing membership and, in spite of its bureaucracy, a team of people working to engage with planners in a continuing discussion about the coming blueprint for the new town of Wye. We were still a couple of lone guerilla fighters on the wings, able to make some very loud explosions almost instantly when needed but independent of everything and intent on staying that way.

Late in the day, when our stream of revelations began to hit their peak, David Brooks Wilson was to wail to a meeting of the village consultation panel, 'Does *nobody* have any control over these people?' It was a ridiculous question, and indicative that the college, like many of its opponents, still hadn't woken up to the era in which we all now lived, one of instant communication, and easy access to information which once would have remained locked in a filing cabinet out of view.

Of course the village had no control over us. We'd run stories that embarrassed Imperial, ABC, KCC and the Future Group too. The parish council had been mightily miffed for a while when Justin had written a verbatim report of their preliminary private discussions with Imperial the day after they took place, a fairly mild story which led the college to think we had somehow bugged the building. We hadn't. Justin had simply walked into the college, parked himself by the door of the meeting room and eavesdropped with a pen and notebook in hand, nodding hello to a passing security guard who'd wandered past at one point.

His success led to an instant increase in security across the Wye estate. An internationally renowned scientist who'd moved on from Wye after the Imperial take-over, Mike Blatt, was astonished to find himself apprehended by Imperial security guards while ambling around Withersdane on a weekend trip back to the village. He was told he could no longer wander around the estate as he used to because of 'the terrorist threat'. Justin, meanwhile, fired by his earlier successes, tried to eavesdrop the second consultation meeting by getting Beth to 'dress him up as a scientist'. This, she later explained, 'entailed putting him in green and brown clothes and a pair of glasses, messing his hair up a bit (not too tricky that one) and giving him some pieces of paper and a "serious-looking" book to carry.' Strangely enough, this attempt didn't work. After the embarrassment of the first story, Imperial had battened down the hatches, locking doors, placing guards everywhere. This was a shame because I would have been interested to have learnt whether any of their security people would have spotted that Justin was carrying a folder with the words 'Dr Science' scrawled in a suitably spidery hand down the spine.

We were renegades on the loose, hitting whatever targets we thought would make interesting reading for save-wye's fast-growing audience. Newspapers ran stories on the basis that they were of public interest. We did the same. If they upset people, that was tough. The public interest invariably outweighed the subsequent trouble. Disclosure was at the heart of what we did, and we did it frequently. The Future Group spent more than three months producing an extraordinarily lengthy and jargon-ridden written constitution. In that time we'd broken innumerable stories, some of which were becoming key to their campaign and being cited as sources of a possible judicial review. This was fine with us. We were producing this information for people to use. Why on earth would we allow ourselves to be constrained by anyone?

There were still those who were determined to work by the rules alone and increasingly they found us an annoying distraction. Early on the Future Group had been joined by a villager with intimate experience of the planning process. Diana Pound ran a small company that embraced all kind of new age jargon guaranteed to raise the hackles of hardened, language-conscious journalists like us. It worked on 'stakeholder involvement' in the 'management of sustainable environments and ecosystems' requiring 'complex and integrated thinking'. Nine months on I read her web-site once again and I still didn't have a clue what they did. The company was called Dialogue Matters, which summed up her attitude towards Imperial and their council cohorts, people who, in our view, seemed to have very little interest in real dialogue at all.

Diana was a keen and enthusiastic member of the group and instinctively loathed the idea of confrontation. She became incensed – if being incensed was a condition she allowed herself to feel – by our approach. For her this wasn't a battle but an engagement in which sensible, rational argument, using established procedures, would, after a suitable period of time, and probably a lengthy public inquiry, bring a result. Probably, in our view, a compromise at best, and perhaps defeat all round, years of blight and uncertainty leading to yet more years of construction work. We weren't there to engage with Imperial. We were there to expose them. Perhaps even engineer their defeat, if that was at all possible.

When the Future Group found the money it turned Diana into a paid adviser and took on board a professional consultancy company at her request. The paperwork and bureaucracy increased. We were receiving leaked e-mails that appeared to be written by people whose mother tongue was a language I had never learned. The group quite rightly decided to launch a money-raising walk around the Devil's Kneading Trough, both to increase funds and an awareness of what was at stake. Diana felt moved to circulate a 'risk assessment' so that everyone understood fully the dangers of talking a stroll on the North Downs in late May. This rated snow and dog bites as medium hazards. Thankfully the dangers of attacks from other people and infection from dog crap were low, but only in the latter case if walkers remembered not to touch any stray faeces – along with any hemlock and deadly nightshade plants – they happened to encounter.

I never met Diana until the night of the party for what villagers now call VI day – for 'Victory over Imperial'. She came up, bought me a beer and said, 'I know we've had our differences…' She was charming and highly dedicated. She also drove me nuts at several key moments of the campaign, at one point leading me to the verge of shutting down the site entirely and finding something sane and rational to do with my life.

As a 'chartered environmentalist', Diana had a mantra for every occasion. One dictated that campaigns such as the Future Group's went through three phases, 'Forming, Storming, Performing'. We had absolutely no idea what that meant. When her efforts and those of a paid outside consultancy finally resulted in a 'planning and environment report', paid for from Future Group donations at no small expense, the publication was placed on the web for all, including Imperial, to see. It was effectively a list of the conditions the college would have to meet in order to get its way. Nowhere did it state the obvious: the village didn't want to become Imperial's 'new small town'. The entire exercise did nothing to oppose the Imperial case whatsoever.

We had one more habit that irritated Diana too. We felt this was a battle that an entire community ought to wage, publicly, together. She and her fellow professional planners wanted to keep everything within the 'proper channels', meetings with fellow 'professionals' from the other side, 'ongoing consultations' and yet more expensive reports couched in language a million miles from everyday English. In Diana's view of things, the common touch was to be avoided. She explained this when, after someone complained about a lack of coverage of WFG's activities on the site, I observed that this was because we never received any information from the organisation (except, though I omitted to add this, through the constant stream of leaked e-mails and I was damned if I was going to write up their activities from those).

The opening line of one article was guaranteed to get her going: 'Wars – and make no mistake, the battle for Wye is a war of a kind – can be fought in several ways'. Immediately she was on the site to observe...

Whilst I fully understand the desire to protest and take strong action it is not always the best strategy. Sometimes staying outside the system and shouting at it works well – but this tends to be national campaigns not specific planning proposals.

Even the major Environmental NGOs now acknowledge that agitating for change is not the same as entering the discussion to have a real say in the outcome, and whilst they may not want you to know it, they are more busy these days getting round the table than scaling buildings with banners.

...If others would like to put either their money or time where their mouth is, they could make a real difference to the outcome, but there are rules to this game and if you want to stand a chance of winning you need to know them and use them with great skill.

And on that note I must sign off because I have just those sorts of actions to take , (as well as some punishing deadlines in my day job and some kids whose names I barely remember!!)

The punishing deadlines didn't keep her away for long. The following day I ran a story about some of the protected wildlife that would be threatened by any Imperial development. Everyone knew the area was rich in fauna and flora. The college had been forced to pay for an environmental assessment as the prelude to a planning application. Naturalists had spent long nights out in the fields, principally watching ponds for signs of the Great Crested Newt, a protected species which was appearing in huge numbers and would require considerable management in the event of any construction project.

Diana was soon back on with a comment again...

Having just said that I didn't have the time to write anymore here I am already... I am all for using iconic species and inspiring people to care more for the natural world (what about 'Naff off from our Newts'?)

But her heart wasn't in it. At the same time she was sending out a supposedly private e-mail report to WFG pessimistically predicting that any number of endangered and protected species would not, in the end, stop Imperial's bulldozers. We never thought they would. I highlighted the threat to newts and nightjars, hares and rare orchids, because by doing so I hoped to allow ordinary people to visualise what Wye Park might mean in practice. Diana Pound defined her priority at this moment as 'concentrating on making submissions on the Regional Spatial Strategy and the various parts of the Local Development Framework'.

I had no idea what these were. One, in the end, was to turn out to be crucial, but in part because the very public that Diana thought should stay silent rose up in extraordinary numbers to protest vocally about it through writing letters to their local council. She had argued vociferously within the Future Group that individual letters from ordinary member of the public were counter productive and might actually annoy local authority officers who received them. Her Indigo unit at one stage had its own 'letter-writing group' which, that May, had, after due consideration, penned a missive to both Richard Sykes and Professor Borys asking for a meeting, both to no avail.

Diana was also writing in secret to KCC's Pete Raine, citing her contribution to save-wye as one reason why she ought to be allowed onto the controversial environmental group he wanted to chair to look into the Wye project, even though he'd already said very vocally in public he was behind the plan and 'it *will* happen'. On April 19th, after a brief correspondence which had included other environmentalists, among them the Campaign for the Protection of Rural England and English Nature, she sent an e-mail which began, 'Thought it best to send this separately – not copy to everyone on the other e-mail.' In it she mentioned a story we'd carried about Raine's planned environmental group...

> The article written by save-wye was questioning whether or not it was suspicious for you to convene and chair an environment group to help with the proposal in time paid for by the tax payer. At least I think that was the gist of it – the articles seems to have disappeared from the site – perhaps because my response prevented it from developing into a good story... As I said some comments complementary and sincerely said, but I also raised some questions challenges to you as you will see.

The piece hadn't disappeared under pressure from Diana; it was simply a victim of some ham-fisted editing on my part. Raine was only too happy to grant her request, offering her a scat on the group that same day on the proviso that it be kept small 'so that the fact you should be on it doesn't open the door to the rest of the world', that it wasn't a substitute for 'wider consultation' and remained focussed on the environment, and that it operate under 'Chatham House rules', so that its proceedings could be reported but not be attributed. Diana's case, made in her first letter to Raine begging to be allowed on board, was...

> I am advising them (the Future Group) that it is better to engage in the planning process rather than keeping outside the process and protesting. I am also trying (though not always successfully) to get press releases, letters etc. to quote what is known rather than rumour and speculation.

The last part was clearly directed at us, since we were the only ones writing regularly about the story at this stage. But what Diana regarded as 'rumour and speculation' often turned out to be well placed and worthy of discussion. Given the paucity of information trickling out of Imperial, Ashford and KCC, it was entirely understandable, too, that people would speculate about what was really going on.

This disregard for public opinion appalled us both, and we weren't alone. The group had been bank-rolled in the beginning by a number of very generous donations, mostly private, but one coming from the county branch of the CPRE, a relatively staid environmental body with a mainly elderly and conservative membership. The CPRE kept us at arm's length throughout, distantly supportive of our efforts but I think a little taken aback at some level by the ferocity and speed of our approach at times. But it broke ranks on the letter-writing subject in the end, pointing out that it wholeheartedly supported the idea that the public's opinion should be heard and sparking a change of heart among Diana's colleagues who grew to like the idea that a sheet of paper and a postage stamp might have some role to play.

The difficulties that lay between the Future Group and save-wye were fundamental, and probably could never be resolved. While we stayed on friendly terms with many members, some of whom supported us quietly throughout, our aims and methods were essentially incompatible. We wanted victory and would do anything legal to get that. They were part of a process of polite, middle-class complaint – protest would be too strong a word – and determined to follow the rule book, failing to appreciate that Imperial and its pals had already thrown it in the bin long ago.

It was a beautiful end to spring. One day I ran nothing but a set of pictures of the gorgeous countryside over which Imperial's planners were now poring day by day, working out the fine detail of what would go where. These images and the sense that they might soon be lost forever seemed far more important to me than the Regional Spatial Strategy, whatever that was.

We had no idea at the time, but the hottest July on record was approaching, and with it the most difficult, challenging and enthralling months of save-wye's brief life.

The Dog Days

The Countess from America

From former spook Ian Cooling to the unlikely opera-loving would-be property developer David Brooks Wilson, this saga has more than its share of colourful characters, many of them tied to that chummy group of councillors, businessmen and quango members who make up the corpocracy that runs the county of Kent. Justin's sniffing around the ragged edges of the story soon turned up another in the unlikely form of an American aristocrat who seemed more at home in the pages of some tragic Mills & Boon romance than in the world of high finance and planning intrigue.

Phyllis Kane lost her first husband only six and a half weeks after their marriage, but later, as her press bio states, 'was given a second chance of happiness when she met and fell dramatically in love with a handsome, swashbuckling Englishman in New York.' His name was Henry George Herbert, the Fifth Earl Sondes, heir to the Lees Court estate near Faversham which had been owned by the Sondes clan for several centuries. In 1900 the holding amounted to a staggering 85,000 acres of farmland, encompassing two entire villages. When the former Miss Kane inherited it on the death of her second husband in 1996 it had fallen to some 4,500 acres. Thereafter Countess Sondes – who preferred to be called *The* Countess Sondes to distinguish her from her husband's first wife, a busy New York socialite who continued to use the same title – pursued the solitary existence of an aristocratic widow, dividing her time between the family home in Kent and a house in Belgravia.

On the surface her estate appeared much like any other in rural England, renting out pheasant shoots in season and employing two full time gamekeepers to look after the birds. But the former Phyllis Kane had got the environment bug too. She had created her own line of fragrances and cosmetic products under the brand name the 'Wheat Essence Collection'. This was based on her own personal philosophy, which she summarised as believing that 'experiencing one's life as a Romantic Adventure is every woman's birthright – and that the spirit of Romantic Adventure begins with proper care and nurturing of the senses'.

On her web-site the Countess invited other women 'to experience the adventure and the pleasures of a life imbued with Ro-

mantic Vision. Using rich seed-oils from the crops of her cher-
ished Estate, she is creating unique products designed to heighten
the senses and inspire the spirit of Romance'. Just in case they
hadn't got the message she added, with a touch straight out of
Wuthering Heights, 'Surrounded by nature on this land as I am, is
like being embraced by my husband. Our love affair continues.'

As I read all these details, kindly passed on by Justin with the
latest story he'd just filed, I was more than a little alarmed to realise I felt no surprise whatsoever that Phyllis Kane should be an
important and integral part of the bizarre story of how Wye Park
had come into existence.

Countess Sondes's interest in environmental matters did not
stop at turning her wheat into romance-inducing candles and
body lotions. She still had contacts in New York, in the United
Nations no less. In concert with them she had developed a broad
interest in 'non-food crops', agricultural products destined for
cosmetics, pharmaceuticals, even, on occasion, car panels. And
fuel. Bio-fuel. Diesel from the fields. The selfsame product
Imperial's Professor Borys had stood up in Wye and boasted
about with such pride on January 9th, citing its world-friendly
credentials as one more reason why the scheme deserved local
support.

Justin had been on the phone, to New York, to Countess
Sondes's office, and to contacts within Kent County Council.
What he'd discovered was astonishing. The proposals being put
forward didn't come, in the first instance, from Imperial at all.
They were the idea of the former Phyllis Kane, in concert with
the original leader of KCC to sign the first concordat, Sir Sandy –
now Lord – Bruce-Lockhart. The centrepiece of Imperial's 'vision'
had been 'borrowed', blended with Imperial's own ambitions for
some large-scale property development in Wye, then resold and
spun as the college's own project.

This was Sondes' baby all along. Bruce-Lockhart confirmed
to Justin that he had flown with her to New York early in 2005 to
pitch to the UN for siting an office in one of the spare Imperial
buildings in Wye. It was not a big deal. There was to be no research, only a small administrative team that would field information on developments in the area and act as a central information
hub for scientists around the world. Though it would carry the
grand title of the 'Global Non-Foods Crop Centre', the most it
would employ in the beginning would be around four people,

perhaps rising to ten if it were a success. Bruce-Lockhart put Sondes in touch with Imperial and the college took a seat on the board of the project, principally because it was to be the new landlord.

Soon it was muscling in on the impressive credentials Sondes had built up through her contacts. When Richard Sykes was selling Wye Park after the second concordat he crowed, 'We are forming a partnership with Kent County Council to take this forward with a global centre for non-foods research'. Not so, Bruce-Lockhart told Justin. The two projects were entirely separate, and there was no 'bilateral agreement' which meant one implied support for the other.

In an interview in May with *Felix*, the Imperial student newspaper, Professor Borys was banging the same drum, saying, 'This is a direction that both the United Nations and other major organisations are advocating. In fact we are in discussion with the United Nations. He went on to add that 'in the face of the international importance of the project, it seemed unlikely that local opposition could stop the plans'. Countess Sondes and her team were certainly in discussion with the UN, but about the low-level funding of a small administrative team which would deal with field research conducted thousands of miles away overseas. This was nothing to do with the thrust of Imperial's science park plan. As we were to discover later, the bio-fuels complex it wanted to build was entirely separate, and based on commercial funding alone.

Justin's story was quite unlike any we'd ever carried. It was detailed, incisive and, I suspect, a little too subtle for some save-wye readers, who simply wanted us to carry knocking copy day in and day out. We weren't helped either by Sondes's resolute insistence that she wouldn't clarify her own position, sometimes to the concern of others involved in her project who felt the college was using her good intentions and contacts for its own ends. This helped Borys and Brooks Wilson conveniently blur the lines between her plan and theirs, in ways that were to fox everyone unnecessarily for months to come, and label Sondes, perhaps unfairly, as an Imperial stooge trying to clear the path for a development she would never have countenanced on her own much larger estate. Not for the first time the parties in Wye Park communicated very badly indeed, though it's difficult to escape the conclusion that, on Imperial's side, people were quite happy for the confusion to continue.

Why did the college need to obfuscate their plans in this way? The principal reason was a practical one that threatened to derail everything. No-one had ever successfully created any major incursions into the thirty six Areas of Outstanding Natural Beauty in England, although the CPRE nationally were to complain in July 2006 that they faced increasing threats from development, citing Wye as one of the most serious. There were supposed to be huge obstacles to be overcome before any such building would be allowed on protected countryside. Imperial believed it had determined how it could get round those obstacles. All it needed to do was prove that its research park would be of 'national importance' and the permission would be forthcoming. Associating the UN with its plans – however flimsy the basis – and touting earth-saving technologies such as bio-fuel would, they thought, help prove their case.

I read Justin's piece and realised once again that Borys and Brooks Wilson were flying this so-called £1 billion project by the seat of their pants. Countess Sondes might remain politely silent over calls for her to distance her small administrative project from the gigantic ambitions of Richard Sykes's team. But the small scale of her genuine venture meant some kind of support from a large institution or corporation for Imperial was going to be vital. BP was one name in the frame. It was looking for somewhere to house its own bio-fuels research unit, backed by £275 million of funding, and Richard Sykes was chasing the contract. If the oil giant went elsewhere or turned down Wye as a base, the centrepiece of the project announced with such confidence only at the turn of the year was dead.

No wonder Imperial was worried. No wonder we were now to discover that one computer, in the estates department of the college, was fast becoming the single most frequent visitor to our site.

A wobble among the politicians

We were having a great time even if the democratic process wasn't. Charles Findlay, the county councillor with laryngitis, had proved to be on predictable form at the annual parish meeting, a public event at which elected representatives are able to offer a report of their activities to their constituents. Wye Park, the largest project ever to affect the area he represented, received not a single mention in his 'review of the year'. He was, however, forced to respond when a villager demanded, 'When are our councillors going to get up to speed and start representing us.'

Findlay stuck to the official line: since there were no plans, he could not express an opinion. Then he added, with the kind of pomposity that was becoming horribly familiar among local Tory party representatives, 'I will take a view whether I go along with the village. I will listen to all the views. There are wider aspects here – Brook, Mersham and Aldington are part of me. It is wider than Wye.'

He was indeed the member for more than the village, but the plan – a real one, not some hazy blueprint – that had already been assembled within Imperial would affect much more than Wye. When finally we got our hands on it we could see it spread as far as Brook, and might one day join the area to Ashford in a continuous line of concrete if other developers jumped on the bandwagon to 'infill' the few remaining green fields left in its wake. Saying it was impossible to form an opinion because no public blueprints existed was like refusing to express a view on Hitler before he'd actually invaded Czechoslovakia. I couldn't help but wonder what his late father-in-law Chippy Barnard might have thought of such prevarication.

Elsewhere in the Conservative party, though, there were distinct rumblings. Ashford's MP was Damian Green, a former journalist I'd once worked beside in the business department of *The Times* before I escaped to the real world of news. Green was an amiable mid-level Tory member who could usually be guaranteed to pick up a shadow cabinet post. Up until the early summer he had been almost as silent on the subject as Charles Findlay, though both Justin and I had pressed him repeatedly. We knew that Green was active behind the scenes, and was taking part in village meetings as well as briefings with Imperial. We both had the impression that he was somewhat unhappy with what was going on. But he was in possession of one of the safest Conservative seats in the country. Unlike his Labour counterpart in Derek Wyatt in Sittingbourne who was hanging onto a slender majority, Green could comfortably afford to shed huge numbers of votes, the entire population of Wye if necessary, and still be returned to the House of Commons with a very safe margin. This showed in his silence and reluctance to be brought into the growing controversy.

Then, in early June, Green finally found his voice. He gave an interview to *Kent on Sunday* – not us, naturally – in which he confessed to being 'very frustrated' by the lack of basic information on Imperial's project. Clearly citing articles we had run about the way costs and statistics concerning Wye Park seemed to vary from day to day, Green wailed, 'Where does this £1 billion figure come from? Where does the £400 million figure come from? And is building on the AONB the only way to raise the money? These are all basic questions that have not been addressed, let alone answered. I continue to believe that they have not been effective in communicating with the people of Wye. Perhaps Imperial College genuinely does not think they need to explain simply because of who they are.'

From such a cautious man these were fiery words indeed and yet another sign for us that the college's project was in trouble. Green was also involved in a farcical series of events concerning a lunch for some of Kent's most important networkers, designed to engender free and frank discussion about Wye.

This was organised by Alan Willett who lived just a few miles away in Chilham and was a senior member of the county's elite. Born the son of a tea planter in India, Willett was a key player in many of the quangos and institutions where the men who invented Project Alchemy first met. Over the years he had variously been a director of Locate in Kent, chairman of the regional development agency SEEDA, and member of several other industrial development agencies. Since 2002 he had been Lord Lieutenant of Kent, a kind of super High Sheriff, the Queen's own representative in the county. It was a position that allowed him to mix freely with friends. He could count among his deputy lieutenants Edwin Boorman, Bobby Neame, of the brewery family that owned the New Flying Horse, and the former pollster and TV pundit Sir Robert Worcester, who also happened to be a director of Boorman's Kent Messenger group and another former Locate in Kent man, alongside Brooks Wilson and Pete Raine. Worcester was also the incoming chancellor of the University of Kent, the very institution that was now taking over Imperial's undergraduate courses in Wye.

In this small world lunches matter. Willett had called one for his home on May 23rd to chat about Wye,. Included on the guest list were Imperial's Sykes and Professor Borys, former and current KCC leaders Carter and Bruce-Lockhart, ABC's Clokie, Damian Green and two people from Wye: Ian Cooling and Charles Findlay. To give the event some environmental credentials he had also invited Dr Hilary Newport, director of the Kent branch of the CPRE.

Justin found out, of course, and wrote a story about the coming chin-wag. This had unforeseen consequences. Willett then realised that the project had been discussed in the House of Commons, by the Sittingbourne MP Derek Wyatt, when, probably with a little prompting from Imperial's PR people, he had suggested the controversial Kent Science Park on his doorstep be moved down to Wye. Upon discovering this Willett cancelled the lunch, declaring, 'It has come to my notice that the proposed development at Wye has been debated in the House of Commons. In view of this, it is no longer appropriate for me, as the Lord Lieutenant of Kent and therefore HM the Queen's representative in the county, to host the proposed luncheon for those concerned with this matter.

'I trust all the invitees will understand that to go ahead with the luncheon would now prejudice my and, therefore, the Queen's total neutrality on all political issues.'

This was a very odd decision because, in one more instance of Kentish synchronicity, it turned out that Derek Wyatt, though a Labour member, was actually the son-in-law of the very Conservative Alan Willett. There seemed to have been a lack of communication within the family somehow.

Still, the threat to the Queen's integrity didn't last. The lunch did take place but on neutral territory, at County Hall in Maidstone. It took a while but eventually Justin got a report of it, one that was to propel save-wye into an entirely new controversy. I had managed to convince myself that the site was in for a quiet period. The summer was approaching. People would be going on holiday. We had been warning readers to expect the tempo of articles, which had often been around one a day, to slacken off soon. I had my own reasons. At the end of the month I would be flying to the US for three weeks, for book promotion, to teach at a writing school, and, hopefully, to finish the first draft of a new novel. The way save-wye was set up I could stay in touch throughout, and edit the site if I wanted. But I needed a break, and so did Justin if only he could tear himself away.

We were making progress. I'd given up expecting much of a contribution from others in the village. I'd certainly abandoned the idea of finding alternative viewpoints, people who thought there was merit in Imperial's vague proposals. They hadn't come forward in public anywhere; the general view was that serious supporters of the college simply didn't exist. This was a source of constant and nagging argument with Ian Cooling whose contributions had diminished, and were usually caustic and critical when they came. He was adamant we were wrong about the absence of other viewpoints. There were those in the village who liked the idea of development but they were, he said, too scared to come forward. I found this ridiculous. Then he came online with a comment I thought deeply offensive to the community at large. Cooling wrote...

> One of the villagers who discussed affordable housing with me said that s/he would not be at all worried if some of the greenfield land was used to build some affordable houses... Sadly, s/he went on to say 'but don't tell anyone I said so or I'll get a brick though my window from the antis.' That villager spoke to me in the way s/he did because s/he knew I could be trusted not to blab the name around the village. Trust built in this way can be of help to a wide range of people in a wide number of ways. Once broken it is gone forever and in all ways.

I'd only ever lived on the fringes of Wye but I'd known the place for more than twenty years. My children had gone to school there. It suffered the small problems of vandalism that any modern community did from time to time. But the idea that there might be conscious intimidation directed at someone because of their views was incomprehensible.

This anonymous comment, just like another reported by Cooling earlier, of the villager looking forward to 'jobs for his kids', provoked widespread bafflement. Most people simply could not understand why any Wye resident would say such a thing, except as an aside in rather poor taste.

What I failed to appreciate was that our borough councillor was throwing a few metaphorical bricks of his own. They were coming in our direction and aimed with a single intent: to convince the world at large that save-wye was an inaccurate and unreliable source of information, filled with negativity and wild conspiracy theories, a damaging place best avoided.

He wasn't the only one to feel that way either. Some of the burning resentment felt in one small corner of the Future Group, an organisation we supported, though not unconditionally, was about to explode in a way that would make Ian Cooling very happy indeed.

Turf war one...

By the beginning of June the Future Group's planning unit had settled into 'engagement' with anyone who would talk to it. We were never included naturally, though most of their reports quickly found their way to us. Diana Pound, she of the 'forming, storming, performing' theory, was closely involved in the discussions, many of which involved Ashford's planning department under its head Richard Alderton. Much of the talk was about planning jargon which we thought too tedious to cover, though we were genuinely pleased to learn that the group was using material we produced on save-wye as the basis for their questions. This was exactly why we existed: to publish information others could use to their advantage.

On June 9th Justin ran a story about an e-mail despatched by Alderton to every Ashford councillor after each of them had been contacted by Ben Moorhead. The letter repeated the council's position that there were currently 'no specific proposals of any sort' for Wye and advised members of the planning committee that they should express no specific views, to the Future Group or Imperial, until the 'relevant information' was available.

It was a fairly routine story, and its main point was an important one. Alderton, who wasn't criticised personally in any way, may have been interpreting current local authority practice in offering such advice. But where did this leave Paul Clokie, leader of the council, ex-officio member of the planning committee, and signatory to the two concordats, both of which pledged support to Imperial? Why he was allowed to be partial when everyone else was told to keep their mouths shut?

For Diana Pound this rather anodyne piece proved the breaking point. She went on the site using the pseudonym Danny M and stormed...

> I wish you two would find out more about how the planning system and local authorities work – you guys seem able to read the most suspicious things into everyday happenings and I get concerned about the worry and anxiety this causes to other people in the community. As well as the hostility it generates towards the planning process and professionals concerned... Come on guys –

bone up on planning procedure and the way councils have to work under the 2000 and the 2004 acts and then be a bit more careful and responsible about deciding whether or not something is suspicious.

All of this happened on a beautiful Saturday morning when I'd been hoping to mow the lawn. I was bemused by her remarks. Firstly because she made them pseudonymously, though it was clear to us who she really was. But mostly because she had missed the point of the story altogether. This was nothing to do with the acts she cited. It was a conflict between common council practice over planning issues and the highly uncommon, if not unique, decision of Paul Clokie to sign the concordat. She was also deeply wrong about our generating 'hostility' among the professionals. When Wye Park was over both of us had the chance to speak to people like Richard Alderton off the battlefield as it were. Council officials were extraordinarily nice to us considering how rough a ride we'd given them. Many were fascinated by a campaign that was quite unlike anything they'd experienced before, and several confessed they missed the site, which they'd come to visit every day.

Bemusement did not describe Justin's condition when he saw Diana's comment. Journalists are accustomed to being told their work is inaccurate. Ian Cooling was whispering the selfsame thing to anyone who would listen at this time. Sometimes reporters do get things wrong. We had only one complaint of inaccuracy throughout the entire life of save-wye, from Pete Raine, over a story I would have been happy to correct if he had clarified his rather vague complaint, something he declined to do. I'm sure we got more wrong than that, and that we interpreted events in ways we now regretted. Journalism is written without the benefit of hindsight.

But on this occasion Justin was bang on the mark, and naturally determined both to say so and identify Diana as the author along the way. We never discussed this. I had qualms when I saw what he'd done but by then it was too late. People who commented pseudonymously undoubtedly felt they had the right to keep their identity hidden. We'd never exposed anyone before. Yet anonymity could work against us. Here was the Future Group's own planning expert using a false name to accuse us,

Saved

wrongly, of an inaccuracy. It was unacceptable behaviour, and it got unacceptable behaviour in return.

Justin replied...

> I'm sorry, Diana, but it is not David and I that need to 'bone' up on planning law it is, rather surprisingly given your self-appointed role acting on behalf of WFG in drawing up the village's 'response', you who needs to get out the planning revision books.
>
> The gagging of local councillors across the UK is a recent phenomenon and has nothing to do with any of the revisions to the Local Government Act. It has nothing to do with declaring a pecuniary or non-pecuniary inter-est, something which is enshrined in law.
>
> As I said in the original piece, which you seem to have failed to notice, it is all to do with councillors somehow holding what are described as 'pre-determined' views on potential applications. This was drawn up in John Pres-cott's infamous Code of Conduct for councillors and it has no standing in law. It is enforced by the Standards Board for England and Wales and I am happy to note that many councillors across Britain are openly defying this anti-democratic nonsense.
>
> I'm happy to point you in the right direction if you are having difficulties with this. Given your role, it is impor-tant that you don't start negotiating with Ashford from a position of weakness.

Diana Pound's firm belief in the importance of dialogue and con-flict resolution was about to go out of the window, and my lawn would stay unmowed. She came back with a wholesale onslaught on save-wye itself, one that could only, I felt, reflect what she per-sonally thought of us.

> Your stance is losing or has lost influence with some of the great and good who are now tending to dismiss your site and what you say as inaccurate and misinformed (though they still check it out). It is undermining the value of working with the planning/environmental decision making system to protect the village (if ICL do proceed it is via this system that the argument will be won) – and to

win this way we need people to believe the system can work in our interests and it is worth putting resources towards that. And your site is causing others in the community to feel defeated and disempowered before we have even really got into the fight and they are giving up – and there is lots that can and must be done.

Justin was justifiably outraged. He'd been spending weeks patiently working on contacts and sources inside this entire project, people who were slowly leaking us material, but in ways which meant we had to be very guarded about its origins in order to protect their identity. This was, always, the problem with journalism at the very edge; it was often impossible to prove that what you were saying was true. He wrote back...

I'm afraid to say that you are as misinformed about the 'great and the good' as you are about planning procedure. Where do you think we get this stuff from? Thin air? Who do you think talks to us? If the 'great and the good' are losing interest then I find it strange indeed that we regularly get calls from people at the heart of this process responding to stories we have written and giving us information and new ideas. Who have I been talking to all this time, I ask myself? Martians?

I had a different concern though. What if Diana was right? What if our aggressive approach really was making the community feel 'defeated and disempowered'? No-one I talked to felt that way. They may have believed we went a bit over the top from time to time, but that was one of the strengths of the site. We were aggressive, we were funny, we personalised stories and didn't pull any punches. Was I suffering from the curse of all ambitious journalists, over-sophistication? Did the real audience, the average villager of Wye, feel differently about us?

There was only one way to find out. While Diana and Justin hissed and spat in the comments column I put together a very straightforward story that repeated her accusations then added, 'We are keen to know if this is the general opinion in Wye. The site is a lot of work frankly and if it seen to be a bad thing it should stop. You can express your opinions in the comments below and in a poll which will be available shortly.'

It was now midday and the site was humming. We'd carried polls before. This one would simply tell us whether many people agreed that we were damaging the cause. If that was the case, I would have had no hesitation in closing the site. Sometimes journalists can become distanced from their public. A reality check from time to time was no bad idea. The early comments we got were utterly one-sided... in our favour. The poll was scarcely under way when Diana was back on the e-mail again in an entirely different mood, contrite, complaining about the stress she'd been under, pleading for everything she'd said to be taken down immediately. In a way I think she genuinely felt we had bullied her into this position. Her original statement that we were damaging the Wye cause and making the community feel 'defeated and disempowered' seemed to have slipped her memory.

I was fed up with the whole thing. I killed the new story and the poll, but turned down her request to remove the original comments. Plenty of people had seen them by that stage and if I took them off someone was bound to say this was censorship on our part. Justin and the Two Connies thought I'd been overly kind, and that Diana should have been left to deal with the consequences of the quite serious accusations she made. Looking back I realise they were right. Diana Pound genuinely believed what she said and had a right to say it. Others ought to have had the right to respond with their views. I was weak in falling victim to a spot of emotional blackmail. But the entire episode left a nasty taste in the mouth. The journalism of the site, our efforts to disclose what truths we could find about Imperial's plans for the village, had never felt in better shape. We had been brought down by someone else's words, not our own.

From this point on I would ban all anonymous comments, something I should have done from the very start. They created unnecessary work and stress, and allowed people who didn't have the courage to say nasty things in public the ability to utter them from behind a mask. Even so the wider remit – to generate different viewpoints and encourage debate – still felt out of kilter somehow.

Diana Pound had let a little genie out of the bottle, one that said we weren't to be trusted. It couldn't be removed from sight simply by acceding to her requests to tone down the very coverage she had instigated in the first place. Ian Cooling was to make sure of that.

Turf war two...

A clearing house for different opinions can only achieve its original intent if different views do actually exist... save-wye has actively encouraged opposing views to be expressed as has Wye Parish Council but if these views are virtually or wholly non-existent then the ageless axiom "you can't get blood out of a stone" is so true.
Kerry Bethel, June 24th, 2006 at 11:43 am

On June 22nd Justin ran an article from a briefing he'd received about the private lunch run by Alan Willett for the great and good interested in Wye Park. It revealed that Richard Sykes said the college wanted to retain total control of the project, and as a result would not be seeking government or European funding to support the development, confirming, in the eyes of most observers, that the venture would be paid for by the construction of large scale housing estates. He also reported...

Sir Richard and Prof Sir Leszek were told by some of the guests that the overwhelming majority of people in Wye and surrounding villages are in favour of the scheme. They were also told that Wye Future Group is a vocal minority made up of 'middle class nimbies' who can safely be ignored, that save-wye.org is, in the main, riddled with inaccuracies and is run by 'a couple of amateurs' and that Wye Parish Council is 'floundering around' with no clear idea of what it is doing.

Imperial's leaders were also told that the first 'community workshop' run by architects Skidmore, Owings and Merrill earlier in the same month had been dominated by the vocal 'minority'. The views expressed there – that Wye's relative isolation because of poor road links and the long waits at the level crossing were things worth preserving – were 'nonsense' and that sorting out transport had been a priority long before Imperial had persuaded KCC and Ashford to sign two 'concordats'.

Ian Cooling, who had been at the lunch, immediately weighed in to say that he didn't recognise this report of an event he had at-

127

tended, a sentiment that would later be echoed in very similar words by David Brooks Wilson when he spoke to the village consultation panel. Cooling, perhaps mindful of the kerfuffle over Diana Pound, went on to add, 'I also reported my view (not necessarily the village view) that the negativity and cynicism of more than a little of the content on this site is in no way typical of mainstream opinion in the community. That remains my view.'

Unfortunately for him and Imperial, the county's one decent newspaper, *Kent on Sunday,* was on the case. They followed up on our report with Dr Hilary Newport of the CPRE, the one clearly uncommitted attendee at the lunch, who told them 'she agreed with the save-wye version of what was said'. Cooling was not to be deterred. The brief time during which he was content to be a contributor to save-wye alongside us was, for whatever reason, over. Now he was a man with a mission... to tell the world not to believe a word they read on the site.

The following week he addressed the parish council. Two different members told us he used words to the effect that save-wye 'reads like the script of a Christmas pantomime'. We were, I soon realised, struggling for our credibility, and, though I'd failed to notice, immensely vulnerable. The site remained the work of two individuals, neither of whom lived or worked in the village. Our sources were, we knew, impeccable, but their identities couldn't be revealed, which naturally lent our stories a hypothetical tone from time to time.

Worse, Cooling was now regularly attempting to post comments on the site that cast further doubts on our veracity. Just as Diana Pound had done, he was using save-wye's own facilities to undermine our ability to carry on with our work. For the second time in two weeks I found myself wondering whether the best thing wouldn't be to pack in the whole thing and let the Future Group and Cooling do their best... or worst. Then it struck me. What was wrong here was the site itself. Our original mission statement was fundamentally flawed. We couldn't represent all voices, nor could we allow our own liberal approach to comment to be abused by those who simply wished to damage what reputation we had. What we needed was a relaunch, and a new, redefined mission.

On Saturday I posted an article explaining what was about to happen.

Why this 'pantomime' will close on Monday
Saturday, June 24th, 2006 in News by David Hewson

I started save-wye.org in January with the naive hope that it would be a focus for different opinions and a forum for reasoned comment about the very real threat to Wye from Imperial College's Wye Park proposals. Sadly, that idea has proved a failure. While the readership of this site has grown from strength to strength and recently passed the 25,000 mark, we have failed to find contributors who bring different opinions to the debate, and the coverage we have carried has fallen very much on the shoulders of Justin and myself, and the busy army of supporters and researchers who have burrowed out material for us.

Our original intention of providing a central clearing house for different opinions on the controversial Wye Park project has proved mistaken and lately we have come under considerable whispering criticism, led by Wye's own borough councillor, for negativity and 'inaccuracy' (by which he seems to mean carrying articles with which he disagrees). For this reason, save-wye as you see it will cease to exist on Monday.

Ian Cooling, in one of his many diatribes against this site, wondered here (we have printed an awful lot of his opinions and gave him his own logon to write them) whether we asked ourselves why no alternative opinions came forward. The implication was, I imagine, that people are somehow afraid to express an opinion in support of Imperial College. In an earlier posting he quoted an anonymous villager as saying he feared he might 'get a brick through the window' if he did so, which I frankly find hard to take seriously, and think is an outrageous slur against the village he represents.

We have come to a different conclusion for this lack of 'balance'. The reason no-one is standing up to support Imperial – Cllr Cooling apart – is that no-one in the village wants the very bad part of what is on offer. While there is widespread support for a renewal of the existing college and the decrepit buildings which have been allowed to rot under Imperial's reign, there is absolutely zero backing for turning over the Area of Outstanding Natural Beauty to commercial development or allowing Imperial to line its coffers by transforming Wye, in its own words, into 'a small town'.

There may be those who, for their own reasons, wish to portray this as a minority view. They have their heads in the sand. Wye Future Group has 230 members; two very well known and respected villagers put their names to the 'no incursion into the AONB' position here only yesterday. You have to be blind or very, very biased to think this is the 'tiny minority' some people would have us believe.

Nevertheless, it is clear that the original vision for save-wye is redundant. We have asked for alternative views until we are blue in the face; they're not coming in because they simply aren't out there. It is futile sticking to our original remit, 'This is a non-partisan web-site designed to encourage discussion and the sharing of information about plans to bring new development to Wye, Kent.'

In truth, this is now working against us, because it allows someone like Ian Cooling to badmouth our efforts in private then come on here to try to do it all again under our own banner. On Thursday night he was telling the Parish Council, save-wye 'reads like the script of a Christmas pantomime'. The following day he attempted to post a stream of comments on this site, two of which we deemed unacceptable. One accused us of allowing a correspondent to post under a false name, in spite of our new rules (the truth is that M. Sorken is a real person, in fact, one of his own constituents). The second tried, once again, to rubbish a report on the fact that the UN do not wish to fund Imperial. Cllr Cooling wished to argue with this on the grounds that it was possible '(no more)' that they might after all. It is possible 'no more' that Elvis will be found working behind the bar of the Tickled Trout. We are, frankly, bored with dealing with this constant tide of unsubtle propaganda aimed at discrediting the work done here without ever coming to a specific point.

We tried, but save-wye as a forum has failed. For that reason, this site in its present form will disappear on Monday, and be replaced by one which maintains the previous content but has a new 'mission statement', one which we hope is clear and unmistakable. From Monday the job of this site is to...

• Oppose all attempts to turn over any part of the AONB to commercial development

• Call for this huge project, one which would change an entire community forever, to be discussed fully in public, not negotiated away in secret lunches between chums

• Examine and question fully and publicly, and open up to debate, every statement and proposal issued by Imperial, local authorities and councillors

• Seek to be the first and most reliable source of news and information on the future of Wye

We do not aim to represent the village. We wish Wye Parish Council and Wye Future Group well in their praiseworthy efforts. We are a news and comment service and a place where people can raise questions, comment on what they see here, and hopefully go away better informed. That said, we think we are somewhat closer to the majority of opinion in the Wye area over this issue than certain public representatives, judging by the constant messages of support and even money we receive constantly.

As to the 'other side'... if this is a pantomime, one can't help but wonder where Councillor Cooling will find someone to be the front half of his horse.

Our enemies wanted us closed down. There was only one way to respond, and that was by giving them more of the coverage they hated so much in the first place. Over the weekend I worked on a redesign. One of the joys of blog software is that at heart all we were publishing was a database that thought it was a web-site. In a system like this stories are stored as records, entirely separate from the design of the site. I could remake save-wye in an entirely new fashion simply by importing and tinkering with a new Wordpress template. I made the type bigger, the headlines bolder, the navigation structure simpler, and put at the top of the right hand column the unambiguous message, 'This site exists to fight the destruction of the countryside and community of Wye in Kent, England'.

When we relaunched the following Monday the comments were universally welcoming, and not a word was heard from Ian Cooling. Cliff Whitbourn, now landlord to our campaign headquarters, a place I used for internet access when the files were too big for my own stretched system, and the principal distribution point for our publications, wrote in a comment, 'If you sit on a fence for too long you will fall off. It would appear that both our elected Borough and County officials have fallen into the Imperial nettle bed.'

I never felt we'd been sitting on the fence, and it came as a shock to realise others did. Cooling and, in her own way, Diana Pound had done us a huge favour. By attempting to paint us into a corner where we might linger sidelined and unread, they had forced us to focus on what mattered – the journalism – and to redouble our efforts to make it better than before.

Four days later I left for Arizona feeling happier about the site than I'd done for a while. Justin and I were freed of the burden of feeling we needed to take account of a broad church of viewpoints that didn't, in all honesty, exist. Finally we had a role we both could understand, and a target too.

I had no idea as I made my way across the Atlantic that the endgame was about to begin.

Reporting off piste

I'd been a reporter. I'd been the boss of reporters. Some you need to keep on a short leash constantly. Others simply choke if you do that, and never pay their way. Since we were both doing this for free – or more accurately at our own expense – the latter wasn't a problem on save-wye, but I learned early on that it was best to leave Justin to his own devices and wait to see what came out. That first unexpected, unwanted and so far largely unexplained phone conversation we'd had in Venice proved it, and I was now to discover what my late-night yelling at him at that moment had prompted.

Justin had woken me in my apartment in the Campo Sant'Angelo to ask for a favour. He wanted to know if, during my time as a technology journalist, I'd worked out how to crack a secure big company web-site, and if so could I pass on the secret.

While I was dining off over-priced seafood and giving talks to readers in my appalling Italian, he had received a message out of the blue. It was from Ashford Borough Council to say some documents he had requested under the FoI Act more than a month earlier were now ready. Like me Justin was down in the dumps at the time and had forgotten filing the request. The call had perked him up. Perhaps there was something good there – even something as important as the secret first concordat released to us by KCC a month and a half before.

But there was nothing, no silver bullet, just a collection of documents we had seen before: letters from Hill to the great and the good extolling Imperial's plan, a crawling missive from Ashford council leader Paul Clokie to housing minister Yvette Cooper and some meaningless copies of something called the 'Quickplace User Guide'.

Beth, once a news editor herself, went through the package. Although she'd decided not to get involved directly in save-wye, she had supported Justin with it since January and knew every inch of the story. 'Look,' she said while poring over the documents at the kitchen table, 'isn't this the Project Alchemy website?'

She was right. On the front page of the Quickplace User Guide was the secret address for the Ernst & Young secure site where the three parties to the concordats – KCC, ABC and Imperial – had worked on their plans in secret long before the December announcement. Justin could scarcely believe it. On the other pages printed out from the User Guide, the web address had been carefully blacked out. But inexplicably somebody had missed it on the opening folio.

He rushed upstairs to the computer and typed in the address. There it was: the logon screen for the Project Alchemy Quickplace, the secret treasure trove at the heart of this story, a place that contained all the documents Imperial didn't want us to see. Perhaps, even, the one we needed most: a plan.

And that was why he'd woken me up at 11 pm in Venice. Could I please tell him how to obtain an authentic logon and a password for a site run by the gigantic international consultancy Ernst & Young?

Of course I could. You found some hacker who could negotiate a way past E&Y's security system. Or you peeked at the computer of someone who was authorised to go on the site and stole his or her identity. There was just one problem with all these solutions. They were illegal. Highly illegal.

I told him that in Venice. I told him it back home when I was sitting once again at my desk, trying to write a thriller based around a mysterious Caravaggio painting, and interrupted, when I least wanted it, by a maniac who seemed to think Wye was worth a spell in jail.

'It's in the public interest,' he complained.

'So is the bank account of every corrupt politician in the country,' I retorted. 'That still doesn't make it OK.'

'But we could crack everything!'

I took a deep breath.

'Listen,' I told him. 'You could go to prison. I could go to prison. You could lose your job. Your career. Your house. Everything. *It's against the law, Justin.*'

'But...'

'Fine, then do it,' I finished. 'But I'm telling you now. If you obtain anything illegally, I will *not* run it. Start your own web-site. Find your own way to jail.'

Of course we had to crack the story. I had no objection to using methods that were shabby, underhand, immoral, deceitful and thoroughly reprehensible to decent, normal human beings who lived by the standards of civilised society. If I had qualms about those things I would never have become a hack in the first place. But you had to draw the line at the law, particularly when it came to computer security. Would-be property developers could lie and scheme through networks of the unelected and the privileged with impunity. The government had brought in some draconian measures that could and would jail someone just for taking a look at other people's information, in the public interest or not. Justin had to understand this.

I thought I had made it all clear. No. I *hoped* I had. It was like talking to a brick wall, of course, and I knew it. So, several months later, with Wye Park truly dead, I invited my co-conspirator to tell me what he really did after my several lectures on the matter. Here is his confession...

The Tiger Inn at Stowting is one of my favourite pubs, *writes Justin Williams*. I can be there in under 10 minutes from home but it is so far off the radar that I can virtually guarantee not to see somebody I know from Ashford or Wye in there.

Late in April I arranged to meet Bernard Ginns, the editor of *Kent on Sunday*, for a quiet beer in The Tiger. This ex-*Mail on Sunday* man (*note the career path – DH*) had supported save-wye from early on, following up some of our stories and always crediting us. This was at a time when the *Kentish Express* was pretending that Wye had been wiped from the map. Ginns, in his early 30s and softly-spoken, had not been in the job long when save-wye finally got off the ground. He had brought a serious touch to a paper which was short on staff but long on ambition.

When I arrived at the pub, Ginns, drinking bitter and hand rolling his cigarettes, was sitting with somebody else. He introduced his friend as a geek. I had no idea why he had brought this guy along – he had nothing to do with the paper, Wye or Imperial College. Even today I don't know whether he was there because Ginns, who was on the side of the white throughout the battle with Imperial, had unilaterally decided that we needed extra help to defeat the college or whether he had just 'happened' to bring Tom, as I'll call him, along. We've never discussed the matter. Like so much to do with the manner in which we ultimately defeated Imperial, it has remained unsaid.

After a few minutes of chat about save-wye and Imperial, Ginns asked me where I thought the story was going. I think I told him that we were running on fumes, chasing shadows and that I was getting intensely frustrated with pursuing a single issue with the barest of information.

'You need a break, in other words,' he said.

'Yeah, we need an in to the heart of the operation if this is to go anywhere.'

'And how are you going to get that?' asked Ginns sucking on his roll-up. It's rare for journalists on different papers to discuss works in progress like this, but I decided that I would share my ideas with Ginns in the hope that he would tip us off to anything that he picked up about Imperial.

'Well, I need to spend some time mooching around Imperial's South Kensington campus making some contacts there but that'll take a week when I can disappear from work for a few days and ...'

I hadn't discussed the Project Alchemy web-site with anybody beyond David and Beth but I saw a kindred spirit in Ginns – a hack who was only really interested in chasing the big story and using all means necessary to get it. I breathed deeply, thought about how angry David would be about this and decided to go for it. I felt very strongly that David was wrong, that we had to use all our journalistic skills to go for Imperial, just as they had used every deceitful and underhand weapon at their disposal to get Wye Park to the point it was without a single word of public debate. 'There's this secret web-site, it's a Quickplace site run by Ernst & Young, who are consultants for Imperial, which the three parties to the concordats are using to get round the Freedom of Information Act. You won't find it by Googling it, you won't find it through Ernst & Young's public site. It's secure. As far as we know, it's got everything on it from early last year when they started discussing Wye Park. I've got the address, I need somebody with access to it.'

'That's funny,' said Ginns motioning to his friend across the table. 'Tom worked for Ernst & Young until last month. Perhaps he knows somebody there who can help you.'

And without any further prompting, Tom said: 'I need the web address for this Quickplace.' I knew it off by heart and scribbled it on a napkin for him – a 32 character code that I would never have guessed if somebody at Ashford council had not failed to black it out from the print-outs I'd received two weeks before.

I found myself catching my breath. This was either an extraordinary coincidence or Ginns was taking a much keener interest in Wye Park than I had realised. He must have known about the Project Alchemy site because David had written of it after we'd received the first FoI releases from KCC in February. But had he really deliberately brought Tom – sitting there in a green anarchist T-shirt and already on the phone to his mate in E&Y's systems department – along to help me?

'Obviously, *Kent on Sunday* would be interested in running any story to do with Wye Park which takes this further,' said Ginns.

'Yes, obviously,' I muttered, reeling from the synchronicity of all this. I had yet to do any real work on this story and it seemed we might be on the point of something big.

Tom broke off from his phone conversation. 'Have you got a card or something with your mobile number?' I gave him my business card. He read the number out to his former colleague and then hung up. 'You'll get a call if he can help, I don't know when because my friend doesn't work in that section of IT. But he knows plenty who do. Be patient. E&Y is a big organisation, it leaks like a teabag.'

Reading all this later, in the cold light of an autumn day with Imperial's mad scheme dead and buried for good, I briefly toyed with the idea of resurrecting the now-slumbering save-wye and reinstating Justin as its principal investigator just so I could experience the immense pleasure of firing the bugger good and proper once and for all. For the record, no laws were broken in pursuit of the truth about Wye Park, nor, to my knowledge, were any animals harmed. But it came damned close at times, on the legal front anyway, and he did well to hide these facts from me.

Not long after this he started lurking around the Imperial headquarters in South Kensington. Justin calculated that 'the idea that the Imperial HQ itself would be vulnerable to a journalistic attack had not even entered their heads. They were far too busy expending energy keeping KCC and Ashford quiet and working out ways to avoid Freedom of Information requests.' He was absolutely right. His contacts were telling him that Borys, Brooks Wilson and the number two in the estates office, Nigel Buck, were regularly reading save-wye and, in Justin's words, 'laughing at us'.

This was a red rag to a bull. Somehow – I do not know, I do not *wish* to know – he discovered a way inside this vast, teeming, bureaucratic organisation.

'Sykes had achieved a lot with Imperial since taking over from Lord Oxburgh,' he went on when I finally got all this out of him. 'He'd closed down agricultural sciences at Wye and sent a generation of lecturers to the scrap heap, plunged the whole institution, which on his ascendancy had not owed the banks a penny, £150 million into the red and managed to alienate many of the leading academics at South Kensington with his ruthless corporate approach to academia. Those academics, many of them senior ones, were tenured – meaning that they could not be sacked – and were deeply unhappy. Some of them were close to the people who sat on the college's management board, the group which approves or rejects its plans and meets quarterly.

'What I learned about Imperial during the spring and very early summer was that it was not a happy ship – from top to bottom there were people with gripes and axes to grind. Many were alarmed by what the college was proposing to do to Wye. Some were willing to talk to us off the record. A tiny number of people with access to the very top were prepared to risk their careers and give us the ammunition we needed to bring Project Alchemy down.'

From a journalist's point of view, sprawling, unhappy, mismanaged organisations are a godsend. For one very good reason. They leak.

A few days into my stay in San Francisco, happily settled into a small house in Cow Hollow, walking distance from the pleasant shops and restaurants of the Marina, I got a message from Justin. We had to talk. It was important.

I was intrigued. The tenor of his message didn't sound remotely furious, despairing or homicidal. It seemed distinctly cheery. Something was afoot.

A Bumper Harvest

Killing it once

At last we are getting to the heart of the matter... Since the merger, many friends, neighbours and fellow Wye College Alumni have asked me if Imperial College had acquired Wye College in order to 'asset strip'. How wrong I was to reply that it seemed highly unlikely because that is not what UK educational institutions are about. I could not conceive that the legacy of the last one hundred years, not to mention the last five hundred years, would be systematically dismantled in order to serve the purposes of an organisation which has embarked upon an exercise in 'asset value transfer' which leaves the host community with so few benefits and such catastrophic outcomes.
Francis Huntington, August 10th, 2006 at 3:07 pm.

Diana Pound had whispered to her Future Group contacts at the beginning of June, 'I have been told that ICL are meeting at the end of June to deliberate over whether or not they proceed and they will then announce this decision a few weeks later in July.'

She was out by a mile. The crucial decision was to be taken on June 12th, just six days after she sent this e-mail, by Imperial's management board and property advisory committee, in circumstances of the utmost secrecy, and kept that way for months. Or so they thought. The college's so-called partners, KCC and Ashford Council, knew nothing of this deadline, though increasingly their planners were becoming baffled by the lack of hard information coming from David Brooks Wilson about the detail of the project. He had a good reason to be quiet. Trying to turn the vague, sprawling ambition of Project Alchemy into some kind of reality called Wye Park had become a nightmare.

On almost every front – planning, the environment, design, funding – Imperial had run into huge problems. Costs were running out of control everywhere, particularly in the environmental studies into such local residents as newts. Specialist consultants were questioning the entire economic base of the project, trying out a variety of models – schemes of different sizes – and finding that none of them could work, primarily because Imperial insisted any solution had to give them a near-instant 'endowment' – profit in anyone else's vocabulary – of £100 million from the out-

141

set. Planning experts, too, were shaking their heads and warning that some of the fundamentals simply wouldn't work. In particular, there were serious doubts that any government would, when this vast scheme reached it after a public inquiry, be willing to allow so-called 'enabling' housing development in an Area of Outstanding Natural Beauty. In other words, Imperial might be allowed to build essential homes to house its workers on site, but it would never be permitted to raise money for the project as a whole by speculative commercial housing, and there was no other easy way to that magic £100 million 'endowment'.

Worst of all for Imperial, the oil giant BP had no intention of of establishing its bio-fuels research centre in an outlying part of east Kent. The college was now desperately trying to persuade the company to take up accommodation in its London headquarters instead. Wye had moved off Richard Sykes' radar screen. It wasn't going to be any kind of world class research centre at all. The academic part of Wye Park was dead, and Justin had the information to prove it.

I listened, delighted, and worried too. For a few weeks now we'd both been coming to think something of this nature was on the cards. I wasn't much of a chess player but the idea of the endgame for Wye Park had intrigued me for some time. It seemed to me we were going to face some unique and very difficult problems when it came to closing down this story for good.

I never mentioned them. Justin was on a roll. He'd worked incredibly hard and now he'd got his reward. I would be back home soon then he would go on a deserved holiday to France with Beth. The end was in sight... for the project and for save-wye.

On July 12th Justin's story went live. It was all well-sourced and would be proved to be absolutely accurate. Yet it filled me with trepidation, through no fault of his own.

Imperial prepares to scrap its Wye Park "vision"
By Justin Williams in News

It has cost hundreds of thousands of pounds, blighted Wye and its surrounding area and led to a run down of the college's operations in Kent, but Imperial's plan for a research institute, science park and thousands of houses is virtually dead, save-wye.org can reveal. A combination of cost overruns, poor planning and the announcement by BP of a £275 million bio-fuels research programme in conjunction with a major UK or US university has all but killed Imperial's Wye Park vision. Work on the project – apart from the masterplanning by Skidmore, Owings and Merrill – has stopped.

The news will both delight and worry those in the village who fought the college's plan to build the research centre, science park and thousands of homes on the Kent Downs Area of Outstanding Natural Beauty but wanted to see the campus regenerated. The end of the Wye Park plan raises the possibility that Imperial will now attempt to break up its Wye campus and sell parcels off to developers.

Officially, the Wye project is still active but save-wye.org understands that the college's management board put the scheme into cold storage at its June 16 meeting. The board agreed to grant Wye Park an extra £100,000 to finish the masterplanning process but a source within the board has told us that it is 'extremely unlikely' any further money will be given to the project when it next meets in September, effectively ending a process launched at the end of 2004 with the first tentative discussions between Imperial College and Kent County Council.

The crisis has been sparked by two separate events. The project has run out of money. We understand from two of the main contractors that they have been pulled off the scheme and that all work on site has stopped. Only SOM is still actively engaged on Wye Park. Waterman Group has been told to stop its habitat surveys – necessary before a planning application can be made – meaning that the deadline for a planning application of spring 2008 has been thrown out of the window and no new date has been fixed.

In June, BP announced that it was going to spend $500 million setting up a bio-fuels institute attached to a UK or US university. A source within BP has told save-wye.org that Imperial is one of several British institutions bidding for the centre and that Wye does not figure as part of the Imperial bid. Furthermore, we understand from Whitehall sources – and as was revealed by Sir Richard Sykes, the college's rector, at the infamous May 23 'working lunch' – that Imperial has not had any discussions about government funding for Wye Park. Therefore, the BP project leaves Imperial with a dilemma: if it wins, the institute would be based in London and the raison d'être for Wye Park vanishes. If it loses and the project goes to another university, the college would struggle to attract industry or government finance for a second British bio-fuels institute at Wye.

The demise of the project will come as a bitter disappointment to the other parties to the concordat – Ashford Borough Council and Kent County Council – who were promised up to 12,500 jobs across east Kent in return for permission to build thousands of houses. Where it leaves those who have invested so much public credibility in a project which would have set a precedent for destruction of protected countryside, remains to be seen.

The news was greeted with delight by Ben Moorhead, chairman of the Wye Future Group, who said it was 'fantastic' that Imperial had scrapped its original plan. Mr Moorhead added: 'I had a feeling that this was not going to happen.'

save-wye.org also understands from tenants at Wye College that some have been told that leases can be renewed to the winter of 2010. Under the Wye Park plan, leases were all to end by October 2008 and no renewals offered but the new position appears to be further confirmation that the scheme is in deep trouble.

Delegates at last month's workshop with SOM were left with the impression that the project was drifting and no dates were given for further workshops. It is unclear whether these will now continue to allow SOM to complete the masterplan only for it to be mothballed the moment it is published.

The village went mad. This appeared to be the day of the great victory. Someone e-mailed me and said, 'I wish you could be here... there's people want to carry you two down the street on their shoulders.' Alan Paterson, a former chairman of the parish council, a man who was raised in Wye and had constantly championed our case, occasionally with some difficulty, inside the Future Group, wrote for everyone when he put up a comment that said, 'I shall get up tomorrow morning and look out of our bedroom window across to Brook Church and upwards to the Crown (albeit now hidden by trees) at the view my late father saw when he came here for a job interview in 1937 and never left, but see it all in a more promising light.'

Everyone was over the moon. But only for a day or two. Then the doubts set in. Justin thought – 'naively' in his own words –

that Imperial would simply roll over after our story and confirm that the project was all but dead. Not directly through us, naturally, but to *Kent on Sunday* or even the *Kentish Express*. He was wrong. Their PR people put out a disingenuous press release which stated that the masterplanning process was continuing and that the college would only make a decision on the future once that had been completed. Sebastian Hanley, the PR man brought in to handle Wye Park on the college's behalf, fudged the issue of the BP institute and the removal of all contractors from the project. Nothing was expressly denied, but nor was it confirmed either.

We went from heroes to zeroes overnight. Justin later revealed, 'John Hodder phoned me to ask if the story was "actually true". Did I have any documentary evidence? Hodder, whose calm leadership during the early pandemonium caused by the signing of the concordat had steadied the village, was probably the one man whose opinion about the web-site mattered greatly to me. I was deeply disappointed when he concluded our conversation with the words: "I think we'll have to wait for a statement from Imperial before breathing easy." I desperately wanted to tell him who my sources were but I couldn't.'

I got the same on my return. Alan Paterson, one of the nicest, gentlest men in the village, couldn't look me in the eye and said simply, 'It's not over yet.' Someone else came up and asked, 'How are things? People aren't being too horrible, are they?'

They all thought we'd screwed up. We knew we hadn't. But we couldn't prove it. Had this been a story in *The Times* or the *Daily Telegraph* then Imperial would have been forced to respond more directly. If I'd been the journalist writing it for one of those papers I would have sat on the phone until they did, and walked round personally to bang on Richard Sykes's door if anyone messed me around. Real papers had real clout. They could run speculative stories based on accurate information safe in the knowledge that the people they exposed might one day throw up their hands and confess. That was how the system worked. Big newspapers could exert massive amounts of pressure.

But the big newspapers scarcely took any interest in a £1 billion plan to rip the heart out of some of England's most precious countryside. Two blokes with a web-site did and our clout was limited. We had the painful, annoying sting of a gadfly, nothing more. *Kent on Sunday* did their best but no-one was talking to them either. The *Kentish Express* swallowed Imperial's bland, misleading press statement and acted as if we were exactly what Cooling and Diana Pound had been implying all along, rumour mongers raising then dashing the hopes of the village at will.

I was glad Justin was away when this happened, gladder too when I discovered he was in a little hotel on the Lot river where the stone walls meant his smartphone didn't work unless there was a rare westerly wind. He'd had hell chasing this story. He'd had hell in his day job, with the *Sunday Telegraph* losing its second editor in six months.

People were very glum, and they blamed us. Things would only change if we could come up with visible, undeniable proof of the scale and scope and enormity of what Imperial had been trying to foist upon Wye. If we could find the plan.

Instead we carried the routine, somewhat lame story media organisations do in these circumstances, one pointing out as loudly as we could that Imperial had not actually denied a substantive word of our original article. I don't think it did us any good. It sounded a little shrill and unconvincing. People wanted proof, nothing less. Deliberately I scarcely communicated with Justin that week. He and Beth needed their holiday. It had been a difficult, exhausting year.

When he returned he was, I soon saw, hurt and upset by the response to a story that he knew to be true, and which had cost him much in time, stress and personal effort. I tried to summarise our position in an e-mail: 'According to Richard Honey (a local lawyer helping the Future Group) Imperial's line and that of ABC is that, yes, the planning has been scaled down but they haven't abandoned the idea and will resume it if it decides to go ahead in the future. RH and WFG too seem to think that, while one analysis of the present situation is that the original plan is dead, another interpretation is that they're merely behind schedule and determined to press ahead later once it's in the LDF. This seems to be the predominant belief within WFG which presumably explains why Alan Paterson was a bit glum the other night. In short people won't believe it's dead from us alone, but only when Imperial says so, and they all think that isn't going to happen for a very long time if ever.'

As usual he was one step ahead of me. On the fourth or fifth day in France the wind had changed to the west, sending low cloud and drizzle up the Lot valley from Cahors. It also brought a faint signal from some communications mast hidden further downstream. His phone had synchronised with the server back in Canary Wharf for the first time in four days. There were sixty unread e-mails there.

Many of them were from colleagues at work documenting the continuing uncertainty at the *Telegraph* where rumours of further severe cutbacks and job losses were gaining credence. But most were from a contact at Imperial and documented the pit that Wye Park had gradually fallen into since May. The project had been in deep trouble before the June management board meeting. An e-mail exchange between Brooks Wilson and Buck showed that Imperial did not have enough money to keep its environmental consultants working on the plan. It meant that it wouldn't be able to conduct an impact assessment this year – so there could be no planning application until 2008 at the earliest.

One message offered the entire management board presentation when he got back. Another suggested that we might like to investigate a little local issue near Milton Keynes where Brooks Wilson was said to have objected to a neighbour cutting down a small tree. There was also the offer of a copy of a letter sent by GeraldEve, Imperial's richly-rewarded planning consultants, warning that the entire project was not financially viable even if the Ernst & Young model from 2005 was used, and that had envisaged 390 acres of housing.

It was astonishing stuff, explosive material. Not least because inside that management board presentation, he was promised, lay a map. The final blueprint for the future of Wye, one which revealed that the college's dream involved building four thousand houses, quadrupling the size of the village, destroying the community and countryside we all knew and loved, just as we had suspected all along.

This was the start of the final act, the moment when we began to glimpse the heart of the matter, the smoking gun that would surely blow Wye Park to pieces one day. It landed on Justin's lap just at the very moment that most of the village thought we were a spent force, a pair of overambitious hacks who'd led them up the garden path of a false dawn only to discover there was despair and endless uncertainty at the end.

Jargon time

There was a riddle here, though. If Wye Park was dead why was Imperial pretending it still breathed? We knew from the documents which Justin had obtained that the college had clamped down on all unnecessary spending as part of its determination to put the project 'on ice'. In a letter to contractors on June 27th, it had told them the management board on June 12th had agreed 'to complete the master plan work and to then undertake a period of review and therefore to place the project into "economy" mode'.

But if BP weren't coming – and they weren't – what was the point? There could be no vast global centre of research excellence and by implication, or so it would seem, no Wye Park. The answer to this puzzle lay in the arcane workings of local government and, in particular, something called the Local Development Framework (LDF). This was a blueprint for the area which Ashford had to produce as part of its planning obligations, an overview of what it expected to happen in development terms within its boundaries over the coming decade.

If some son-of-Wye-Park construction project were to emerge, its possible construction had to be included in the LDF in order to justify any planning application. The LDF was there to set out what the area needed for the future. Any building scheme of the size Imperial had in mind could only stand a chance of success if the LDF mentioned that there was a plan and a need for such a venture. The grandiose idea that Professor Borys had so casually outlined in January might fall apart. But the fact remained that Imperial continued to own a large estate in Wye, one which could become extraordinarily lucrative if only the college could persuade someone to buy at residential or commercial prices land which it had picked up for a song as agricultural fields in the first place.

David Brooks Wilson's estates department was now focused on getting a mention of Wye Park into the borough LDF at any cost. If he succeeded then some kind of money-making development scheme, perhaps even one that entailed new housing and yet another business park alone, just might be possible to reclaim a rich profit from the disaster that had gone before. The college had frittered away some £1 million on experts and consultants to try to lift the wingless bird that was once Project Alchemy off the ground. A mention in the LDF was rapidly looking like the last possible opportunity to get back some of that wasted expense.

A measure of how desperate Imperial was to claw its way into the area plan was contained in the string of e-mails that Justin received on his return from France. One minuted a meeting of the Concordat Group – a quasi-official body consisting of Imperial, Pete Raine from KCC, Hugh Bullock of GeraldEve, Dan Ringelstein of Skidmore, Owings and Merrill and Richard Alderton from Ashford. The minutes were only short but clearly showed that Imperial's consultants had been busy writing the Wye section of the Local Development Framework draft alongside Ashford's civil servants. This was something that many planning experts found extraordinary when we revealed the actual documents.

There was nothing wrong with a would-be developer discussing issues such as the LDF with the council. Consultation of that kind could save time and money all round. That was not what appeared to be going on here. In the wonderful way that sometimes happens when people forget that computers have long memories, the editing trail of the actual document Justin had obtained was still in place. It revealed who had changed what and when. Through GeraldEve Imperial managed to water down the draft's original demand for 'proven national interest' to merely 'public interest'. A paragraph on the role of the local community was made less demanding after college objections.

It was technical stuff, but enough to convince people that something was going wrong with Wye Park, and our original story may not have been the red herring many had come to believe. Justin was also able to cite documents which showed that relations between Ashford planners had deteriorated seriously around June as the college piled on the pressure to get some mention of its development in the LDF.

But there was a much more interesting possibility raised by these revelations too. It was apparent to us that the LDF had taken on a crucial importance for David Brooks Wilson and his team. It was the last chance to gain any profit out of the still, cold corpse of Wye Park. In his presentation on June 12th, Brooks Wilson hadn't even considered the possibility that the project might not make its way into Ashford's area development plan.

Yet, as relations deteriorated between the authority and the college, that seemed to be a tantalising possibility.

Some time soon, probably by October, Richard Alderton's planning team would write the finished version of the LDF. If we could cause so much fuss, embarrassment and noise that the project never made it into that document, Wye Park would, surely, be dead for good. Conversely, if the project did scrape its way into the LDF, then years of blight and bureaucracy might lie ahead. We couldn't begin to contemplate that. I wasn't even sure we had the time and energy to keep the site up and running until October.

Finally, we had a target. Two months in which to bury Imperial's monster, in public, with a full and frank death certificate provided by the college itself. Or else admit defeat, pack up and leave everything to years of slow and expensive 'consultation'.

The Big One

There comes a time when stories grow too large even for an accomplished lone wolf reporter to handle alone. That time was now. When I sat down and began to sort through the information Justin's various moles and contacts within Wye Park had leaked to him I understood his bewilderment about how next to proceed. Investigative journalists rarely work with the full story in front of them. In my day as a reporter we mostly dealt with snippets and fragments, a glimpse of a document and the invitation to scrawl down a note of it, or a brief, unauthorised chat with some unhappy employee, a man or woman nursing a grievance and willing to share it, usually over a beer in a pub.

This was, as I kept reminding people, the 21st century. Everyone worked by e-mail now, and the subtle task of leaking illicit material had taken on a new dimension. All you needed to do was get a copy of the original, as a word processing file, a spreadsheet or a presentation, then forward it somewhere. Provided you could evade the internal security screens – and they seemed very flimsy indeed across Imperial's sprawling network – the job was finished, with a speed and efficiency I could only have dreamt of back in the 1980s.

Justin had received an enormous amount of material from inside Wye Park. It ranged from reports on finance and viability to detailed studies on planning and environmental concerns. He also had a stream of confidential e-mails between the principal officers of the college and outside parties that revealed a bilious, bickering atmosphere which explained, in part, why some of those on the inside were willing to send all this precious information our way.

And he had the Holy Grail too. A map. *The* map. One so clear, so unambiguous we knew it was the final version, the blueprint that would one day go forward in a planning application as Imperial's true 'vision' for Wye. It was horrifying yet in a way comforting too. Staring at it on my computer at home, on page forty seven, 'The Land Use Plan', of the document the college's management board had approved on June 12th, I realised that our innate fears of the scale of the development had been justified all along. This was what everyone instinctively feared, because we knew the lie of the land of our community. When we walked our dogs on the ancient footpaths behind Withersdane we could imagine how acres of boring modern housing might spring up over the fields of wheat and the meadows where cattle now grazed. Looking at the neglected greenhouses and abandoned laboratories behind the college's grimy and neglected modern library we could see, too, the logic of sweeping them away and replacing them with offices and industrial units, stretching all the way to the foot of the hill.

This was the new Wye that lived at the back of our imaginations. Patrick Keegan, a local architect who had lived in the village for years and was familiar with developing large housing estates, had come to dinner during the summer and, with a typical Wye sense of humour, rolled out for me a spoof blueprint he had drawn himself for the new town to come. This ran from close to Brook to Wye and beyond, reaching the foot of the Downs, homes and offices and factory units spilling all the way down the gentle hill into the village. A new road stretched from the M20 through to Jane Austen's former home in the hamlet of Godmersham, replacing the existing A28 as the principal route between Ashford and Canterbury. At the eastern end of this new dual carriageway's run past Wye, Keegan had thoughtfully drawn in space for a supermarket and a service station, with another site for what he had labelled 'McDonalds, Olantigh' by the side.

Looking at Imperial's actual blueprint two weeks later I realised that, with his architect's eye, he'd got it spot on. The only part missing was the new road, and that had been slyly slipped into the county planning process separately earlier in the year at the KCC meeting attended by Charles Findlay who had, naturally, not said a word.

If you knew Wye you only had to look at Imperial's secret blueprint to understand it was the real thing. The map was highly detailed, marking contours and field boundaries, with housing in yellow, the research institute in blue, and the 'cluster park', essentially a business and commercial estate, in red. Everything fitted in with the inner perception of the village we all possessed already. Imperial hoped to build 250 acres of housing in all, stretching from Olantigh in the east, up to the Downs, then past Withersdane on to its existing holdings at Silks Farm and Amage in the west, and around the ancient farmhouse of Coldharbour at the foot of the road to the Crown. Two new roads would feed in to these estates from either side of the village, cutting through the network of solitary paths so popular with locals and visitors alike.

The business park would run south from Olantigh Road through the flat crop fields above, ending at the foot of the steep rise to the Crown, and amounting to thirty seven acres in all. The so-called research institute, which was meant to be the reason behind the plan in the first place, amounted to just twelve acres in all and would be built on either side of Scotton Street, the road to the Downs, part in front of Withersdane and the rest in the fields across the road. We knew now that this institute would probably never take place, since BP had ruled out Wye as a possible location. If the broad scheme still worked its way into the planning process the likelihood would be that the college would attempt to use this for other purposes, perhaps by extending the business park or, more likely, the amount of land used for housing, the one quick and simple way any developer had of raising large sums of money through building in the Ashford area. As if to emphasise that cash and housing was at the heart of the project, Imperial had also marked in yellow two plots of land in distant Brook which it owned, signalling their intent to turn them into small housing developments too.

It all made sense. When we finally published the map the entire village looked at it, on the site and in masses of printouts from our samizdat press, and knew this was the real thing. Alan Paterson, who had seemed so gloomy when I met him after Justin's first story, rushed to be the first to post a comment...

> In haste as we must catch ferry!
> What can I and my family say but thank you again to David and Justin for this ammunition that so greatly helps the formal opposition to Imperial's Vision for Wye.
> Anyone who has until now been sceptical will surely be persuaded by the weight of evidence you have amassed. Thanks too to your brave 'whistleblowing' sources from all those of us who care about the future of Wye. Keep it up.
> *Alan Paterson, August 10th, 2006 at 9:37 am*

But that was in the future. First we had to get all this mass of information into a manageable form and decide how to present it. The problem was the size of it, report after report, every one of them a gem demanding a story in itself. We were determined not to diminish the power of these astonishing leaks by rushing them onto the site simultaneously, drowning readers in information. I soon realised how important this was to be. We were still, in some quarters, deeply mistrusted.

On August 8th I fed in one more story from Justin's leaks. It was a report on the environmental implications of the proposed development. Imperial's plans were so large that they would have to meet new strict guidelines on energy sustainability – including the generation of electricity. Existing utility services in the area couldn't possibly cope with the power demands. Imperial would, said a report from a group of professional consultants they'd hired, have to generate their own. A combined heat and power plant would need to be built close to the village, burning 'friendly' fuels. And at least two wind turbines, each fifty metres high with a blade diameter of twenty metres, would have to be erected too. It was a hot story. The local press ignored it, which didn't surprise me. So, to an extent, did the village. The idea seemed too far-fetched. Someone asked me if it wasn't some kind of a bad joke. We were still, in the eyes of some, a couple of jesters.

Doubts like these could not be allowed to happen with the principal revelation still waiting in the wings, the masterplan itself. Up until now we had simply written stories as they came in, rarely even checking each other's copy because we didn't have the time. That was no longer good enough. I needed to step into the role I'd been shirking all along, that of editor, and set out what was going to happen and how.

Justin, never a selfish journalist who wanted to hog things for himself, seemed relieved. I mapped out a plan for six articles to appear simultaneously first thing on the morning of Thursday, August 10th, with a simultaneous print publication for download and to be distributed through every possible channel we could find, the New Flying Horse, Wye News, and all the available people our samizdat network could reach. This was designed to be the killer blow and I was determined we would get it right, presenting readers with hard evidence direct from Imperial's own files, as much as we dared without compromising Justin's sources.

The final breakdown of the pieces ran like this. *Not dead yet... but it's struggling.* An assessment of the state of Wye Park in 'economy mode', and how Imperial were trying to slip some mention of it into the LDF as a way of keeping the project alive. *And now there are political heads on the block.* A run around some of the political implications of the information we were revealing. *The real cost of Wye Park (and it's peanuts).* Some internal financial numbers from Imperial's reports, ones which showed its initial portrayal as a '£1 billion project' was far from reality since Imperial's private estimates forecast that the real price tag was closer to £175 million. *Wye's countryside: a cash cow to be unlocked.* An examination of Imperial's attitude to its estate at Wye, with documents that showed its principal interest was raising money from land sales. *Imperial rebuilds Wye... as a town of 10,000.* The fine detail of the vast and ambitious building scheme which had been approved on June 12th.

The covering introduction summarised what we were now making public in a concise, easily digested form. Six articles were too many for one person to write, not least because Justin was once again embroiled in the continuing turmoil at the *Telegraph.* I offered to help but I didn't want to steal his thunder. This was his story and I felt uneasy having my name on it. In the end he suggested we run joint bylines on pieces which involved both of us, and that is how most of the substantial stories carried by save-wye during its brief remaining life were handled. I wrote the intro, the politics and the finance, and a two page print newsletter, while Justin worked on the rest.

This time we read everything very carefully, including each other's copy. At seven thirty on the morning of August 10th I called Justin on his way into work to say I'd gone through it all one more time and we were ready to go. One of us, I can't recall which, said the words, 'Unleash the hounds' and with a few clicks of the mouse it was done. The biggest set of stories save-wye had ever produced, the result of months of intensive work on his part, not mine, went live.

Secret no more: the nightmare vision for Wye
Thursday, August 10th, 2006 by David Hewson and Justin Williams

We've been told for months it was nothing more than an idea for civilised discussion, and certainly not a plan. Now save-wye can prove this charade to be the gross and indefensible lie we've suspected all along. Today we publish extracts from the secret report that went to Imperial College's management board on

June 12, almost two months ago, which discussed the detailed blueprint the college had already assembled by that stage, one which would mean the death of the Kent village of Wye forever.

Click on the picture of the map and you will see the enormity that Imperial wishes to visit on the village, and all so that it can fill its coffers to pay for more facilities in London… not Kent at all. This is the detailed plan Imperial College, Ashford Borough Council and Kent County Council hoped you would all never see until it was too late and the destruction of Wye so insidiously ingrained into the local development process that only a miracle could stop it. The reality would be as bad as anyone could have feared… a sprawling mass of offices, scientific buildings and houses that would quadruple the size of the present village, wreath the area in construction work for years and end Wye's heritage as a historic rural jewel of east Kent once and for all.

And just to rub it in Imperial hopes, as it has promised, to skip construction in the Area of Special Scientific Interest – for now anyway – but plans to send the bulldozers beyond it, to build new housing on land it owns in the village of Brook too. It is a vast and cynical exercise in property development that would cause a furore anywhere in the country. But the idea that such a plan could be visited on an Area of Outstanding Natural Beauty is simply breathtaking… and explains the extraordinary lengths to which the college and its placemen in Kent's local authorities have gone to hide the truth from the very people this gigantic scheme would affect, economically, socially and culturally for years to come.

Today we can throw off a little of that shroud of secrecy. Click on our summary on the right to get a brief overview of the spin machine that has been foisted on the Ashford area for the past nine months. In separate longer articles below you can find out how…

- The detailed plans for the village and outlying area would involve construction across huge swathes of beautiful countryside and stretch halfway to the village of Brook

- The prospect of BP going to London instead of Wye has thrown a huge question mark against the project, and turned it instead into a potential moneyspinner to pay for college development in London

- The publicly quoted costs for the project of £1 billion to £1.5 billion bear no relation to the real and much smaller estimates used in private by Imperial, quotes that appear to include the college taking £100 million in 'profits' for work in London the moment it goes ahead
- Imperial's own private documents boast about how local politicians have helped them formulate their plans… with potentially dire consequences for those involved
- Imperial assesses the risks it believes could bring its overweening ambition crashing to earth

These are the most detailed revelations about Imperial's ambitions and the way it has played fast and loose with the public to date, and they tell the story, for the most part, from the college's own secret internal records. We hope to bring you more of the same in the future.

The effect was electrifying. Imperial had already been carrying out an internal witch hunt after our earlier revelations. When these stories appeared the college went into meltdown. Innocent staff were dragged into meetings and grilled about their loyalty. Those in the inner circle of the project looked at one another and wondered if it was one of them doing the leaking. It was all enormous fun, not least because the college's lieutenants clearly had no idea how much information we truly possessed. The leaks we had published earlier that month, about the environmental report and the influence the college had sought in writing the LDF, had been bad enough. But these six stories showed our penetration of their organisation was much deeper than they could ever have feared.

We had enough material to produce another six such stories the following day, and the day after that. I refrained, for two good reasons. I wanted to let the impact of the current revelations sink in locally, and get followed up by the two newspapers that would surely take an interest. And we knew this string of good luck wouldn't last. Justin's moles were only human. They would be caught up in the panic inside the college and realise they had to go quiet if they were to keep their careers. That was only to be expected. They had risked more than enough already. But the rotten truth was that, by going for broke with the most precious information we had, save-wye was writing its own death warrant. Our sources would dry up. We had run out of Freedom of Information requests to give us new revelations. We would, like it or not, be faced with the prospect of returning to our initial role as a distributor of informed opinion, not hard news. It was clear by now that there was only one viewpoint current anywhere in the village: this project must stop. How many times could we say that yet again?

Over the next few days we slipped in some more of Justin's luscious leaks, detailing, in revelatory internal e-mails, how close relations had been between Imperial's developers and Ashford's planning team, the 'key messages' script that Ernst & Young had written for everyone, including councillors, to read whenever they were asked about the project, and the existence of Plan B, an escape route by which the college would recover its costs for a failed Wye Park simply by selling off parts of the estate to anyone who would have them. This last article revealed the actual worth of Wye College: £17 million for everything, college, Withersdane and the farm land at real world agricultural prices. It showed exactly how much extra Richard Sykes and crew hoped to extract by converting those fields to housing, with an instant profit of £100 million for nothing more than a simple change of use.

Kent on Sunday took its usual interest in the story. The *Kentish Express* scarcely touched it, and never printed the tell-tale map, a gift for any real local newspaper, at all. Justin offered it for free, in print quality high resolution, to the editor, Leo Whitlock, only to be told the paper had no space to print it. There must have been a lot of bouncing baby pictures or school kids with chickens on their heads that week.

And from Imperial? Scarcely a word. Nor from our councillors or the local MP Damian Green. We'd produced the detailed information which the college had drawn up in secret and never even hinted at in its so-called 'consultations' with the village. We'd blown apart the myth of Wye Park completely and the Kent power network still didn't understand how to respond. To my utter amazement, David Brooks Wilson was about to brazen it out one last time.

Terrorists

By this stage the village was in a very jolly mood so it seemed time for some light relief. Justin had exactly the right thing in that e-mail he'd received on his return from France detailing some little local planning difficulties David Brooks Wilson had been experiencing in his second home in Milton Keynes. It was a lulu of a tale, which we headlined, 'Environmental activist comes out of the closet'.

A neighbour had wanted to chop down a cherry tree on the rather ugly modern redbrick development where Brooks Wilson lived with his wife. This infuriated the man who was now trying to squeeze four thousand homes onto the beautiful rolling fields of Wye, a very far cry from the urban canal-side location of the Brooks Wilson home. So that we might prove that last point on the site, one of the Connies had taken some photos of the area nearby so that we could illustrate the gulf between Brooks Wilson's version of desirable countryside and ours.

His letter to the local council opposing the loss of a single cherry tree was a classic of pompous hypocrisy, just the kind of Nimby attitude Imperial had been trying to throw at their critics in Wye without success.

My wife and I have lived in Woodley Headland since 1987 and consider this application would have an adverse effect on the character and amenities provided to all residents by the location of the said cherry tree. It should be noted that with the exception of one tree which was destroyed, it is believed, due to illness, that every house in the road has a cherry tree in the front garden and, indeed, it was part of the overall nature and quality of the original development that called for the location of these trees which are now beautifully matured.

My wife and I consider the removal of this tree will make the area into much more of an urban landscape and not be in keeping with the requirements of the original covenants in the title deeds to the said properties in Woodley Headland.

It follows that we both believe that the removal of this tree will have a severe impact on the appearance of the area and indeed the overall character of the street bearing in mind that all the houses contain such a tree. It is also felt that the removal of this tree could be the catalyst for the removal of further trees thus causing a major deterioration from a country landscape fronting the canal into one of an urban nature.

Justin set a photo of the Downs, with the Crown on the top, next to a shot from the passing Connie of Brooks Wilson's distinctly mundane corner of Milton Keynes. Down the farmers' market that weekend people spoke of little else. John Rogers, a well-known and popular local figure, summed up their feelings with his short, pithy comment on the site, 'What a wonderful story! Hypocrisy rules and blind greed prevails.'

Brooks Wilson was not so amused. Justin and I had discussed in detail exactly how much we intended to reveal about this key figure's home life. While there was no legal reason we couldn't print the man's address, and we had photos of his actual house, we decided not to do so, and used generic pictures of the area instead. This spared readers the sight of the man's front garden which contained some of the most hideous garden furniture either of us had ever cast our eyes on, parked on the tiny Brooks Wilson lawn for all to see.

This article got us the only official letter we ever received from Imperial. Its director of human resources wrote to us...

Whereas the College would defend the right to your opinions in a free society we are of the view that the personal details contained in this article transcend normal lobbying activities. The contents of your article breach Mr Brooks Wilson's right to privacy as well as copyright and data protection rights. We would, therefore, ask you to take immediate steps to remove the pictures of Mr Brooks Wilson's home in Woodley Headland; the details regarding the address of his private residence; and the reference to his property in east London 'being occupied during the week'. We are confident that you will appreciate the security and privacy issues raised by the contents of the article which could have a very serious effect on the personal safety and security of Mr Brooks Wilson and his family and their right to a private life.

Fortunately Justin got in a reply to that one, a polite refusal, before I had the chance to respond in a far more intemperate fashion. It was wonderfully understated, much more than I could ever have achieved.

Dear Sir,
Thank you for your email of August 22, 2006.
Mr Brooks Wilson's letter to Milton Keynes council is a matter of public record and is available to any visitor to the council on request. It is, therefore, in the public domain. He is at the centre of Imperial College's highly controversial plans for its Wye Campus – plans that involve building on hundreds of acres of protected land and which directly affect the lives and futures of hundreds of residents of that village. His objection to the removal of a tree preservation order is, therefore, a matter of legitimate public interest.

As to your concerns about privacy and safety, save-wye.org made a decision not publish a picture of his house or detail his addresses in Woodley Headland or London. There are no copyright issues involved, nor any data protection issues because Mr Brooks Wilson chose to write to Milton Keynes council, thereby making his view about the cherry tree a matter of public record.

Imperial and Brooks Wilson were living on another planet. We hadn't identified his house, we hadn't breached his 'right to privacy' – not that such a thing exists in English law – nor had we endangered his security in any way whatsoever. We had simply pointed out that his private actions failed to be consistent with his very public ones, which is something the media have done for years and hopefully will for many to come.

When Brooks Wilson turned up for the next consultation panel he was still utterly livid about this article, decrying us as 'terrorists' and asking if no-one could rein us in. It was Damian Green, Ashford's MP, who put him straight, pointing out that people who chose to live in the public eye had to live with the consequences. As Green observed, everyone knew he had a house in the Ashford area and one in London, and that, as an MP, he spent most of the week in town. That didn't represent a security threat. It was how things were.

The hypocrisy didn't end there. Word reached us several weeks later that Lord Bruce-Lockhart, signatory to the first concordat, former leader of KCC and now chairman of the Local Government Association, a man who was apparently happy to see Wye disappear for good, had been personally offended by our treatment of Brooks Wilson and was complaining loudly about it. He told Ben Moorhead that the story we ran had been a gross invasion of privacy and 'utterly unacceptable'.

I was astonished. If we'd actually printed a photo of Brooks Wilson's ghastly garden furniture or his gross and tasteless private villa in Tobago – both of which we possessed – he might have had a point, though we still would have been within our rights. But we didn't. I couldn't believe a man like Bruce-Lockhart who had managed to reach the summit of local government in the nation could fail to understand the basic workings of the media over matters of public interest. Or rather I couldn't until I reminded myself that he came from Kent where newspapers meant the tame little creatures owned by his friend Edwin Boorman. Like all the others in his circle, he never expected to have to deal with rough boys like us.

Brooks Wilson had something else to say about us at that consultation panel, and it was a statement so astonishing it would bring this whole story to the boiling point. We had now, in our own eyes, delivered a fatal wound to Wye Park twice, once in July, when Justin had revealed it had gone into 'economy mode' after the college decided to try to tempt BP to London instead, and a second time on August 10th with our six-part revelation of the fine detail of the project, and the tell-tale map, both firm proof that the 'this is only a vision not a plan' line was just plain wrong.

To my amazement the man was still determined to brazen it out in the desperate hope of squeezing some mention of Imperial's development into the forthcoming development framework. The map we published, he told those present in Wye that night, was just one draft out of twenty seven or so, and had never made it into the presentation to the board. It was the old Cooling line we had heard so many times. We were just a couple of chancers, make-it-up artists, two lowly hacks who had deceived the village once more.

I couldn't believe it. We had to kill this thing all over again, and this time in a way that left no-one in any doubt it was gone for good.

Letters galore

Before we could turn to Imperial's masterplan for one final time, we discovered there was urgent work to do. On Friday, August 18th I received one of the usual round of leaked e-mails from inside the Future Group. Though I had no way of knowing it, we were now just three weeks away from the crucial borough council decision that would scupper Wye Park entirely. The message was from Ben Moorhead and confined to the inner members of the organisation who were still, to my astonishment, being reached through an e-mail system resting within wye.org, not the new and rather desultory web-site they now had.

The missive was a call for everyone to send a letter to ABC to ask for Wye to be left out of the LDF altogether. This was, Moorhead said, a 'crucial moment in our effort to protect Wye and its countryside from Imperial College's bulldozers'. And nobody even thought to ask us to be involved in publicising an effort which, as things turned out, would prove to be one of the principal daggers in the project's heart.

What happened next illustrated the difference between the conventional, 'decent' mode of campaigning typified by the busy, dedicated men and women of the Future Group and the new, anarchic, instant form of action which Justin and I had come to invent by accident over the previous eight months. Time was short. The LDF was to be settled some time over the next eight weeks, and letters urging the removal of Wye Park had to be on the desk of the council's planning officer Richard Alderton quickly ahead of a planned decision on September 11th, though in the event it would all happen much more quickly.

The Future Group had by now lost any reticence about asking people to pick up their pens to contact their councils, partly in response to the CPRE's objections to Diana Pound's attempts to stifle an earlier letter-writing campaign. Moorhead wanted desperately to get a good and informed response from his members. This heartfelt and praiseworthy aim was to be greatly, potentially fatally, hampered by the organisation's own bureaucracy and its lack of a fast, easy way to communicate well with the outside world.

He had written a great letter though. Had they simply come to us and suggested we run it as a story I would have done so. But since they didn't I decided to do what came naturally: nick the idea and develop it ourselves. Everything we had built since January was now to come into play: the site's facility for instant communication and feedback with the public at large, the distribution scheme based around the staff and the busy bars of the New Flying Horse and the counter of Wye News, our little samizdat system for getting A4 publications out from our hidden printer in the village through the volunteer courier network. I never envisaged any of this. It just happened then, when the occasion arose, fell naturally into place.

Printed material was crucial to what we were trying to achieve. We needed to reach our own readership, but we also needed to spur them into persuading their neighbours to sit down and write a letter too. So I stole then adapted the best part of Moorhead's message and created our own plea for people to write something, whatever their opinion, and quickly.

The print version was headlined 'Will you write a letter that could save a village?' and covered both sides of an A4 sheet, with the copy beginning, 'The battle for Wye has been joined.' The article was timed for release on the following Monday. We'd learned early on that the site's readership fell substantially at weekends when people, naturally, had better things to do. Also I wanted to ensure there was a constant supply of the printed versions available in Wye when we went live. I wrote...

Here's your chance to make a difference

One of the great myths of the Wye Park saga is the idea that the opinions of ordinary people don't matter, that the question of whether a content rural community should be destroyed forever is to be decided by the experts on both sides of the argument.

We have long argued here at save-wye that this is a grave mistake, and pretty downright insulting for those who don't have time to take part in long meetings and campaign groups. The power of public opinion is real, provided the public can be bothered to express it. Well, now is your chance. For the time it takes to write a letter and the cost of a postage stamp you just might help bury Imperial's monstrous masterplan to destroy the Wye we know forever.

That opportunity comes with the approaching finalisation of Ashford Council's 'core strategy' document, essentially a plan for the whole of the borough against which Wye Park would be judged should Imperial try to proceed with it. I'm sure many of you glaze over when you see jargon like this popping up over this site. We do too, frankly. But the core strategy – which incorporates the local development framework we hear so much of – is important, and could prove a final hurdle across which Richard Sykes and his construction crew fail to leap. As a local resident you have a right to express an opinion on it, and if enough of us do that, in one obvious direction, then we will be hard to ignore. Remember: ABC is still trying to tell everyone that only a handful of nimbies oppose Wye Park. Now you have the opportunity to prove them wrong.

Just so that you understand a little of the background let me summarise some of the stories on this subject you will find elsewhere on this site. First, a draft core strategy was produced by the council earlier this year, but since that date the council has added – without anything approaching proper consultation – a clause to help Imperial get planning permission should it try to go ahead with Wye Park. They have also allowed Imperial's own advisers to write parts of the document directly, letting the college's adviser succeed in downgrading one of the key requirements any eventual planning application would have to overcome.

This is outrageous, undemocratic and sadly typical of this shambolic local authority. But you can do something about it. You can write to Richard Alderton, the head of planning (at Ashford Borough Council, Civic Centre, Tannery Lane, Ashford TN23 1PL) and register your opinion. We're not going to tell you what to say, because an individual letter means much more than some photocopied round robin.

But here are some points you might like to consider. First, how about urging that Wye should be removed from the core strategy document altogether? It hasn't been subject to proper consultation. There is no need to rush it through, since Imperial could still make a planning application even if it isn't included. Its appearance in the core strategy appears to show nothing but bias on the part of the council and you may feel free to tell them so.

You might want to remind the council of a few of the things that make Wye special, such as the Area of Outstanding Natural Beauty. Wye Future Group, which is also urging its members to write to ABC on this subject, also suggests bringing up the national policy guidance which demands that AONBs only be built on if a matter is in the 'national interest'. How can thousands of homes and a relatively modest office and science park be in the national interest?

You might want to question the jobs figures. True, Ashford has been tasked by the government with creating a lot. But the plans which have been leaked so far show that the initial 12,500 jobs figure is a myth, and the reality would be much smaller.

Finally, you could bring up the clear evidence that there are abundant alternative sites for such a scheme with planning permission already. When large parcels of existing development land in and around Ashford are empty, and often have been for years, why should new building take place in protected countryside?

Ashford Council is in a deep, deep hole over Wye Park. It has behaved with outrageous partiality, and without the full facts of Imperial's intentions. If enough of us bombard the civic centre with polite, reasoned letters of opposition, who knows? We might just persuade someone in this council that the best thing to do is drop Wye Park from the core strategy altogether, and give the authority the chance to recover a little of its reputation after the secretive shenanigans of the last eighteen months.

And if that happens, we can all pop the champagne for a while. The future of Imperial's holdings in Wye will not be solved by a victory like this. But it would be a win for the angels. And don't we deserve one right now?

The council won't tell us how many letters it's received for an interminable amount of time. But if you'd like others to see yours just cut and paste it into a comment form here for all to see. And don't delay either. Time is short.

We'd never tried this kind of direct appeal before. I wondered whether readers would really want to make public on the site their own thoughts and a letter to the council. The English are funny about private correspondence sometimes. At first I thought I'd blown it. The day I posted the article we had just one response, from Kerry Bethel, a busy, committed villager who'd followed the campaign throughout and could always be relied upon to do his bit. But we needed a lot more than that.

Then the trickle slowly turned into a steady flow. Ordinary residents, former parish councillors, local doctors and scientists, people who'd worked with Richard Alderton before... they all started writing, and sharing their correspondence for the world to see through the web-site. What was astonishing was the quality. These weren't Nimbyish, whining tomes of complaint. They were heartfelt, intelligent, argued reasons for leaving a vast construction scheme in Wye out of the development programme for the coming decade in Ashford.

One, in particular, stood out, a letter written by a civil servant who addressed the issue in clear, professional terms couched in the language of a planner, though not so opaquely that the rest of us couldn't understand. This message raised issues that went to the very core of the decision, questions about alternative sites, those targets set by John Prescott, and the long term sustainability of Imperial's presence in the village. The author's job precluded our mentioning his name, but it didn't stop me highlighting his letter in a separate article which I ran a few days later to jog more responses.

At the same time the printouts were flying off the bars of the New Flying Horse and circulating round the village thanks to our volunteers. Responses were coming in from Maidstone and Canterbury and beyond. One night in the bar when I was talking to our principal courier, a local teacher, Judy Ellis, a couple at the next table heard our conversation and asked what it was all about. We told them. They were from the Midlands, on their way to cross the Channel, but promised to write too. Something remarkable had happened. It was no longer just Cliff who would talk freely and openly on the subject to anyone who passed. The pub itself had become a nerve centre of the operation, with the young staff happily handing out leaflets and chatting to customers about what was going on. It had struck me throughout that the voice of protest against Imperial had been predominantly middle class and middle aged. It never seemed to touch anyone much under the age of thirty. Now that had changed. Something was happening, and I think we all knew it, even if we couldn't quite put a finger on what had changed.

Richard Alderton was on holiday while all this was going on. When he returned he found his desk at ABC covered in hundreds of individual letters demanding Wye be left out of the LDF, virtually every one different, well argued, and with good reasons. As Alderton and his staff sat down to look at their inbox they realised they were witnessing a public response quite unlike any they had ever encountered or, we were told, heard of in any other similar circumstances. This was the true voice of the public, ordinary people horrified by the plans which we had leaked and the idea that Wye might be destroyed simply for greed. Those letters were to bear heavily on Alderton's decisions in the days to come. Under the procedures used for developing the LDF, he knew he would have to declare them all to an independent inspector. Even if he wanted to – and everything we were to learn later suggested this was not the case – Alderton could not bury them without a second thought.

Just to hammer home the point, Justin had a few highly personal leaked documents for Ashford's planning head to read on his return, ones that showed exactly how Imperial, the council's so-called 'partner', felt towards him. They formed part of an exchange between David Brooks Wilson and fellow Imperial estates officer Nigel Buck after Alderton had asked Imperial's planners for an update on the masterplan 'in view of the long period of silence'.

Our files positively bristled with brusque e-mails despatched by Buck. Earlier, after we had asked Imperial's PRs for a copy of a graphic produced by Brooks Wilson at a consultation panel, he had stormed back, 'No. They can pay for their own f******g masterplan.'

On this occasion he was in no mood to accommodate Alderton who, along with his fellow planners, had been growing distinctly uneasy about the college's prolonged silences, and now politely sought further information.

To: David Brooks Wilson
From: Nigel Buck
Date: 19/07/06
My personal suggestion is that we should not respond at all to richard… he was at the last concordat and was told what he needed to know then.

If you produce anything in writing it will immediately become part of the public record so I am advising against such a move.

> He should be spending time getting the LDF out not wasting the tiem (sic) of consultants we are paying for and he isn't!

We'd known for ages that Imperial had been desperately trying to avoid putting anything on paper in case it worked its way out under a Freedom of Information request. Key documents had been deleted from its own systems and placed on those of its consultants which, as private companies, were exempt from the act. This message confirmed this dubious policy. To us, too, it showed the attitude Imperial had developed towards its so-called partners in the concordat. They were there to facilitate what Imperial wanted. Nothing less. Certainly nothing more.

While our letter-writing campaign was being taken up by all and sundry, the Future Group had fallen victim to its own internal bureaucracy. On August 21st, when we went live with the letter request, the group was mulling over whether to send Moorhead's own excellent missive on the subject – the one which first gave us the idea – to 'the whole mailing list'. The first circulation was apparently very limited. Two days later they were debating whether a single letter with multiple signatures was acceptable, or, in the eyes of Ashford, a petition. Someone pointed out it would be a good idea to act soon since save-wye was already doing something similar, oblivious to the fact we'd stolen their idea in the first place. None of this was easy for them. While we had our friendly samizdat laser printer based in the village, capable of being fired up the moment we posted a publication, the Future Group relied on an outside print shop and conventional deadlines. By August 26th, three days before Richard Alderton was due to return from holiday, copies of Moorhead's letter were finally going out, though it would take three more days to complete.

It all got worse. On September 5th the group discovered that its e-mail network had failed. The organisation wanted to call members to a meeting a week later and was unable to do so. It was reduced to trying to notify 750 members by post, the letters arriving only days before the event to which they were being invited. Hours of manual labour, long days spent trekking around the district, and much last-minute toil went into trying to get Moorhead's letter out to the masses. We know from our own experience that it took two to three days for most people to get around to writing a letter. The Future Group's creaky communications system meant that by the time most of the responses it could prompt arrived at Ashford's council offices they were too late. Alderton already had a weight of evidence on his desk pushing him to drop Wye: the visible masterplan, which we would now make available in its original form for everyone to see, hundreds of articulate letters of protest, and proof of the college's own imperious attitude towards the authority and so-called consultation.

The Future Group played a pivotal role in the defeat of Imperial College. Its quiet nagging at Alderton's team over months of meetings had, with our coverage and the paucity of genuine information from Imperial, been leading him to doubt the plan for some time. But it was the flood of intelligent letters and the visible, unmistakable presence of the masterplan that pushed him over the edge. The Future Group was comprised of good, dedicated people who would work long hours in support of a cause about which they felt deeply. The episode of this crucial letter was proof for me that good intentions meant nothing if your message was incapable of being communicated to the public quickly and efficiently.

The game had moved on by the time the group was beginning to get its distribution process into gear. Notice that it had entered a new phase would come from the most unlikely of sources, with the most unlikely of public gestures. Ian Cooling was about to come out publicly and very visibly on the side of the angels. To us, that could only mean one thing. Wye's borough councillor had come to realise the war was over, and was now desperate to make sure he was standing in the victor's territory when the armistice was finally declared.

Cooling had little time to get into position. On August 25th, four days before Alderton's return, with the flow of protest letters aimed at him now flowing steadily, we had made our final attempt on the faltering life of Imperial's masterplan. This time we were both determined the thing would stay down for good.

Talking statues

The problem we faced over our revelations of August 10th was simply a variation of the one we'd been hampered with all along. They were a report of an event, not the event itself, thereby allowing Brooks Wilson to tell people we'd only seen a few scraps of worthless information, and used those out of context to scare people once again. To prove our case we had to reveal the original documents, not extracts from them, however substantial the latter might appear. With the masterplan presentation produced for the June 12th meeting we had no difficulty over sourcing. It was completely untraceable. What gave me concern was a line that appeared at the foot of every slide in the PowerPoint document, one that said 'copyright Imperial College, London'.

We'd scrounged some free legal advice from a media lawyer who told us what we half suspected already. This was a copyright document. We could argue for breaching that copyright if we could prove that to do so was in the public interest. That wouldn't be hard, and in the end would probably be successful. But if Imperial wanted they could still come at us with lawyers in the meantime, forcing us into court to make our case. A big newspaper faced with a situation like this wouldn't think twice. It would publish and be damned. Big newspapers possess money, full-time legal staff and friends in high places. We had none of those things. If Imperial sent the men in wigs our way we would find ourselves dragged before the bench, faced with huge expenses, and trapped in a legal procedure that might freeze the site for weeks or even months, just at the moment when we had the most to achieve.

I'd no doubt the village would rally round to help out with any legal bills. After all we'd never asked for a penny to support what we'd done. Still, the idea of being unable to cover this final, crucial stage of the story was simply unthinkable. We needed a way to publish this vast document, running to 20 mb as the original presentation file, too large for a conventional download, and at the same time escape any immediate legal consequences.

I'd had an inkling for some time that we might end up facing this sort of dilemma, and a possible solution. Strangely enough it stemmed from the very novel I'd spent that year writing, when I wasn't engrossed in save-wye.

I've lost count of the time I've spent in Rome, yet still it's a city that fascinates me. Every time I go there I find something new. Researching this latest book I'd come across one more fascinating detail. From the sixteenth century on, when the Vatican ruled the city with an iron grip, quashing all opposition, people had discovered a very Roman way of getting round the censorship rules. They chose several well-known and prominent statues in the city and used them to start 'conversations' discussing local politics and personalities. Each night an anonymous message would be posted on a statue announcing some news or outlining an opinion. A day or two later a message or counter observation would appear on a statue elsewhere, couched as a reply. It was a way of spreading dangerous information without getting caught. The most popular 'talking statue' was Pasquino, close to the Piazza Navona, which is still covered in political diatribes today.

I always maintained two or three web-site accounts as a way of testing out new designs for my own. That was why I was able to move save-wye so quickly when we were crashed by the denial of service attack earlier in the year. With no great forethought, I'd also, shortly after starting save-wye, obtained a domain name for one of them, www.talkingstatues.net. This was housed behind an address firewall which hid my identity entirely, and told anyone who looked up the site records that it was under the control of a company in Oram, Utah. I could post the entire copyright Imperial College masterplan to talkingstatues without a single footprint back to me or save-wye.

It wasn't a perfect situation. If the college's lawyers really wanted to come at us they might have gone to court and sought some kind of order to examine my computer and see if I had any link with talkingstatues. That would have given the game away. But it would also have been expensive, time-consuming and rotten publicity for them. So it was a risk I was willing to take.

The question then became: how do I make it available? A 20 mb PowerPoint file is a lot for anyone to download, and I suspected many of save-wye's readers wouldn't have bothered. The net provided its own solution. PowerPoint will happily export a presentation as web pages. I'd never done this before but it was easy. In less than a minute Brooks Wilson's secret presentation had been converted into a 57-page web site, with navigation menus and graphics – including the maps – all in place.

I'd long since exceeded the usage limits on my own net connection. So I took my laptop down to the New Flying Horse, paid a modest sum to access the local wi-fi network there, bought myself a beer, and uploaded the lot to talkingstatues, making it a sub-directory of the main site so it could all be reached through the address talkingstatues.net/WyePark/wyepark.htm. I did nothing at all to the front page which stayed the same, dull template design that basic Wordpress came with. Nor did I change the date on the one and only story it contained. There was no explanation of the site, no contact form, no indication why talkingstatues existed at all. Just a story that said...

December 31, 1969
A building project in England
Filed under: Uncategorized – @ 5:00 pm
There is some controversy about a building project in Kent, England. We have agreed to host this report on the project as a result of public interest. Please return to this site from time to time to see what other interesting documents we may have found around the world.

People clicked on the link and got the very full and highly detailed document that had been approved by Imperial's management board on June 12th, unedited, in all its horrifying glory. That was enough for me. It turned out to be enough for everyone else too.

We then needed some way to guide readers from save-wye to this mysterious site in Utah. Under the headline 'That Imperial College presentation in full' Justin produced a very straight news story ostensibly to clear up any confusion that remained after Brooks Wilson's remarks to the consultation panel in which he said the map we published earlier was 'one draft out of twenty seven'. He wrote...

We didn't publish the entire presentation because we felt it was unnecessary and the size of the file is enormous. The extracts, we thought, spoke for themselves. However we have now discovered that the entire document is freely available on the internet through a web-site in the US, www.talkingstatues.net, where it has been converted into an ordinary site which can be viewed much like this one. We have looked at this site and can verify that the document is indeed the final version shown to the board at the June meeting which also proved the basis of our reports.

Finally, just to emphasise the point, he pulled out a killer e-mail from his treasure trove. It was from the office of Richard Sykes himself, sent out to contractors in June, and contained the key phrase, 'At the presentation to the Management Board/Property Advisory Committee, on the 12th June, a preferred option for land use was agreed which will feature in the completed master-plan document.'

A preferred option for land use. Not one of many. Not a draft, or something that would change later. This was the 'preferred option', and all people had to do in order to see in detail what it entailed was head off to talkingstatues.net and read, in full, the long and highly-detailed secret internal document which revealed in full Imperial's ambitions for the village.

I looked at what we'd done and thought: *they're dead.*

Later, in the village, someone came up to me, full of thanks and praise as usual, and said, 'Those talkingstatues people seem very nice, don't they? How *kind* of them.'

Quite a few people didn't have a clue it was us all along.

'Yes,' I replied. 'They must be.'

Wye gets on the telly

For months now Ian Cooling had been remarkably silent in public on the subject of Wye Park. This annoyed everyone. I was determined to do something about it, tempting him out into the light of day in a way I knew he could never resist, not that I had any inkling this was to generate our first true sign that the Imperial ship was about to sink below the horizon.

I'd given Ian Cooling free access to the site and he'd abused it, fomenting arguments between me and Justin, privately briefing Imperial on us, and trying to persuade council officers not to answer routine information requests we'd made. The flood of leaked e-mails revealed he had also, on at least one occasion, checked a contribution to save-wye with David Brooks Wilson, discussing the answers he gave to the questions which arose from our coverage of the secret lunch he'd attended at county hall organised by Alan Willett, the Lord Lieutenant. This was the point at which he declared very publicly, in words to be echoed by Brooks Wilson, that he didn't recognise Justin's report, only to go silent once more two days later when Dr Hilary Newport of the CPRE, who'd also been there, told *Kent on Sunday* she thought we had got it right.

The e-mail Justin had uncovered showed that the synchronicity between Cooling and Brooks Wilson's approach to this interlude was no accident. Cooling, the elected councillor for the village, wanted his chums in Imperial to understand how very much engaged he was. Brooks Wilson told him afterwards, in a message we possessed, 'Very wise and very well worded Ian. I congratulate you. How about lunch again? DCBW.'

The crazy thing was that, while a few in the village thought that Cooling was in this for nefarious reasons, neither of us believed that for a moment. I'd known the man for years. He had worked hard at the tedious task of being a borough councillor, taking on mind-numbing chores most of us would have avoided at all costs. Perhaps there were old IntCorps habits that proved difficult to suppress. Perhaps it was simply the curiously secretive style of covert politics which went with membership, albeit junior, of the Kent Tory party clique convinced it owned some god-given right to rule the county. Whatever the reason, clear unequivocal statements never came easily from him, or sometimes at all. Ian Cooling had been courting both sides in the game. People had to begin to understand this because, when the contest was won, as it soon would be, I knew for sure he would be elbowing his way into the celebrations and trying to stake his claim of the 'credit'.

I have to say it again because it's important. We were about full and honest disclosure. Not much else to be frank.

Television coverage of the threat to Wye had been dire throughout. So had that in the national press for the most part too, given that this was a pivotal event, the first real attempt to break the formerly cast-iron protection guarantees that AONB status was supposed to bring. The Future Group's lack of a full-time press officer since Tatiana Cant resigned was partly to blame. Ben Moorhead had taken on the role himself, along with far too much other work. But Imperial's barmy adventure was a saga that could not be described in three words, each of one syllable, so for most modern television it was much too complicated a story to tackle.

Wye had, however, been selected to take part in a BBC 4 series entitled *The Perfect Village* in which the restoration architect Ptolemy Dean travelled the country describing a variety of different rural communities before, at the series' conclusion, deigning to declare one the most 'perfect' in the land. It was like some dismal reality TV effort where the contestants wore ancient bricks and mortar instead of botox and lip gloss.

Ptolemy Dean grew up in Wye and clearly retained a great deal of affection for the place. He spoke to the parish councillor, Richard Bartley, who was allowed to give a brief, much cut overview of the threat to the community from Imperial's plans. The programme also included interviews with Professor Borys and KCC's Pete Raine. The deputy rector knew by this stage that the grand plan was doomed. Perhaps that was why he seemed so deeply miserable on camera, frozen, robotic and exceedingly unconvincing. Raine, the strategy man for Kent, was still in the dark about the mire into which the project had sunk but this didn't stop him crowing smugly about his enthusiasms over a pint in the garden of the Tickled Trout, then adding, 'If I was living here and I was in that situation (in other words facing up to Imperial's massive development scheme) I would be very concerned.'

Raine's argument was astonishing. The area, he said, needed the jobs. Dean never questioned this ridiculous notion on camera;

the jobless rate at the time in Ashford was 1.6 per cent, effectively full employment. The local council was privately admitting that if any would-be factory owner turned up in town looking to employ two or three hundred people they would have to try to import the labour from somewhere in order to fill the vacancies. Dean gave Raine a much harder time during the entire interview, but all the tough stuff wound up getting cut. It was a nice programme for nice people you see, and heaven forbid that any rancourous note of disagreement should be introduced into a friendly chat between decent chaps in a lovely garden next to the tinkling waters of the Stour.

The sight of this oleaginous, overpaid KCC apparatchik trying to pull the wool over everyone's eyes made my blood boil. There was, though, a more local target on hand, and, as I began the article, I was determined not to forget it. After lobbing deserved abuse in the direction of Raine and Borys I moved onto the real reason I was doing all this, the one that justified the headline 'Where are the councillors when we need them?'

> On a larger point, I can't help but wondering why this vast development, one which Raine, on an earlier occasion, compared to the Channel Tunnel Rail Link, seems to be something that only the non-elected are now allowed to discuss in public. Why did not a single democratically chosen public representative appear in this show? Why are their voices so absent from everything to do with Wye Park everywhere? From what source came the astonishing case of prolonged laryngitis which seems to have afflicted our councillors on the subject of what could be the largest single development project in the Ashford area in decades?
>
> Until an election comes along there's precious little you can do if public representatives decide they are going to sit out the most crucial development in their neck of the woods. But you do wonder whether they should continue to claim the public money they receive from our taxes and which now supports their silence on this issue.
>
> How much is it exactly? Under the member allowances which ran from April 1 last year to March 31 this, Charles Findlay, Wye's county councillor who has yet to say a meaningful word in public about Wye Park, re-

ceived a total of £19,562 in allowances and £847 in 'mileage, fares and other authorised payments' – a total of £20,409. Wye's borough councillor Ian Cooling has been steadily climbing the ranks of the most highly remunerated on Ashford Council. In the last financial year his travel expenses alone came to £2,138.53, not far short of his leader Paul Clokie's £2,679.10. But at least Paul Clokie's travel expenses seem relatively static over the years; Cllr Cooling's rose from a mere £20.70 in 2003/4 to £770.18 in 2004/5, and then last year's personal best of £2,138. In total he received £12,552.59 for his Ashford duties. Between the two of them, Messrs Findlay and Cooling have trousered over £32,000, which is a lot of money for keeping quiet.

It's only fair and reasonable that councillors should receive the authorised remuneration for their work. But isn't it fair too that in return we should expect them to find their voice on such an important issue from time to time? We elected them for that reason.

No-one elected Pete Raine or Prof Borys to come along and destroy our community just because one of them happens to think it makes a worthwhile exercise in social engineering and the other sees it as a way to line the pockets of his college with grubby millions in ill-gotten gains. Their dismal, duplicitous performances on this short TV show make me wonder, not for the first time since this dreadful saga came into being, what on earth is happening to democracy in Britain today.

This was bound to get Cooling out of his lair, itching to put up a response I could predict virtually down to the very words. As I wrote, Richard Alderton's desk was piling high with more letters demanding all mention of Wye be removed from the LDF. Ashford's planners, whose dissatisfaction with Imperial had been growing for some time, were finding some good solid reasons to start thinking about turning back the clock on the concordat that had haunted them throughout the year. By the time he was halfway through dealing with the flak this article would send his way, Ian Cooling knew the game was finally up.

Our councillor changes tack

Politicians can rarely resist an easy pop at their enemies. When I asked the question 'why were there no councillors on Ptolemy Dean's dismal TV programme?' I knew the answer already. No-one had asked them. Had Ian Cooling been offered the chance to get his face on camera I doubt even the prospect of a frosty lunch with David Brooks Wilson could have stopped him charging in to grasp the opportunity.

So it came as no surprise to discover that, for the first time in ages, a familiar mix of whining and pomposity was back on the site two days later, stating what I knew to be the obvious. He was never approached to be interviewed by Ptolemy Dean. 'Had I been invited, I should have been delighted to accept. But I wasn't, so I couldn't.'

There then followed a staggering eleven hundred words – more than the original article – of self-justification and aggrandisement, detailing how his payments were justified, and his workload of late had included toiling for the local business association, dealing with hooliganism on buses, a church booklet on heritage, and 'keeping an eye on the new warden arrangements at Luckley House following Veronica's retirement', before adding, 'I'd better stop there anyway, or the two guys on the other side of the hill will start accusing me of blowing my own trumpet.' Not that he did end there; he rambled on for another three yawn-inducing paragraphs.

It was exactly what I expected. I rubbed my hands then came back and made the point I'd planned to introduce at this juncture all along: I was never accusing either him or Charles Findlay of doing *no* work. My gripe was that one of them, Cooling, had scarcely said a word in public about the big story in their constituency since March, and the other not a worthwhile thing *ever*. Didn't he understand that TV programmes chose their interviewees on the basis of research and cuttings? And that if anyone looked for people who were vocal on the subject of Wye Park the names of Cooling and Findlay would never enter the frame? They hadn't been invited because they hadn't been publicly engaged in any debate on the subject. As far as any outside observer would be concerned, they simply didn't care.

Cooling responded with the briefest, oddest comment he ever made: 'Quick (short!) reply David – to confirm that rightly or wrongly I think my views are irrelevant. What matters is the views of the residents of Wye, which I have been regularly gathering and using as the basis of my arguments for changing minds. Only time will tell if I am successful.'

After that the site started to get very lively indeed, with comments that hit home because every one now came with a real name attached, a face anyone in the village could recognise. Cliff Whitbourn, who'd bravely refused to be anonymous throughout, summed up the mood as usual: 'Dear Ian. You were elected because of your views and perceptions of need within the local community. If you now consider your views irrelevant, stop faffing around and resign. Yours, with ever decreasing respect. C.H.W.'

For the first time the man really looked as if he was on the ropes. When he posted a follow-up at twenty to midnight on Saturday September 2nd I knew that something big was happening behind the scenes. For weeks now we'd been running a poll on the site asking whether people thought there ought to an independent inquiry by the local government ombudsman into the secret deal of the concordat, one that looked at the roles of ABC and KCC in signing up to such a huge project without the slightest consultation, even within their own ranks. A couple of hundred people had voted in favour; a handful, mainly from within Imperial – we could tell this from the trail of tell-tale IP addresses, internet footprints, they left – had voted against.

The prospect of an independent inquiry caused grave concern for many of those involved. There were firm rules about how close local authorities could come to developers. Ashford had already had its knuckles rapped once before after admitting that it had allowed one house builder to pay for officers' time on a planning application. They didn't want that happening again.

Yet in his late-night return to the site to make one more thousand-word ramble around the lamp-posts Cooling at the close of his comment decided, quite deliberately, to drop a bombshell.

'I was originally sceptical about the value of an enquiry by the Local Government Ombudsman,' he wrote. 'I now believe that there is so much rumour, counter-rumour, accusations, conflicting information, disinformation and lack of information, along with a degree of unfamiliarity with what is and is not permitted under planning law, that such a process is now needed as a catharsis.'

He was calling for an ombudsman's inquiry into his own council, run by his own party. He could have done this at any stage in the previous six months. The catalogue of revelations we'd produced, of secret deals and doubtful planning practices, was enough on its own, and he knew that. Yet now, at twenty to midnight, at the end of the week Richard Alderton had come home to face a pile of resolute letters of protest and firm proof of Imperial's masterplan, he had finally found his voice.

I didn't see the comment in the approvals queue until seven the following morning when I got up. It went in immediately. Shortly afterwards I spoke to Justin. We were, as usual by now, of one mind, and he had just made his public in a comment.

> I take it that when such an astute operator as Ian calls for an inquiry into Ashford's conduct or joins the clamour demanding that Wye be dropped from the LDF, it's like Gerry Adams calling on the IRA to start decommissioning: something must be afoot.
> Justin Williams, September 3rd, 2006 at 11:37 pm

Ian Cooling was too astute an operator to have made such a bold and unexpected statement without good reason. A decision had been reached. Imperial had lost, and now he was scrabbling to get on the right side of the border before the news finally broke.

Ashford hammers in the stake

The following Monday Justin put in some calls. The news was all encouraging. Richard Alderton had brought forward the date of the meeting to decide on the LDF, and it seemed certain that the outcome was going to be bad for David Brooks Wilson and his fellow would-be property developers in Imperial. The decision on what to include would now take place in a week's time on September 11th. On that first day we were unsure whether the college plan would be ejected from the LDF altogether or simply watered down. As the week wore on, our confidence grew. One phone call from within Ashford, more than any, convinced us the game was up. It said that the masterplan map and the 57-page report which we'd published furtively on talkingstatues.net had proved the final straw. Ashford had tried to get some sense out of Imperial about the status of the documents we'd released and failed. There was no confirmation of them, and no denial either. What partnership there had been between the local authority and David Brooks Wilson's team was now fractured altogether. Alderton's planners knew that leaving Wye Park out of the LDF would kill the project entirely. That was exactly what they planned to do.

We still had some stories left in our must-run pile and two in particular seemed appropriate for that limbo week before Alderton's new LDF meeting. Justin made the most of it. One leak detailed the original 'frequently asked questions' drawn up for the project, which now seemed so far from reality it was difficult to believe Imperial had paid consultants to write such drivel. The scheme would, for example, be partly government funded, from the UK and Brussels, which was never to be an option. There was also the wonderful line: 'Will you clash with the community? In fact, [our] interests are the same as the residents: we sense that the points of *agreement* on what Wye should look like are far greater than our points of *difference'*. Fine words, and all of them written before anyone had spoken to a single villager.

There was another telling e-mail from the keyboard of the pugnacious Nigel Buck, one we published because it was wonderfully illustrative of the attitude this distant London college had towards us meek country folk. There had been a discussion between Diana Pound, the Future Group's planning adviser, and local Imperial staff about whether she could take some office space in the college for her company Dialogue Matters. All she wanted was 'four desks, four bookshelves, a couple of filing cabinets, some storage, light and airy, loo nearby, access to drinking water for tea and coffee. Good decorative order, phone line/internet access or reduced rental to reflect the need to have it put in'.

This inquiry found its way to Buck who thundered back to his minions in Wye, 'You may feel differently but my first impression is that this provides succour to the enemy and should not be countenanced!'

We made the e-mail public, naturally, and the news that, in the end, she had been offered space in a building that was notorious for its rack and ruin, with the advice that it would need to be redecorated and was 'a bit sub standard'.

So we were the 'enemy', not residents whose 'points of agreement' were far greater than our 'points of difference' after all. Ian Cooling, now boldly wearing his new robe as champion of the village, came on to save-wye to bellow in a comment, 'This is grotesque. Buck has a lot of explaining to do, preferably on his way to collect his final pay cheque.' Not that anyone was fooled by his rapid Damascene conversion.

As usual I was in the wrong place when momentous decisions were made. On the Monday night of the crucial meeting I was near Bristol at a two-day publishing event and talking at a public library. Once again I lived off my smart phone and left all the hard work to Justin. We spoke that Tuesday morning. He'd had a briefing from Ashford. It was everything we'd hoped for. Richard Alderton had looked at the mass of material that had landed on his desk over Wye Park – the protest letters, the leaked masterplan, and the constant nagging from the Future Group – and decided enough was enough.

Justin headlined his story 'Imperial's vision is dumped from the LDF', and made clear this was the end of the road. Even the *Kentish Express* seemed to realise they had a significant story on their hands, bizarrely bundling up the 'possible' collapse of Wye Park as a local disaster along with that week's news of cuts in the Eurostar service from Ashford and delays in a large council building project. The paper, brainless as ever, didn't seem to realise that the 'lost 12,500 jobs' it was lamenting never existed in the first place.

I got back on the Wednesday morning wondering if Brooks Wilson would try to brazen out this one. We knew the college had a management board meeting scheduled for the end of the month. The earliest any formal decision to kill Wye Park publicly could be made might well be then. Equally the rejection of the plan by Alderton's committee still had to be rubber-stamped in council, which wouldn't happen until October. If the people concerned wanted to be bloody-minded they could keep this corpse on life support for months to come. I was exhausted and due to go back to America for more promotional work around the time of that management board meeting. We needed an end to this now.

I talked to Justin and we decided on one more article, a piece that called on the college to tell Wye its masterplan was dead. Just for good measure we slipped in a couple of embarrassing leaked e-mails too so that they understood our treasure trove of nasties was not yet entirely exhausted, and we might delve into it again should the need arise.

It's time for Imperial to do the decent thing.

Wednesday, September 13th, 2006 in Opinion by David Hewson and Justin Williams

The tanks are still on our lawn, their guns spiked, their turrets empty. The Sykes army has all but departed in silence, knowing the war is lost and wondering what to do next. Imperial College's grandiose and extraordinary ambitions for the green fields of Wye now lie in tatters, waiting only for someone to come along and sweep away the torn remains of the so-called concordats. And then?

If there is a shred of decency remaining in this aloof London university, a recognition somewhere that communities and indeed Imperial's own employees in the village deserve, finally, consideration and respect then, surely, this: Imperial must face reality and start to tell us the truth.

In spite of the spin that has been reeled off to local authorities and gullible politicians, Imperial has been planning its exit from Wye for some time, since it long ago decided it would not provide what we wanted most of all: an active university college in the village. What we know now is that this departure will largely be on our terms, not its. Instead of leaving with £100 million in its pockets, it will scuttle back to London with its tail between its legs and whatever quick profits it can glean from selling off easily disposable assets. Today, for the first time, we can reveal this retreat has been under consideration from Imperial for some time.

The exit strategy, which was being discussed among the college's coterie of would-be property developers as early as May, is this: recover the costs of a failed Project Alchemy/Wye Park by selling off certain assets, such as the main college itself, and 'land bank' the rest of the estate in the hope that at some point in the future, Ashford council might include it in the borough's development area. With hindsight, that may look rather naive but then everything that Imperial has done to date has smacked of ineptitude and naivety: did it really think the local community would swallow its ideas if it promised to sort out the level crossing problem? And did anybody in David Brooks Wilson's office seriously believe that simply not talking about the real motivation behind its plans – grabbing £100 million by flogging off land for 4,000 houses – would go unnoticed? Delegates to the next Skidmore, Owings and Merrill (Imperial's masterplanners) workshop on October 16 will know that the college is still up to its old tricks with the invitations specifically ruling out any discussion of housing when we all now know exactly what it has been planning from the very start.

From the beginning of this farrago Imperial has been playing fast and loose with an institution with 900 years of history behind it. In May, Mr Brooks Wilson – who, in his own words, thought there was only a 50/50 chance of getting Wye Park through – had a discussion with Robin Worthington, Cadbury Schweppes property chief and a member of Imperial's property advisory committee. There was clearly concern on the committee that Wye Park was a massive gamble given that nobody – no university, no house-builder, no landowner – had ever achieved what Imperial was setting out to do. After the conversation, Mr Worthington e-mailed Mr Brooks Wilson to suggest that perhaps it wasn't such a gamble after all given that the college had got Wye at such a knockdown price in the first place and could recover its costs – which might rise to £4 million if it went all the way to the High Court – by simply flogging off some of the silver:

From: Robin Worthington
Sent: 31 May 2006 09:44
To: Brooks Wilson, David C
Subject: Wye
David,
Following on from our telephone conversation yesterday,
three ways of saying the same thing -
1. Is it fair to say that £3/4m in fees is not a punt, as we're
bound to get at least that much back?
2. Is it more akin to investing in Premium Bonds than the
Lottery?
3. I did ask Nigel some time ago whether there (are) any
surplus properties at Wye which, if push came to shove,
we could sell for £3/4m.
      Robin

Mr Brooks Wilson agreed. If it did go 'belly up', he said, there
were several surplus properties that could be sold. This 'seriously reduces the downside risk'. In other words, it's worth using
public funds and public goodwill to attempt this gamble because the college could simply recover the costs – however
large. Wye College, punted backwards and forwards over recent
years, has become a chip in a giant game of roulette:

From: Hutt, Claudia on behalf of Brooks Wilson, David C
Sent: Mon 05/05/2006 10:47
To: Robin.Worthington
Subject: RE: Wye
Dear Robin,
Many thanks for your note below.
As ever you have hit the nail on the head. Were this to go
belly up there are several surplus properties at Wye which
we could sell for £3-4M whilst retaining the rest of the
land bank for future use.
In my view that very seriously reduces the downside risk.

As Imperial surely appreciates by now, the fight against Wye
Park was based upon reality and genuine horror at the scale of
their extraordinary proposals, not some Nimbyish desire to stop
all new development at any cost. Time and time again, villagers

have told the college that we would welcome modest, sustainable and mutually agreed renewal of the brownfield sites that have been allowed to go to rack and ruin under Imperial's ownership. That position has not changed. But nor should anyone pretend that the last nine months have not happened.

There is a growing sense of shock now emerging well beyond Wye about the duplicity with which this huge and wealthy London university attempted to bring a swathe of commercial development to the Area of Outstanding Natural Beauty under the guise of scientific research. Had it succeeded, some of the most beautiful countryside in Kent would have been lost forever. And Imperial itself would simply have pocketed the profits and left Wye to its own devices, retracing its steps to London to invest the fruits of its property development there.

This was scandalous behaviour on the part of a body financed by public funds. Those councillors, officials and local authorities who swallowed Imperial's line may well have not heard the last of this saga. But nor have we. The biggest single land owner in Wye wants to get out of the village and make some money on the way. It will, one way or another, do this. But it must surely appreciate that the success – and ultimately the profit – of its departure will depend on how much it can recover its shattered relationship with the community it has treated so badly for the last nine months.

If Imperial remains secretive, manipulative and duplicitous in its intention towards the village, we will respond in kind, in a way they should surely recognise by now. Professor Sir Leszek Borysiewicz may have thought he was addressing a bunch of bucolic idiots when he stood up at Withersdane on January 9th, all that time ago. He surely knows differently today. If the college wants to embark on another round of confrontation with the village, we can promise that it will meet with a response that is more effective, more informed and even more determined than it has been on this occasion. We have no illusions now, and we will have the local development strategy on our side.

If, on the other hand, someone in Imperial's headquarters sees sense and finally begins to engage with the village in conversations and negotiations that are genuine and meaningful, not the sham we have seen to date, then it will, in spite of past events, find a community willing to listen and attempt to reach a mutually beneficial solution. The ball is now in Imperial's court, and we will be watching closely to see how it is played. In the first instance, the college can do itself and us a favour by making the following clear.

- That it will not be proceeding with the masterplan to build the science park and housing
- That it will not seek to develop any part of the estate except the existing dilapidated brown field areas
- Its long-term intentions towards the farm, Withersdane and the college itself

We know from our own sources at the very highest echelons within Imperial that these are questions the college could answer easily over the next few days. We hope there is some voice of reason somewhere within the management of the college which realises that honesty and openness are the only way forward for it from now on.

We hope too that local politicians, many of whom have served their constituents appallingly over this saga, will support this call and demand immediate clarification from the college on these matters. Had they been more sceptical and responsible towards their duties of care, the Wye area would not have been plunged into the difficult and painful times it has experienced over the last nine months, for no other reason than Imperial College's desire to make millions of pounds out of something it bought for a pittance. It may be late in the day but if Paul Clokie can apparently start to find an independent voice on this matter – for whatever reason – then surely there are others who can summon up the courage too.

Did this article make a difference? I honestly don't know. Paul Clokie, who had started to issue dark noises about being duped by Imperial, was in London at this time, engaged in a difficult meeting with college officials who told him they were so incensed with the obstreperous, awkward people of Wye they wouldn't build anything there, ever. When Clokie was finally to find his voice on this matter, that was his tone too. By defeating Imperial's plan to turn our small country village into a new town we were the real losers. People would listen to his words in disbelief. If this was a drubbing, it was the kind we'd take any day of the week.

We knew nothing of what was going on behind the scenes at that moment. Then, late on that Wednesday, I discovered the college planned to issue a statement at an undisclosed hour on Friday. In less than thirty six hours we'd know whether our work was done or not.

The great day

We haven't just saved Wye, we've struck a blow for the English countryside. We've helped to show that the protection of beautiful landscape in any AONB or national park isn't to be trifled with: even if officials are slow to defend it, the residents are not. I hope the next institution that wants to raise hundreds of millions of pounds by wrecking an AONB will draw the most important lesson: never underestimate a small English village. I for one feel very proud of ours today.
Nick Dunlop, September 15th, 2006 at 9:33 am

That Thursday remains a blank to me. On Friday I'd fixed an appointment at the village barbers, Smiles, for 9.30 in the morning, and knowing the wonderful sense of timing and location I had employed throughout this nine-month assignment, I fully expected I was going to be in the wrong place at the wrong time yet again.

I would have been too if Imperial's PR people hadn't for once stuck to their word and delivered something on deadline. At seven that morning the e-mail containing the press statement from Professor Sir Leszek Borysiewicz, deputy rector of Imperial College, and the man who had been charged with rebuilding Wye after Imperial's own vision, dropped into my inbox.

Still only half-dressed I read it, phoned Justin, gave him the details then said the words I'd been longing to utter, 'You are *so* fired.'

Borys had announced Imperial's unconditional surrender. Not only was Wye Park dead, nothing would replace it. The 'scientific vision' would no longer be pursued, there would be no expansion of research and development, nor a search for a replacement for 'the vision project'. No swift decisions on Wye's future were imminent and the current level of academic activity, with the growing presence of the University of Kent as a tenant of Imperial, would continue.

I'd been prepared for a week. A new header for the site, with the word 'SAVED' in giant letters over a beautiful view of the countryside by the renowned photographer and Wye resident Steve Bloom, was already in place along with a template for a

191

print newsletter. By just after eight the story, headlined 'Imperial makes it official: Wye Park is dead', was leading the site, and the print version was there too. I had time to pop in to the Co-op for some milk before my haircut. John Hodder, now retired from the parish council and soon to move out of the area, was there, still a little dizzy from the news I thought. None of us had expected everything to collapse quite so quickly. None of us knew what the day would bring.

Hodder was full of thanks for our efforts. I returned the compliments, got my hair cut and came home to see the site getting more hits than it had ever received in a single day before and the comments queue beginning to stack up with message after joyful message. Some were serious, some silly, some a little tearful, a few seeming to indicate that the champagne corks may have been popping before lunchtime in a few places. Richard Bartley, the parish councillor whose comments had been so mangled in Ptolemy Dean's miserable TV programme, summed up my own feelings with the words, 'Who would have predicted such news nine months ago?' No-one. Not a soul.

Ben Moorhead was there quickly too, in typically kind, self-effacing fashion, saying, 'WFG, myself and everyone concerned for Wye send their renewed thanks for everything you have done to help win this battle. When we were down you cheered us, when there was a gap or uncertainty you found new angles and stories to plug it. You found the plan, the single most important revelation to date. I cannot thank you both enough. It's been a fraught journey with a joyful end.'

We deleted only one comment, the third that Diana Pound posted that day. The first two were OK but when this one landed in the moderation queue...

> You know I think we should give a big thank you to Imperial – I have lived in and around Wye for about 20 years and I have never known such a strong sense of community – right across ages and backgrounds – I've made loads of new friends and gained a whole new social life of green and multicoloured meetings. Its often been v stressful and pressured but there has also been lots of fun. I've also gained myself a bit of a reputation – one week meeting different men on 4 different nights in the pub!!

So thanks to Imperial for helping this community come together and for many new friendships.

...it was just a touch too much.

Praise makes me deeply uncomfortable, and I was heartened to realise Justin felt the same way. One thing only concerned us now: how quickly we could close save-wye for good. With Imperial's complete surrender we had no reason to keep it alive. There would be development battles ahead for Wye, as there would be in any rural community close to a hotspot like Ashford. But these would arise in the normal run of events, not as part of such an extraordinary set of circumstances as those which began when the leaders of our councils sat down to sign that first secret concordat in the spring of the previous year. The demise of Wye Park had removed all prospect of any imminent threat to the green meadows of the AONB. What happened from now on would, for the foreseeable future, be confined to the miserable, wrecked brownfield land the college had created in its neglect of the old labs and offices of its own estate.

My instinct was to give people the weekend to celebrate then tell them on Monday that we were packing up our bags for good. The site would stay live for as long as it had visitors. I knew from contacts we'd received in the past that other campaigners elsewhere in the country wanted to access it to see if they could pick up any tips for their own efforts. This was the internet after all. I wasn't printing a new paper every day. It cost me not a penny to keep save-wye alive, frozen in time at the moment of victory, as it will be for as long as people want to visit it.

There were two problems with keeping quiet. There was going to be a village party that night at the New Flying Horse. I would have to be there. People would have to be told. The other, naturally, was Justin. He just couldn't wait for us to shut up shop. By 10.25 he was e-mailing me saying, 'It's already going stale, I can smell it!'

Fine. I thought. I started this damned thing on my own. I was going to close it that way. Besides, I had already sent him an e-mail confirming what I had said in my initial phone call, one entitled, 'You are *so* fired'.

At 11.59, after getting a nice photo of him from Beth, which I ran in the piece, an act I knew would infuriate him, I posted what was supposed to be our final story...

And this is the end for save-wye.org too…
Friday, September 15th, 2006 in News by David Hewson

This is the last substantive article you will read on save-wye… Is the Wye saga over completely? No, but the worst part, the threat to the green heart of our community from a massive housing development, science cluster and research unit, most certainly is. There will be arguments to come about smaller scale brown field development in the village. There will be justifiable resentment among many about the dreadfully lacklustre performance of some of our public representatives over this issue, many of whom will now, naturally, clamour to take the credit for Imperial's downfall.

But it's not the job of an individual web-site to bring these people to account, or to monitor the future of more modest development plans for the village. It's yours, and you have never been in a better position to rise to the challenge. Through the vigourous response of the Parish Council and Wye Future Group, you have proved this small and often sleepy rural community will never again be pushed around by big business – even when it masquerades in the guise of a public body that can pull the wool over the eyes of our gullible councils. There are, though, a few things I need to say before we depart.

The first is a heartfelt thank-you to Justin Williams whose journalistic talents provided the exclusive leaks and revelations which are the principal reason this nonsense has been sent crashing to the ground so quickly. The Parish Council, Wye Future Group and the many individuals who wrote to Ashford Borough Council deserve a huge chunk of credit, but it was Justin's astonishing ability to winnow out the truth from the hype that set the tone of this story from a very early stage.

The old cliché 'without whom it would never have been possible' simply doesn't do Justin justice. I started this site back at the beginning of the year on a whim, primarily, let it be said, out of anger that the coverage of this issue in the *Kentish Express* was so poor I wanted to be better informed myself. I tried very hard to get others involved in writing articles for us, but it didn't work. You are, after all, not journalists, and what this situation required most of all was good, honest tough journalism of a kind you will only get from professionals.

Boy was I – and ultimately you lot – lucky to discover a consummate professional lived just down the road. I'm happy to take the credit for creating this weapon and pointing it in the direction of the dreaded triumvirate of Imperial, ABC and KCC, but it was Justin's extraordinary journalistic abilities that found the ammunition and ultimately pulled the trigger with such deadly accuracy. You will never know the lengths to which he went in order to get those leaked documents out of the heart of those closest to this very secret project. But let me assure you, they were above and beyond the call of any duty, the untiring work of a tenacious, talented reporter of the kind that's rare in newspapers these days. Back when I was a journalist in what used to be called Fleet Street I worked with and learned from some of the most famous names of the day. Justin stands alongside the finest, and it's a credit to his own selfless love of the Wye area that he was willing to spend so many days and nights applying those skills to the most parochial of local stories.

There are others to thank too. Those many anonymous supporters who quietly helped us ferret out information and try to make sure it was correct and capable of being published without revealing the sources. Some people risked their jobs to help tell you the truth about Wye Park simply because they felt, very strongly, that what was happening here was deeply, fundamentally wrong. You know who you are and it's important you now know that an entire community is deeply grateful, alongside everyone who loves the English countryside and feared its protected status would be struck a fatal blow by Imperial's plans. I must also thank our secret little printing press in the village which, with the help of financial support from individuals, has been quietly placing printed material in all the right places, making sure that those who weren't connected to the internet didn't stay out of the loop.

The most important of those distribution points was, of course, the New Flying Horse which displayed our newsletters prominently, week in and week out. That can't have been an easy decision for Cliff Whitbourn. He works for a large Kent company that would have profited mightily from an extra four thousand homes on the doorstep. But Cliff backed our work from the earliest days, was a fearless commentator in his own right, and one who, unlike most, wrote under his own name from the start. I can tell you now that his courage and determination to keep this issue in the public eye kept us going when flak from other quarters made us wonder why we were bothering. Given the dearth of coverage in the *Kentish Express*, it was on the counter of the New Flying Horse and the shelves of Wye News that through a constant flow of news stories and opinion articles we began to spread the message that this was not a done deal, in spite of the £1 million Imperial was willing to throw away on planners and consultants to get it off the ground.

Sometimes things got a little heated. Reporting is like that. Journalism doesn't exist to tell you what you want to know. It's there to tell you what you ought to know. It's uncomfortable, it's aggressive, it sometimes takes no prisoners and upsets people who want to be on your side. That's the name of the game, and one more reason why we now need to depart the scene.

Also, we were making this up as we went along. No-one had ever really run a web-site like this before, least of all us. We invented our own rules, we did what our consciences told us, and if that occasionally caused disagreements and flak then so be it. To paraphrase *The Godfather* we were wartime *consiglieri* and we were willing to do whatever it took to make Imperial's true ambitions public and, with a bit of luck, stymie them.

Until recently we never, in our wildest dreams, believed it would all come tumbling down this early. But then, to be honest, I don't think either of us understood at the outset how bizarre and far-reaching the college's ambitions were, or how much duplicity we would uncover along the way.

We've learnt a lot over the last nine months. One thing I will pass on. This is the 21st century. Things happen quickly and are difficult to roll back. The old methods are important, but they are not the only methods, and if you stick to them alone, hoping you have the time and space to spend months debating the wording of a constitution, you will one day walk out into the sun and discover the world has changed about you for the worse. It is also essential to communicate, quickly and regularly, with the community at large, which in this case was utterly against Imperial's plans, in spite of what a couple of people would have you believe.

I hope the village will benefit from the techniques we developed and the mistakes we made, and come to develop its own web-site, one that acts as a serious and timely forum of communication within the community. This is your job now, not ours. The war is over. Good luck and best wishes for building the peace.

David Hewson, September 15, 2006

At 5.30 I was interviewed by the BBC for the 6.30 news, on which everything I said was cut except for one line about how, if people really wanted to create jobs in Kent, they might do it somewhere like Thanet, where there was real unemployment and KCC had just spent millions buying an industrial estate of their own. At 6.37 I received a snotty, irate e-mail from someone in Thanet saying effectively, 'We don't want the crappy science park you people just rejected.' At 6.39 I went to the pub, on my own since Justin was working and couldn't get there till after nine.

To my intense embarrassment there was a round of applause when I walked in. The beer flowed. I didn't pay for a single pint. It seemed as if every last member of the Future Group was there, people I knew by name only, though many told me how they'd all met so many new friends during the duration of the campaign, and how pleasant that had been. I was struck, as always, by how nice and well-adjusted and reasonable they all were. For all the occasional infighting, they had been drawn together by the same genuine sentiments, a horror at the destruction we all felt would occur if Imperial got its way. Even now, with the battle behind us, I was unsure if they understood what exactly we'd done and why, or that the very factors that drove them to come together – a communal spirit, a need to work through the democratic process in a slow, thorough painstaking fashion dictated by procedure, not expediency – were precisely what a couple of reckless lone wolves like us needed to avoid in order to be of any use whatsoever.

It wasn't a reflective meeting. It was, soon, a rather hazy one. So much free beer. So many people I didn't know who wanted to talk. I couldn't hear well in these circumstances at the best of times. After a while I couldn't talk well either.

The smartphone went. It was Justin, naturally. Cooling was about to make an entrance to the party and, in advance, had sent round what some would regard as the crowning e-mail of his career. Earlier that year he had been lunching with David Brooks Wilson, briefing Imperial on us and others, and offering quiet advice to Imperial on how best to win over the village. Now he crowed, in a message addressed to John Hodder and Ben Moorhead...

> I'd like to pay a very warm personal tribute to the pair of you for your leadership and all your hard work sustained over so many months for the good of Wye. More than a few people have asked why I was not more visible. The reality was that with the two of you so superbly effectively in action, there was simply no need for a third. My job was elsewhere with the long, slow business of changign (sic) minds.

It was too good not to share. I called Cliff away from the bar for a moment and let him read it in the kitchen on my phone. I swear that at that moment he developed a tic I'd never seen before and happily never would after.

When the man the Connies referred to as 'GL', for Great Leader, arrived, Cliff couldn't bring himself to work his way to the end of the counter where our local councillor stood. Nor could I. It wasn't easy in any case. I'd never seen the pub so packed or so joyful.

In the event he didn't stay long. There was an uneasy atmosphere around Ian Cooling by then and I felt it wasn't going to go away quickly. After finding himself staring at rather too many turned backs, which must have felt very odd in such polite company, he was told to depart in no uncertain terms by one local who found the beer had unlocked sentiments he might have kept to himself in other circumstances.

Normally that kind of behaviour would have got the chap thrown out. But this was not a normal night. At an hour I do not recall Justin, stone cold sober and staring at me with a jaundiced eye, looked in my direction and said, 'It's time for you to go..'

I stabbed a finger in his direction and retorted, 'You are *not* the boss of me, Williams. And also you're fired.'

'So how *are* you getting home?' he asked.

This seemed a reasonable point. I left, musing on the thought that I would never again have to write another word about Imperial College or Councillor Ian Cooling.

I was, of course, wrong.

One last article

David and Justin,
As you know, I am not normally given to overt expressions of praise. However, you are two of the most tenacious, erudite and honest willed people I have known.

I have yet to cancel my commission for a 'Wicker Man' (especially designed for errant elected officials) however, just in case!
Cliff Whitbourn, September 15th, 2006 at 1:03 pm.

The following morning I went down to the farmers' market, principally to buy something for supper. I felt a touch hung over from the previous night. I felt odd in other ways too. Something that had been an important part of my life was now over. I'd been praying for it to disappear for months. Now it was gone I missed it in a strange way that was difficult to pin down. There would be no more insane e-mails waiting for me when I started the day, no anonymous documents through the post or the dropbox. Most of all, I wouldn't have the pleasure of working alongside Justin any more. We would both go back to the day jobs we'd tried not to neglect during the long, exhausting and occasionally bitter campaign.

Writing's a solitary life but for the nine months of save-wye that realisation – always present among those of us who invent stories and people and worlds for a living – had receded. Through the simple medium of a computer and an internet connection I had been touched by the lives and cares of countless others, and touched a little in return. Now I had to go back to what, in my profession, was reality, which is, in truth, the very opposite.

The market seemed busier than ever. The Future Group had their stand by the Post Office as usual, neatly placed so that nothing encroached on college land. Amazingly, people were still giving them cash; some £70 or so got collected that day, even though those manning it kept telling the givers they really had no idea where the money would go any more. It didn't seem to matter; some simply felt guilty they hadn't given already. One old lady had handed over a bunch of postage stamps. No-one knew quite what to say. They could only look each other and murmur, amazed, 'It's over.'

There was a display with the news of the victory for all to see, and a very generous message saying thanks to Justin and me. I wondered if these charming, decent middle class people had the slightest inkling of what I really thought: that if this battle had been left to their niceness alone the outcome might have been different. We danced around the subject in a couple of conversations and left it at that. They weren't stupid and nor was I. They had reacted in a fashion that was natural for people of their background and beliefs. Unburdened by cynicism, unwilling to work outside the rules of civilised society, they had fought the way respectable, reasonable people did on these occasions. Deep down, I suspect, most knew this wasn't enough, but their decency prevented them from stooping to the measures Justin and I had reached for without a second thought. We were products of our background too.

We'd declared the site closed, though there was still something nagging in our own heads, some unfinished task we couldn't quite pin down.

After I had talked with a few people on the stand I picked up some smoked duck and a few organic vegetables, of a quality you'd never find in a supermarket, and found myself unable to concentrate fully on anything at all. I'd asked, quietly, a couple of people what they thought would happen next, and whether, crucially, they would continue with their demand for an inquiry into the secret, shameful way in which Wye Park had been put together simply to wipe out the small world we all knew and loved and exchange it for a few hundred million pounds to spend in London. Some felt an investigation had to happen as a matter of course. Others...

Averted eyes, the odd murmur about being 'magnanimous in victory'. It was the umpteenth time I'd heard that phrase since the previous morning and I was starting to find it grated, quite seriously.

While I was away Charles Findlay had turned up, Charles the silent county councillor, the Tory party hack who'd been given his orders to turn up to the concordat signing nine months before, had his fill of bread pudding, and said nothing for the duration. It was no secret that the campaign had ended so early that WFG still had several thousand pounds in its coffers. No-one had seriously wondered what to do with that money yet. The death notice for Wye Park was scarcely twenty four hours old.

This didn't stop Findlay walking up and uttering the longest single sentence he was to speak to those who had been defending the village where his wife had grown up in the delightful 1930s ambience of Withersdane.

He looked at these good people and said, 'You'll have to give all that money back now.'

And then he pottered off with his little dog.

I listened to this story and noted it. I took a photo of the lovely display the Future Group had put up, with the nice tribute to us there, and sent it to Justin who was, as usual, hard at work on the *Sunday Telegraph* on his busiest day of the week. Then, when I was home, I called him and found, naturally, that his mind had been working the same way too. A little later I put up a brief notice that there'd been a slight change of plan. We would publish one more article on save-wye, the following Monday.

By the end of the afternoon it was pretty much in place, though we would spend the next day tinkering with it, making sure we were on ground that was as firm as possible if it came to a legal challenge. This was supposed to be our closing statement and like so many of our most important articles it would be a series of questions for others to take up, we hoped, and seek answers. I don't think any of us expected much of a response. In the end, we got one that we could never have predicted, the most extraordinary twist in the tail of this affair, and one that I think sheds a good deal of light on the psyches of the people who got us into this mess.

Early that evening Justin, who would be at work for many long hours to come, e-mailed me, just when I thought I might be able to get Wye out of my head for a little while.

From: Justin Williams
Subject: stuff
Date: 16 September 2006 17:53:00 BDT
To: David Hewson
D,
I wonder whether one (me) or both (much better) of us should think about having a blog on democracy in kent. A new site where there wouldn't be any pressure to keep coming up with new stuff day in day out. I'd happily run it and post when I felt like it but would dearly love to have you on board. Whaddya think?

I stared at the message for a couple of minutes, bewildered. Then, still a little shell-shocked, I replied.

> **From**: David Hewson
> **Subject**: Re: stuff
> **Date**: 16 September 2006 18:35:59 BDT
> **To**: Justin Williams
> I think: no. For me anyway. I tried blogging and it just don't work. Too much effort for too little reward. Also you end up writing stuff for the sake of it not because it begs to be written.

As if that was going to shut him up. I should have known by now. Perhaps it was a quiet night on the *Sunday Telegraph*. Four minutes later, partly typed in capital letters for pity's sake, came the answer...

> **From**: Justin Williams
> **Subject**: RE: stuff
> **Date**: 16 September 2006 18:39:54 BDT
> **To**: David Hewson
> OK – I accept that – I'm only talking about a blog in the save-wye sense but at a much lower intensity. But you may be right – I have these impulsive urges which really need to be reined in.
> BUT SOMEONE'S GOT TO DO IT OR WE'RE JUST GOING TO GET MORE BLOODY CONCORDATS

Richard Sykes and his minions may have missed this point but I'd had it hammered into me from an early age, and repeatedly of late: the important thing about dealing with hacks is to make yourself very, very clear.

I went downstairs, poured myself a glass of wine and thought for a while. It was a beautiful late summer evening, the sky succumbing to that golden evening glow you get when September is starting to slip into the slow, lazy slumber of autumn.

Then I returned to the computer and composed one final e-mail.

From: David Hewson
Subject: Considered opinion
Date: 16 September 2006 18:59:23 BDT
To: Justin Williams
Sorry.
I rushed my answer about your suggestion of a political blog. My considered reply is this:
Are you fucking insane?

A final revelation

The piece we ran was entitled 'Some parting questions for "The Usual Suspects"'. It started with a graphic Justin had produced based on the poster for the film of the same name. The heads of the actors had been replaced with those of the men who were the subjects of this article: Paul Clokie, David Hill, the ABC chief executive, Ian Cooling, Paul Carter, the leader of KCC, Pete Raine, the smug KCC planner who praised Imperial so highly in the garden of the Tickled Trout with Ptolemy Dean, and finally Charles Findlay.

The scheme to kill Wye was not a foundling, discovered on our doorstep, its origins unknown. It had been connived at, developed, worked up and schemed at long beforehand, in concert with the very people we had chosen to represent us and defend our interests. In the way of the world, most would get away with this act of treachery. Still, we thought the least we could do was to leave some important questions on the table so that any interested party, an individual, the parish council, or the Future Group, could pursue each with the relevant party in the future.

We asked Paul Clokie and David Hill why they were now claiming they never knew that Imperial's plans involved huge incursions into the green fields of the AONB, when we had it in writing from ABC's own head planner, Richard Alderton, that a figure of 250 acres of housing, which could only be achieved through such an intervention, had been discussed with him. We asked Paul Carter about a statement he had made to the papers that weekend saying, 'The opportunity to create really significant employment growth and future jobs and prosperity has now disappeared. It is very disappointing news.' Disappointing for whom, we wondered? The friends Carter, a professional property developer, had made in public life?

We wondered why Pete Raine had routinely been copying our e-mails and those of others to David Brooks Wilson without permission, and why a paid council officer, not an elected official, had the right to become the public champion for Imperial College, declaring to all and sundry, on TV and in the papers, how excited he was by a project that would have destroyed an entire community.

Of Charles Findlay we wrote...

No-one can accuse Charles Findlay of wrongdoing. In order for that to happen he would have to have done something in the first place. And, when it comes to vast environmental nightmares on his own doorstep, doing things just isn't Charles Findlay's style. Cllr Findlay lives in the village and Wye Park was the largest potential development project to have occurred in his constituency in history, hopefully ever. And his opinion of it?

Your guess is as good as ours. He said nothing when the concordat was announced. He said nothing when we revealed that a secret version had been agreed nine months earlier. He was silent when his own authority cravenly killed Freedom of Information releases to us on the orders of Imperial College. Not a word escaped Cllr Findlay's lips when we revealed, with detailed maps, the full scale of the horror that Imperial College wished to visit upon the area he represents…

In 2005 Charles Findlay was elected to KCC with a majority of almost two thousand votes out of fewer than eight thousand cast. Last year he claimed more than £20,000 in allowances and expenses from the authority, which means that, at the current rate, he has another £50,000 or so to pocket before, in 2009, the voters of Ashford East have a chance to pass judgement on his performance, if it can be called that.

Our question for Charles Findlay is very simple. What on earth are you *for?*

And then there was Ian Cooling, Conservative member for Wye on Ashford Borough Council. Justin laid out the questions meticulously, backing up each with the evidence he'd acquired. It wasn't a killer blow. But it was interesting all the same. There was a spreadsheet detailing the incredibly complex arrangements made to inform hundreds of people about the concordat signing. Cooling's name was there to do some of the legwork for all this. The document was dated November 8th – a full ten days before he claimed to have been 'brought into the loop' with a briefing by Hill, one which had left him furious. There were incriminating e-mails too, including one which read…

From: ian cooling
Sent: 05 June 2006 10:48
To: Brooks Wilson, David C
Subject: Meeting?
Hi David
I gather that decision-time is looming with key meetings
the middle of this month and next. Any value in us meet-
ing before/after either?
Regards
Ian

This message, addressing Brooks Wilson as David C as only inti-
mates did, was despatched just seven days before the crucial
management board meeting which would approve the 57-page
report Justin had leaked with such cataclysmic results. Cooling
clearly knew something was up. How?

We also printed the list of key contacts Brooks Wilson's out-
going PA had passed to his new assistant when there was a change
in personnel. This listed some very important people, including
the deputy managing director of the lobbyists Bell Pottinger and
the CEO of the developer Grosvenor Estates. But at the top of
this list of 'useful names', just eight in all, was 'Ian Cooling – Ashford Councillor (Wye)'.

Justin left it at that. I wanted more, so I added...

We know of your genuine and heartfelt affection for Wye
and its residents, Ian. We know, too, that you put in long
hours on work that most of us would find too tedious to
countenance. But this was the big one, a threat to our
community and countryside which, if it had been successful, would have destroyed the area we love forever.
Your constituents had the right to expect active, visible,
unequivocal leadership. Instead, when we needed clarity,
you gave us slippery prevarication. When we needed direct, strong public support, you gave us silences or whispered murmurs about 'working behind the scenes'. When
the outcome was certain you found your voice at last and
e-mailed John Hodder, the parish council chairman, and
Ben Moorhead, the chairman of Wye Future Group, to
say you had not been more visible because 'with the two

of you so superbly effective in action, there was simply no need for a third.'

That doesn't wash. You were a member of the authority and a close confidant of its leader as he hatched this plot with Imperial. You had a duty to speak out in a loud, clear and independent voice and you ducked it. We know you'll argue till the cows come home that you were never in the Imperial camp. But do you think it's possible that David Brooks Wilson and his colleagues had, for whatever reason, somehow come to believe otherwise?

We never expected any real answers, although I was certain Cooling would, as always, come back with a lengthy riposte which never addressed the questions asked, and try to obfuscate each clear issue with fudge and bluster and self-congratulation.

It took two days to arrive. I stared at it, amazed. Justin did too. He phoned and asked, 'Is he really saying what I think he is?'

Indeed he was. Ian Cooling, graduate of the Ashford School of Spooks, former intelligence officer, flogger of spare Jaguar car parts in his spare time, couldn't prevent himself making a quiet boast at the end, revealing, in his customarily arcane language, hidden inside a response that was almost two thousand words long, that yes, he had been, in the vernacular of his chosen profession, performing the role of double agent.

The language was so awkward, the connections so deliberately shrouded in verbal murk, that I had to go on the site to point out what he was really saying. In answer to the closing two sentences of the question I posed above, Councillor Ian Cooling, member for Wye, replied: 'If in doing so (dealing with Imperial), I managed to convince David Brooks Wilson that I was one of his most important contacts, then it could certainly be argued that I was succeeding – and that this was a positive for the village and not a negative. It also means that the answer to your closing question is probably "Yes".'

Yes.

In other words, he was happy to confirm what we had known for months: that Imperial were indeed firmly of the belief that our own borough councillor was on their side not ours, for reasons Justin and I understood only too well.

Aftermath

A letter to the paper

The comments got a little heated after Ian Cooling's cryptic confession. Naturally, no further questions went properly answered, by him or anyone else. There was a call for all his correspondence with Imperial to be released to the parish council in order to clear up any suspicion that his double agent activities might have been in any way geared to one side more than the other. He had no objection, he insisted, but if anyone wanted that they ought to put in a Freedom of Information request to Imperial, not expect it from him. Everyone understood the implications... weeks of tedious waiting, with nothing to show at the end.

Not another word about Wye emerged from KCC or Imperial. No-one was moved to resign or found themselves shifted sideways. It was now a story to be buried and forgotten, as swiftly as possible by those who were involved.

The collapse of the project didn't provoke an immediate outbreak of considered, in-depth journalism in our local newspaper either, though it could scarcely be ignored. There was an interview with Paul Clokie which was as tough as it was ever going to get. The reporter meekly asked the leader of ABC if he thought the public deserved an apology for the behind-the-scenes shenanigans of the concordat. Clokie, egotistical as ever, said he thought this 'impertinent'. The paper, nevertheless, in an uncharacteristic show of independence, argued in an opinion column that an apology was indeed in order.

I penned a letter to the editor. 'They'll never run it,' Justin grumbled. He was wrong. They printed every word the following week, and such was the astonishment in Wye that I got several e-mails pointing this out, since I was back in the US on the promotion trail again. Here is what I wrote...

Paul Clokie does owe his electorate an apology for the farce of Wye Park as you state last week. But he's not the only one. This was a deal, signed in secret, by ABC, KCC and Imperial College with the express intention of turning Wye into a small town with an associated industrial development and huge housing estate, all simply to make money.

211

I am at a loss to understand what you are referring to as 'utter fiction' in the coverage of it elsewhere. That Imperial put the whole stumbling mess on ice as far back as June? We've published their own documents to prove it. That it would have involved huge amounts of housing on the protected green fields of the AONB? Proven, with Imperial's own map, which we leaked and you have still never run, even though you have now referred to it twice. This was a concerted attempt to drive through a development that would have destroyed countryside loved by people from the whole Ashford area and beyond. Yet from the pages of the *Kentish Express*, when you did see fit to cover it, one would have thought this was a little local planning difficulty involving a bunch of rural eccentrics. I have to say you let off Paul Clokie very lightly in your 'exclusive' interview (made exclusive, it seems, because you're the only ones he'll talk to). He has yet to answer the crucial question: why did he claim not to know about the 250 acres of housing when his own planning officer Richard Alderton has stated, in public, in writing, that it was one of the options placed on the ABC table by Imperial?

Wye Park was more than a planning scandal. It was an indication that something must be wrong with the state of democracy in Kent because in a healthy political environment deals of this nature, in private by our public representatives, would simply be impossible. A strong, independent questioning press is a part of any healthy democratic process. Yes, Paul Clokie owes us an apology. But for your failure to cover this story in an adequate, inquisitive, intelligent way, so do you. It's very easy to come out on the winning side when the war is won, just as Wye's own borough councillor is trying to do at this very moment. But people are not so easily fooled.

I got back to the UK a week later to discover the *Kentish Express* had briefly acquired some spine. There was the inevitable reply from Clokie to my missive, one that rambled and resolutely failed to answer a single specific point. But elsewhere the editor, Leo Whitlock, penned an editorial entitled, 'Democratic deficit is root of problem'.

After an opening bout of whinging excuses for its pitiful record, Whitlock went on to echo the message that we had been trying to get across through save-wye from the very beginning: something had to be fundamentally wrong with the system to allow a near-tragic farce like this to happen in the first place. The local paper now agreed. There was, indeed, a 'democratic deficit'. What caused this change of heart on their part? A sense that it was time for some real journalism, perhaps, though sources within the KM group had already revealed to us that key decisions on editorial coverage of the Wye story were often referred by the Ashford paper to director level within the group. With luck, the issues Wye had made public had become too large to ignore. When the *Kentish Express* finally did get around to covering it, Clokie and his followers then turned on the paper and savaged it for the mild rebukes it had issued.

Ian Cooling stood up to do his bit for the party, lambasting this exceedingly mild coverage as a 'corrosive drip, drip'. Other loyal Tories rounded on the paper for 'negativity', code-word for 'going off message' or 'printing stuff we'd rather not read'. It was a classic illustration of the truth about a tame media; you will get no gratitude, no preferential treatment, no favoured inside track in return for your loyalty. Politicians know a poodle when they see one, and will kick harder than ever the moment a pet creature they regard as their own has the temerity to utter the meekest whimper of independence.

Three weeks after the collapse of Wye Park it was public knowledge that relations between the ruling clique of ABC and the local paper were at an all-time low, a state of affairs that can only have been sanctioned by more senior figures in the newspaper group, perhaps with the knowledge of Edwin Boorman himself. There wasn't a picture of a grinning infant anywhere either. The paper may have managed to run a photo of Paul Clokie – the third in that issue – above a caption and story about the leader of the opposition Peter Davison, but all in all this seemed a healthy, and much improved, state of affairs.

And yet... our little world was not yet still. The Two Connies whined like mad about the site's state of suspended animation, pleading for its revival, finding other local scandals they thought we ought to be looking at. One evening Brendan Pierce said, only half-jokingly, 'I'm really starting to miss those days.'

I thumped him, naturally.

These things don't end. They peter out, and as summer turned to autumn, one that was gloriously sunny by the time I was back in the country, one nagging question remained in my mind, a crucial one.

What really saved Wye?

I determined to find an answer. Contrary to the beliefs of people like Diana Pound, we had regular if occasionally distant contact with people on the other side of the fence. Many of the professionals in planning and other departments were quietly fascinated by what we did. They could boast about being a part of it to their peers. One of them confided to me, 'Imperial told us so little about what they were doing I used to come to save-wye every day just to find out what was going on. I may not have agreed with everything you said but it was really useful at times.'

With hindsight, and people now able to talk a little more freely, I came to see some of the errors we'd made over the months, and the dead end alleys we'd wandered round needlessly. There were no real howlers, but we had overemphasised some points and underemphasised others, principally because we were almost always working in the dark, scratching around for whatever loose information we could find.

One aspect in particular we had given insufficient weight: the planning process itself. This was my fault; I hate jargon and formal procedure. Terms like 'local development framework' and 'core strategy' turned me off completely. Besides, the Future Group had a team on this already, and paid advisers to tackle its tedious fine detail. What could we have done? Explained it better to others who were baffled by the jargon. No-one else was doing that.

The nagging question, though, was this: did the Future Group's quiet, long chats with Ashford's planners win the day, or our loud, incessant complaints and revelations?

I made discreet and lengthy inquiries. It was obvious from those within the loop that they'd talked about this among themselves already at length, and that they found it a little awkward to discuss outside their usual professional circles. The standard line was that the battle for Wye was won by the combined power of the parish council, the Future Group and save-wye. One of those closest to the issue described it as 'one of the most influential local campaigns I have ever witnessed', calling our group efforts 'one glorious coalition'. I found the last part a bit rich. Most people in the Future Group had been individually marvellous to us throughout, all of them were wonderful in the closing weeks and I knew their work talking to Alderton's team had been highly important. Still, I couldn't forget that we'd never received a single formal document from the organisation since its inception, and their lack of communications skills continued to appal me. By mid-October the web-site they now possessed still hadn't recorded the fact that Imperial's plans were dead, and had notched up just fifteen hundred visitors in all the months of its existence, fewer than we used to get in a single day. On their page on the only other source of village information, wye.org, the latest news story on the subject dated from the previous April.

The victory by coalition idea wasn't good enough. I needed to know. So I persisted. It was obvious that the efforts of the Future Group and the parish council were crucial. But would Imperial have collapsed so quickly through those alone? Would Ashford still have given way to pressure to take the Imperial plan out of the LDF?

It took some persistence, but I got there in the end. The answer lay there already in the archive of stories on save-wye. The key decision had been made during the week of Richard Alderton's return from holiday in the last week of August, and announced, in a typically sideways fashion, by Ian Cooling's abrupt public lurch to the side of the angels with his call for an independent inquiry at twenty to midnight that Saturday, the day the Future Group finally finished the long, laborious job of distributing printed copies of Ben Moorhead's original letter, most of which arrived too late to make a difference.

Two things, we were told, turned the possibility of Imperial being dropped from the LDF into a certainty. The letters that had been prompted by our purloining of Moorhead's letter and swift publication of it, on the site, through the samizdat network and the New Flying Horse, and by pushing it online with copies of actual submissions.

And, more than anything, the map. The glorious masterplan which, when Imperial tried to pooh-pooh the original story, we published in its entirety through the secret, untraceable medium of talkingstatues.net. From our own statistics it was clear that this lengthy and detailed document had been downloaded and copied many times by every party involved in Wye Park, including some people within Imperial.

Would we have won without it, I asked? There was a polite cough, a glance at a watch, and silence. Later I knew for sure. No-one was ever going to say this in public, in part because it might cause legal problems, but this was the killer blow. Without that graphic piece of evidence of the horrific scale of Imperial's 'vision' and the shock it produced, a reaction which in itself helped us generate those early letters for Richard Alderton, some mention of Wye Park would probably have found its way into the LDF. The planners were adamant that this would not have been the end of the story. The masterplan we'd published was what they called a 'developer's pitch'. Ashford would never have given permission for so many houses in the countryside, they said. Whatever followed would have been watered down, and might have fallen by the wayside altogether.

But there would still have been something in the development plan for the area, a note, an intention to build, and sometimes that was all that was needed. The shadow would be hanging over the village for a long time to come. If Imperial had succeeded in clawing its way into the LDF then some kind of planning application would, we were assured in Ashford, have been inevitable. We would have faced a public inquiry, a call-in by the Secretary of State, years of uncertainty, years of work and fundraising on the part of the Future Group on their own, because we couldn't even consider trying to keep the web-site going that long.

It was Justin and his brave-hearted moles who saved Wye and while I felt deeply proud to have provided the means by which they could pull it off I wished, all the same, that it had been different, and that the credit could have been laid entirely at the door of those constant, patient people within the Future Group.

Still I knew I couldn't let it go just yet. Without telling anyone I had put in a request to KCC saying in effect, 'Now the game is up, what reason is there to keep anything secret? This is the last FoI request. I want to read everything.' I also followed up on Ian Cooling's response to our call he make his e-mails public, by asking Imperial College to release them as he suggested, not that I think he thought anyone would bother.

There was to be one last throw of the dice, one final round of stories to be written that would take us closer to the truth.

Some final secrets revealed

Once again I was elsewhere when the results, late on the part of KCC as usual, came through. Two days after I got back to Cow Hollow, San Francisco, to talk at area book stores and work on one last revision of the manuscript for the novel that had taken shape during save-wyc's brief life, the Cooling e-mail file turned up and threw my American schedule into chaos. Not that I minded. Over the next few days we would throw back the curtain of secrecy surrounding Wye Park in ways we could only have dreamed of even a few months before.

I'd asked for all the e-mails from the college between its officers and Wye's borough councillor, and all mentions of us in internal documents. The second request was turned down on the grounds it would be too costly to provide and demand more work than was allowed under the Act, a back-handed compliment if ever there was one. The first generated a small file of messages that showed the relationship between Cooling and Brooks Wilson in particular to have been extraordinarily cosy indeed. We knew by this stage that Brooks Wilson had left Imperial amid the fallout from Wye Park and was pushing his CV around Whitehall and other public bodies looking for a new employer. Was it possible Cooling might be searching round for new avenues for his talents? Not if he could help it. Even as these most damning of messages became public, his position now remained fixed: he wished to 'move on' from questions about Wye Park, and refused to discuss them in the open at all, although he made a few frantic, failed efforts to get others to defend him on the site.

And there was so much more to discuss once we saw these new e-mails. The previous February, at his first public statement on the project, Cooling had described how he went 'ballistic' on hearing of the plan the previous November, adding, 'Could I invite you to think: you feel angry, what do you think I feel? You are certainly not the only one in this village who feels angry'. The January 9th meeting, he added, had been a 'patronising disgrace'.

All of this was now seen to sit very oddly with what he was saying to his friends on the other side. On January 4th, 2006, five days before the Withersdane meeting, here he was confiding to Imperial about what his public position would be when he finally got around to declaring it...

One point I did not mention in my earlier mail, but which you and Professor Borysiewicz (and others?) should be aware of, is my personal line when asked in the village where I stand in all this.

My response has been simple and to the point: It is the community of Wye that elected me, not Imperial College. I see real and substantial benefits to the community in this proposal but not at any cost. I shall be working with all concerned to ensure that the benefits are fully understood; that the downside is also properly appreciated and effectively addressed and that the community is fully involved (not just consulted) at all key stages.
Hope that makes sense!
Ian

I found the line about who elected him decidedly odd. Why on earth would he feel the need to point that out to the college? And how could he see 'real and substantial benefits' in something that he wasn't supposed to comprehend in any detail? Then, ten days after Withersdane, he was back on to the college again. Not to condemn them for the 'patronising disgrace' they had just inflicted on the village, but to offer his advice on how best to sell their plan to the community, and a grovelling apology for being late with his feedback: 'I'm ashamed to say, I have also spotted a note for me to send you a check list of my points for that meeting. With huge apologies for doing so at this disgracefully late stage, I offer the following.'

Between 2000 and 2004 he'd earned nearly £39,000 for 'marketing consultancy' from Imperial. It sounded as if he was back in the job, though this time unpaid.

This post-Withersdane message was marked 'Importance High' and contained eleven bullet points for action. Three of his suggestions – a separate web-site, what was to become the consultation panel, and a local exhibition – did take place, each in a desultory fashion. Cooling also wanted to see a newsletter promoting the scheme, a communications plan for the coming twelve months and 'systematic and continuous analysis of the local media'. In conjunction with the latter he had the most astonishing suggestion: 'Other forms of communications with the community – should there be letters in the local paper to correct the hugely erroneous record that grows weekly – if so, who should write them? Should someone be responding to the blog set up on the village website – http://www.wye.org/. According to the webmaster, there were 10,000 hits on the site last week.'

Here was the local councillor telling a would-be developer of his own community that it ought to start a letter writing campaign, presumably with his help, to sell its scheme to the locality. One that would 'correct the hugely erroneous record', by which one assumes he meant anything that Imperial found disagreeable, such as suggestions that the scheme might be more about money than education, science or research. Not long after this he was accepting my invitation to come and write on save-wye. Was this just one of his many contributions to the Imperial cause? We weren't to discover. Our local councillor stayed resolutely out of sight, and for the first time ever failed to respond when I posted a story about him, detailing all these revelations, and headlined, 'Councillor Ian Cooling, Imperial's little helper'.

There was something else interesting. I'd asked for all of Cooling's e-mails, yet this fairly meagre release failed to contain one we had already received from Justin's moles, the damning message Cooling had sent in June pestering Brooks Wilson for information. Why, I asked Imperial's FoI team, wasn't that included? It took a couple of days but finally I got an answer. Because I hadn't received all the e-mails, only those that had been 'retained'. In other words the ones they hadn't thought to shred. We would never get a full release of Cooling's communications with the college. But, within the space of three days, we'd have something even better.

Justin had put in the same request as I had to KCC. One day after Cooling's e-mails arrived the council's FoI team said it had decided what new documents it would now release, and they would prove so large they had to be posted as a CD, not despatched by e-mail. I wailed about being in California; Justin copied all seventy three files and sent them to me in Cow Hollow. I looked at them and realised I'd forgotten how downright gobsmacking this whole saga could turn at times.

Justin and I shared out the stories just as we did in the old days. It ran to six pieces in all, spread out over several days, all based on the council's own reports and scribbled notes. We merely picked out the juicy parts and pointed up the connections and implications, of which there were many. This batch of documents roundly killed off any notion that the size of the planned development was a surprise to our local councils, however much they protested to the contrary. There was a hand-written memo from Pete Raine clearly dating back as far as 2004 in which he noted, 'IC need development land in AONB. £100m worth.' Around this time KCC's county planning officer, Leigh Herington, in a meeting with Imperial also scribbled...

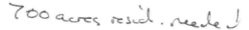

So a vast scheme taking up almost the entire rural Imperial estate and the demand to get £100 million in profits for the college were both on the table from the earliest stages, contrary to everything the village had been told. Why? Herington's hand-written scribble revealed all...

The college told the council it wouldn't contemplate building the scheme on the empty acres of the Thames corridor, which were crying out for investment, because of 'lifestyle' issues. Nor would it take up any of the hundreds of acres of unoccupied development land a few miles away in Ashford because it wanted something that was 'Oxbridge'. It was Wye, Richard Sykes insisted, or, as Herington's note emphasises, 'Imperial **will** go'. In fact, even with its secret concordat signed, the college was privately planning its academic exit from the village within the year in any case. The councils fell for everything they were told, hook, line and sinker, and with an astonishing glee.

By March 2006, another note from Herington had refined the plan to twenty acres for the college, twenty acres for 'research', effectively a business park, and between a hundred and four hundred acres of housing, all aimed at producing Imperial's much-needed 'endowment' of £100 million. That same month Paul Clokie was standing up in public and issuing a formal statement in which he claimed, 'The first key point to remember when discussing this issue, is that no-one has any clear idea of what

Imperial College's plans for Wye may amount to... All we have at the moment is a concept.'

Clearly, if this were true, then council officers never spoke to their elected members over almost two years of meetings with Imperial, all of them on the most chummy of terms. This seemed incredible given that the closeness of these parties was simply breath-taking. Now we were able to read the private letter Paul Carter sent Richard Sykes on November 10th, 2005, a month before the public announcement, thanking him for 'an extremely enjoyable and informative lunch... after a hectic week, it was very pleasant to listen rather than talk'. Carter declared he was both 'very excited' and 'extremely supportive' of the concept, and was keen to introduce his team to Sykes before what he described as 'big bang', the day everything finally went public. One key member Carter wanted to put before the rector of Imperial was the publicly reticent Charles Findlay, billed by Carter as an 'extremely useful ally. He is well connected locally and is a Company Director with a range of experience in both farming and the delivery of large-scale community projects'.

Twelve days later Carter was reaching for his headed KCC note-paper again, writing another missive to his new-found friend in the lofty circles of academia, thanking him for one more lunch. In the margin he scribbled, 'PS. It was so important to get the locally elected members on board. I was delighted by their enthusiasm'.

There it was in black and white, in the words of the leader of KCC. Both Cooling and Findlay had been brought into the loop before Wye Park was public knowledge, and were 'on board' and 'enthusiastic'. The warmth which these authorities felt towards a developer of a project it would one day have to judge 'impartially' was mutual. After the disastrous January 9th meeting, at which Pete Raine had pleaded that 'the lack of plans at this stage was a well-known planning Catch 22', a sentiment echoed by Ashford's David Hill, David Brooks Wilson had been swift to send both a herogram congratulating them on their performance.

> Dear Pete and David. A brief note to thank you, somewhat belatedly, for your splendid efforts last night on our behalf. I think given what we had anticipated, the meeting was a lot smoother than it could have been and I'm

sure that this was due in no small part to your own elo-
quent interventions during the course of the night.
Many thanks for coming to support us. Borys and I have
discussed how we could improve things in future and I
know that Pete and Borys have also been in touch. We
will follow up and improve on the next occasion.

So *that's* why our well-paid council representatives were there? To
'support' Imperial College, not explain things impartially to the
baffled and frightened public of Wye at all. Just to make this relationship crystal clear, Nigel Buck, the college estates employee
who was to succeed Brooks Wilson as estates director, penned a
missive to both KCC and ABC in early February letting them
know exactly where they stood in the pecking order. This was
issued around the time KCC was facing up to the awkward truth
that it had to come up with some answers to the FoI request I'd
submitted a few weeks before, something it, and Imperial, clearly
didn't relish.

Buck wrote a formal and extremely abrupt letter to both
authorities effectively swearing them to secrecy should any prying
member of the public ask to see information pertaining to Wye.
This order was headed, 'Declaration of Intent concerning the
Wye Park Project'. It informed both councils that everything
they would receive about Wye Park, whatever its content,
whether it be by letter, e-mail, note or discussion, would be regarded as 'commercially sensitive' by the college and thus barred
from release under provisions of the Freedom of Information Act.
In other words Imperial demanded, and got, an agreement from
both authorities that they would block every piece of information, potentially for years to come, prejudging it as 'commercially
sensitive' before it was written or even dreamed of. Freedom of
Information legislation is designed with the presumption that
information should be made public unless there is good reason
for it to be withheld. Imperial managed to turn this on its head
by forcing through a blanket blackout, in concert with both
councils, which meant that every future item to do with Wye
Park would be kept from public view, whatever its content.

There was one other wonderful aspect to this letter too. Not
once but three times, Buck used the phrase 'during the current
period of negotiations'. Imperial and the two authorities had
every right to discuss a project of this size in advance of a plan-

ning application. But 'negotiations' were something else. Such a phrase implied that, once the right formula was reached, approval would be forthcoming from both KCC and ABC, something which the college's attitude suggested from the very beginning. If that were the case then all ideas of local consultation and an unbiased process open to persuasion by opponents of the scheme were visibly ridiculous. These three organisations were bargaining over how to carve up Wye and its Area of Outstanding Natural Beauty, and had been for more than a year before anyone outside the loop understood anything was going on.

Who did know? There were clues littered through the seventy three documents KCC released after much pressing, ones that were doubtless even more evident in the eighteen e-mails, notes, maps and project files the council said it would now never make public on a variety of technical grounds, including Imperial's 'commercial sensitivity' agreement. The effort to build Wye Park may have involved more than £1 million of public money, but the project's genesis occurred well away from the glare of open scrutiny. This nightmare began inside the private power circles of Kent, run by men, and occasionally women, who knew one another more through social and political contacts than any apparent sense of social or civic duty.

The signs were there in the secret attempt to build a new road into Wye, directly from the M20 motorway, a project that turned out to be one of the many demands Imperial was making of the authorities, all the while insisting it wouldn't put a penny towards the cost. This idea was first mooted in a note from one Sarah Ward, chair of yet another quango associated with KCC, the Kent Rural Taskforce. On November 22nd 2004, not long after Imperial announced it was closing the old Wye College, Sarah Ward wrote a note marked 'strictly confidential' for her contacts within the county council. In it she told the authority, quite inaccurately, 'Imperial College are prepared to co-operate with Kent and Ashford local authorities on the future of Wye. They do not intend to withdraw from the campus and plans for its future use are still very fluid. They would like to establish a science park based at Wye if an improved transport infrastructure could be provided, making access from Ashford... and the M20 more convenient. They envisage that money would be raised from the sale of a small area of land for residential development.'

This memo set in train a lengthy sequence of events in which KCC, ABC and regional authorities would struggle to find some way to finance, at a cost of £30 million or more, a highly controversial road, one that Imperial and the authorities would lobby for as part of the South East Plan, only to see it dropped when Wye Park collapsed.

And all through a short missive from the chair of a body most people in Kent had never head of. Who was she? Mrs Ward is part of the posh Kent county set, a former Wye College student, and a farmer. In addition, she happens to be a deputy lieutenant of the county, like Edwin Boorman. Her name also appeared on the membership list of a little-known group known as the Kent Ambassadors, run by KCC supposedly for people who can do the region favours by dropping its name at the right occasion. A good number of ambassadors are sportsmen or people in the arts. A good number aren't. Mrs Sarah Ward for example, David Brooks Wilson himself, Sandy Bruce-Lockhart and the grand old man of the Kent Messenger, Edwin Boorman, who all happen to be Kent Ambassadors too.

Curious, I pulled the full list of ambassadors out of KCC, through one more prolonged FoI request. There was no explanation why Brooks Wilson, a man who hadn't lived in the county for years or had any direct connection with it, should have his name on it. But there were a few other familiar figures. Hugo Peel, the beaming PR man with the yellow bow tie at the great signing ceremony attended by Ann Sutherland and John Hodder, turned out to be a Kent Ambassador, though his connection with the county seemed intangible. So was Sir Robert Worcester, one-time boss of MORI, now head of the University of Kent, which took over Imperial's students in Wye when Richard Sykes didn't want them, and a board member of Boorman's Messenger Group *and* yet one more deputy lieutenant.

It even extended to families. Sarah Ward was mother-in-law to the son of Sarah Hohler, a member of a Kent aristocratic family, supposedly descended from William the Conqueror, which had long been active in county politics, to the extent of providing at least one MP in years gone by. Mrs Hohler's contribution to Tory politics in the county was more muted. She had been a member of both SEERA and SEEDA, and on occasion Paul Clokie had substituted for her personally on the regional authority's planning committee. Oh, and she also happened to be deputy leader of

KCC, number two to Paul Carter, so doubtless in the thick of things over Wye Park. None of these people lived in our part of Kent. Some didn't even reside in the county at all. Yet they were all entangled in the effort to bring to fruition Imperial's overweening ambition to concrete over the AONB.

These hydra-headed links went on and on, through all the many quangos that live unseen behind the fabric of local and regional government, rarely, if ever, featuring in a single newspaper article. It turned out someone in the village had produced a flip-chart labelled 'The Brooks Wilson Pinball Machine', since it didn't take much of an effort to see the ubiquitous Imperial man as the key figure that linked so many of those who had a hand in the project. A photo of it was e-mailed to me while I was in San Francisco after I wondered whether we could use it on the site. I stared at the thing in amazement; it would have needed a screen three feet wide to view properly. Watching all these tangled relationships finally work their way into the light of day was rather like stumbling into a familiar room to find a school of octopuses indulging in group sex on the carpet. The tentacles seem to go everywhere, and you could never quite work out which bit belonged to whom.

We placed everything we had on the web-site. The statistics went through the roof again. People were outraged. And then they became quiet. A journalist from the *Kentish Express* spoke to Ben Moorhead about the revelations for thirty minutes, and didn't even bother to phone us. Not a word appeared in the local paper. After the brief storm in October, when the *Kentish Express* had complained of a 'democratic deficit', normal, servile relations had, it seemed, been resumed.

So all we had left was our outrage, and outrage changes nothing. There remained no active opposition on either of the councils in Kent, only the lone voice of Peter Davison, leader of the Ashford Independents, from time to time. Not a single Tory councillor expressed any concern in public. A brief e-mail I sent to David Cameron wondering if he might ask someone to look into the way his party members had behaved in power in Kent was brushed off with a curt reply, 'It's a local matter'.

The options of the village narrowed. There were two courses open to the community. To be 'magnanimous in victory', as the perpetrators of Wye Park hoped. Or to pursue this lingering scandal through the uncertain and time-consuming process of a complaint to the Standards Board or the Local Government Ombudsman. Either one could take years and fail on a technicality. The people who ought to care about this didn't, because they were the ones who got us into the mess in the first place. In a single party county like Kent, where anything usually gets elected provided it wears a blue badge, there wasn't much hope for change. There's a word I never use in my novels, unless someone is ridiculing the idea, and that's 'closure'. The idea that the past can be somehow neatly, safely packaged away and, if not forgotten, at least let go. The Wye scandal is one of those rare occasions when this cliché would be appropriate. All those involved needed do was apologise and resign and then perhaps local government in Kent could start all over again. But it wasn't going to happen. They wanted us to forget, and for one very good reason.

Alan Paterson, raised in the village, a man who felt its possible loss more than any of the newcomers among us could, told me that he'd walked his dog to the Devil's Kneading Trough soon after the victory, sat and admired the view he now knew would not be despoiled and found himself in tears. It was a short conversation, one that moved briskly on to the game of golf he'd just played. This is England after all.

Later I went there myself. Before Imperial's plan became public I'd not been on the Downs much in recent years. We were long term residents, we knew Wye and its beauty spots well. Like most locals we took for granted the place where we lived. When I needed photographs for the site I was surprised to learn that few locals had any to speak of. Even Steve Bloom, the professional photographer who travelled the world from pole to pole capturing shots that took your breath away, admitted he had none too, and swiftly strode off to capture a set of gorgeous images that would adorn save-wye in its closing weeks.

On a cold bright November day I sat where Alan must have done and wished I could have been joined by Richard Sykes and Leszek Borysiewicz, David Brooks Wilson and the perfidious Pete Raine, who had once earned a living defending Kent's natural environment. I would have pointed out Ashford in the distance, surrounded by industrial parks, most of them half empty at best, desperate for the kind of development Imperial claimed it wanted to bring the area, and adjoined too by growing sprawls of new housing devouring the flat land in every direction. I would have looked at the Downs, the nearer countryside, imagining the old road, half hidden from the Kneading Trough, winding down through the woodland beneath the Crown, past Withersdane on towards the village, verdant, alive, unchanged over centuries, home to fox and badger, owl and hare. And people too. Good people who had just endured a terrible year.

I would have asked... how could you?

And they would have laughed at me, as David Brooks Wilson and Nigel Buck had in the early days of save-wye, astonished that anyone believed they could stand up to the might of an institution such as theirs. I was lost in a daydream, which is not difficult high on the Downs on a day like that. Where we saw beauty, they saw opportunity. Where we sought preservation and continuity they craved so-called modernity and change. They were masters of their universe, metropolitan men determined to shape it and profit from their labours as much as was humanly possible, paying lip service only to the environmental and human cost which was, in any case, invisible since they, almost to a man and woman, lived elsewhere. They wouldn't have cared about the pain they caused. We were, to them, throwbacks, people of no importance, obstacles in the way of a greater future of cheap housing and mass commercial development, and money, money, money, most of all.

I wondered what Captain Arthur Davies and his family, once of Withersdane, now lying in a pink marble tomb in Wye's churchyard, would have made of them. And, in a grave nearby, Chippy Barnard, dead in a wartime accident, father to Anne who was to marry Charles Findlay, lover of bread pudding, loather of public statements of any kind, but marked out as 'on board', 'enthusiastic' and an 'extremely useful ally' weeks before any of his fellow village residents understood their way of life and the community they loved was in dire peril. I could, I felt, have talked to any of those dead men and their families and made myself understood. But Sykes and Borys, and Brooks Wilson...

For them this land was a place to possess, master and exploit. For us it was a precious legacy to cherish, nurture and hand on in turn. These superior men of London, distant lords of so much that seemed of little importance to us, knew better. All that mattered was their own brief span, nothing else, not for a moment.

I sat there, seething, not weeping. So many times I'd said to the people I knew in the Future Group, 'Learn what century you're living in.'

There, high on the Downs, I realised I sometimes forgot what truly meant too.

We'd won, but it was in some ways a harsh and Pyrrhic victory. Imperial had frittered away more than £1 million trying to conquer Wye and been sent packing with its tail between its legs. Our combined, frequently fractious coalition had quietly scored one of the most astonishing environmental triumphs of recent years. But we were not the same as before. The agricultural college of such international acclaim, a place we knew and loved, was lost for good, destroyed by Imperial's lack of care, which had so nearly spilled over into the village at large. There was no way of return, no chance to turn back the clock. Our small, happily eccentric academic community, like an Oxford college shrunk to miniature and tied to our beautiful, ancient countryside, was gone for good. Never again would we see tipsy students stumbling through the village in togas and evening dress, queasy from some secret ceremony involving pints of beer and live goldfish, giggling, grateful for a little time in a place that would remain in their memories for the rest of their lives.

Wye's days as a magical place to which young men and women travelled from all over the world to learn the rites and runes of working of land were over. One more piece of Kent's diminishing heritage had been wilfully dismantled in the false names of progress and capital and it would never be rebuilt.

I gazed at the fields below, a sea of green and gold and dun brown earth glorious beneath a chill wintry sun, a harsh, cold certainty growing at the back of my mind. This world belonged to men like Richard Sykes and David Brooks Wilson, men who would look with avarice and ambition at the empty acres below, and rub their soft, uncalloused business hands in anticipation.

Their names may change. But they'll be back, I thought. They'll be back.